THE 66 MINUTE BIBLE

Edition 01-Revision 01

Victor Robert Farrell

The 66 Minute Video Bible

All current
Contact & Sales Information
Can be found at
www.The66MinuteBible.com

THE
66 MINUTE
BIBLE

ISBN Number 978-1-910686-84-3

First published

May 2016 by Whispering Word

All current contact and sales information can be found at

www.The66MinuteBible.com

Printed in The United Kingdom

for

WhisperingWord

The 66 Minute Bible

Dedication

This book is dedicated, very simply,

To the now four most important people

In the whole wide world to me.

My daughter Gemma,

My son Jonathan,

My Grandaughter Ellie May,

And of course,

My wife

Bridget.

PREFACE

I am Pastor, Rev. Victor Robert Farrell, and this '66 Minute Bible' has long since been part of a global vision to communicate the God of the WHOLE Bible in very raw terms to very real people. This is my passion and the reason why I founded The 66 Books Ministry, who, through our 66 Cities project, over the course of the next 25 years, by the grace of God and according to His will and favor, shall be preaching consecutively from each of the 66 Books of the Holy Bible, the Gospel of the Lord Jesus Christ in 16,500 of the most influential cities of the world on an annual and ongoing basis!

US, UK or elsewhere, or, "How do you spell that?"

To be British, is to be somewhat like 'the last of the Mohicans.' The United Kingdom I grew up in is breaking apart. Even so, I am of Irish & Scottish great-grandparents, grandparents and parents, and I was also born in England. Therefore, I am British and a Celt at that. Even so, I love North America. Does this make me a Yankophile, or loving the South and its battle flag, more especially a Dixiophile? Alternatively, maybe I could be an Americophile or a Canameriphile? Who knows? Suffice to say, that as our nations are divided by a common language, America being the residence of the majority of our English readers, I have tried to adopt the spelling and grammar of the Americas. Even so, I have no doubt failed, and in the so doing, both mixed and matched the UK and US spelling and grammatical styles as I have compiled these overviews. I confess that I am a double-minded man, unstable in all my editorial ways. The purists, either side of the pond, I am sure will never forgive me. The rest do not care. Either way I need your help. So, if you spot any 'howlers,' do let me know. Please Email me your corrections on:

getyouracttogetherman@whisperingword.com

Bible Versions & Text Form

Despite calling on statistics form the King James Version, preferring the 'Textus Receptus' or the 'Majority Text,' I have tried to use the New King James Version (NKJV) throughout these overviews.

This book was made to accompany 'The 66 Minute Video Bible' which can be found on line at www.66MinuteBible.com. For these 66 Minute 1 minute video overview of each book of the Bible I really must thank United

Christian Broadcasters who so kindly produced these for our ministry. Thank you UCB.

Thanks also to Jonathan Feinberg and www.wordle.net which is a free online 'word cloud' program from which I have produced what I see not as clouds, but as Word Fingerprints of the Mosh High for each Book of the Bible. I hope you like them, as each one is a unique 200 word signature.

Thanks lastly to John Walkenbach and his nifty King James Bible on an Excel Spreadsheet. It's excellent, I have lifted most of the Word and verse statistics from this free resource.

Rev. Victor Robert Farrell, May 2016, England.

Just a Huckster

Some young preacher will study until he has to get thick glasses to take care of his failing eyesight because he has an idea he wants to become a famous preacher. HE'S JUST A HUCKSTER buying selling and getting gain. They will ordain him and he will be known as Reverend and if he writes a book, they will make him a doctor. And he will be known as Doctor; but he's still a huckster buying and selling and getting gain.

And when the Lord comes back,
HE will drive him out of the temple
along with the other cattle.

A.W. Tozer

(from 'Tozer on Christian Leadership,' compiled by Ron Eggert)

John 3:30 He must increase
but I must decrease.

Prologue

I am told that there are 788,258 words in the King James Bible and of these 14,565 are unique. That's a lot of words! I have been reading the Bible for nearly forty years on an almost daily basis. It still remains to me the most exciting book on the planet, however, it never gets any easier. Bible reading is a spiritual discipline and for me the emphasis is on discipline.

I created this resource to aid you in your Bible reading, it gives your brain a sixty second overview of the Bible, a loose enclosure to herd the narrative of the book into something that can be seen as a whole. It was never created to be a substitute, but an aid. Just saying……

Friends, welcome to the most exciting book on the planet!

Rev. Victor Robert Farrell, May 2016, England.

The Old 100th

All people that on earth do dwell,
Sing to the Lord with cheerful voice.
Him serve with fear, His praise forth tell;
Come ye before Him and rejoice.

The Lord, ye know, is God indeed;
Without our aid He did us make;
We are His folk, He doth us feed,
And for His sheep He doth us take.

O enter then His gates with praise;
Approach with joy His courts unto;
Praise, laud, and bless His name always,
For it is seemly so to do.

For why? the Lord our God is good;
His mercy is for ever sure;
His truth at all times firmly stood,
And shall from age to age endure.

To Father, Son and Holy Ghost,
The God whom Heaven and earth adore,
From men and from the angel host
Be praise and glory evermore.

From 'Fourscore and Seven Psalms of David'
(Geneva, Switzerland: 1561); attributed to William Kethe

Dedication .... **vii**

PREFACE .... **ix**

Just a Huckster .... **xi**

Prologue .... **xiii**

The Old 100th .... **xv**

| GENESIS | **27**

BIBLE SECTION | OLD TESTAMENT - THE PENTATEUCH 27

Total Words | *38,265 (The 04th Biggest Book in The Bible)* *27*

| EXODUS | **29**

BIBLE SECTION | OLD TESTAMENT - THE PENTATEUCH 29

Total Words | *32,684 (The 07th Biggest Book in The Bible)* *29*

| LEVITICUS | **31**

BIBLE SECTION | OLD TESTAMENT - THE PENTATEUCH 31

Total Words | *24,541 (The 12th Biggest Book in The Bible)* *31*

| NUMBERS | **33**

BIBLE SECTION | OLD TESTAMENT - THE PENTATEUCH 33

Total Words | *32,893 (The 06th Biggest Book in The Bible)* *33*

| DEUTERONOMY | **35**

BIBLE SECTION | OLD TESTAMENT - THE PENTATEUCH 35

Total Words | *28,351 (The 08th Biggest Book in The Bible)* *35*

| JOSHUA | **37**

BIBLE SECTION | OLD TESTAMENT - HISTORICAL BOOKS 37

Total Words | *18,853 (The 21st Biggest Book in The Bible)* *37*

| JUDGES | **39**

BIBLE SECTION | OLD TESTAMENT - HISTORICAL BOOKS 39

Total Words | *18,966 (The 20th Biggest Book in The Bible)* *39*

| **RUTH** | **41**

BIBLE SECTION | OLD TESTAMENT - HISTORICAL BOOKS.........41

Total Words | *2,574 (The 43rd Biggest Book in The Bible)*.............*41*

| **1 SAMUEL** | **43**

BIBLE SECTION | OLD TESTAMENT - HISTORICAL BOOKS.........43

Total Words | *25,048 (The 11th Biggest Book in The Bible)*............*43*

| **2 SAMUEL** | **45**

BIBLE SECTION | OLD TESTAMENT - HISTORICAL BOOKS.........45

Total Words | *20,599 (The 17th Biggest Book in The Bible)*............*45*

| **1 KINGS** | **47**

BIBLE SECTION | OLD TESTAMENT - HISTORICAL BOOKS.........47

Total Words | *24,512 (The 13th Biggest Book in The Bible)*...........*47*

| **2 KINGS** | **49**

BIBLE SECTION | OLD TESTAMENT - HISTORICAL BOOKS.........49

Total Words | *23,519 (The 12th Biggest Book in The Bible)*............*49*

| **1 CHRONICLES** | **51**

BIBLE SECTION | OLD TESTAMENT - HISTORICAL BOOKS.........51

Total Words | *20,365 (The 18th Biggest Book in The Bible)*...........*51*

| **2 CHRONICLES** | **53**

BIBLE SECTION | OLD TESTAMENT - HISTORICAL BOOKS.........53

Total Words | *26,069 (The 09th Biggest Book in The Bible)*............*53*

| **EZRA**| **55**

BIBLE SECTION | OLD TESTAMENT - HISTORICAL BOOKS.........55

Total Words | *7,440 (The 30th Biggest Book in The Bible)*.............*55*

| **NEHEMIAH** | **57**

BIBLE SECTION | OLD TESTAMENT - HISTORICAL BOOKS.........57

Total Words | *10,480 (The 27th Biggest Book in The Bible)*............*57*

| **ESTHER** | **59**

BIBLE SECTION | OLD TESTAMENT – HISTORICAL BOOKS........59

Total Words | *5,633 (The 34th Biggest Book in The Bible)* 59

| JOB |..........61

BIBLE SECTION | OLD TESTAMENT - POETRY 61

Total Words | *18,098 (22nd Biggest Book in The Bible)*..............61

| PSALMS |..........63

BIBLE SECTION | OLD TESTAMENT - POETRY 63

Total Words | *42,685 (This is the Biggest Book in The Bible!)*.......63

| PROVERBS |..........65

BIBLE SECTION | OLD TESTAMENT - POETRY 65

Total Words | *15,038 (The 24th Biggest Book in The Bible)* 65

| ECCLESIASTES |..........67

BIBLE SECTION | OLD TESTAMENT - POETRY 67

Total Words | *5,580 (The 35th Biggest Book in The Bible)* 67

| THE SONG OF SOLOMON |..........69

BIBLE SECTION | OLD TESTAMENT - POETRY 69

Total Words | *2,658 (The 42nd Biggest Book in The Bible)*..............69

| ISAIAH |..........71

BIBLE SECTION | OLD TESTAMENT – THE MAJOR PROPHETS ...71

Total Words | *37,040 (The 05th Biggest Book in The Bible)* 71

| JEREMIAH |..........73

BIBLE SECTION | OLD TESTAMENT – THE MAJOR PROPHETS ...73

Total Words | *42,654 (The 02nd Biggest Book in The Bible)*............73

| LAMENTATIONS |..........75

BIBLE SECTION | OLD TESTAMENT – THE MAJOR PROPHETS ...75

Total Words | *3,411 (The 04th Biggest Book in The Bible)* 75

| EZEKIEL |..........77

BIBLE SECTION | OLD TESTAMENT – THE MAJOR PROPHETS ...77

Total Words | *39,402 (The 03rd Biggest Book in The Bible)*...........77

| **DANIEL** | 79
BIBLE SECTION | OLD TESTAMENT – THE MAJOR PROPHETS ...79
Total Words | *11,602 (26th Biggest Book in The Bible)* *79*

| **HOSEA** | 81
BIBLE SECTION | OLD TESTAMENT - THE MINOR PROPHETS 81
Total Words | *5,174 (The 36th Biggest Book in The Bible)* *81*

| **JOEL** | 83
BIBLE SECTION | OLD TESTAMENT – THE MINOR PROPHETS ...83
Total Words | *2,033 (The 49th Biggest Book in The Bible)* *83*

| **AMOS** | 85
BIBLE SECTION | OLD TESTAMENT - THE MINOR PROPHETS 85
Total Words | *4,216 (The 37th Biggest Book in The Bible)* *85*

| **OBADIAH** | 87
BIBLE SECTION | OLD TESTAMENT - THE MINOR PROPHETS 87
Total Words | *669 (The 62nd Biggest Book in The Bible)* *87*

| **JONAH** | 89
BIBLE SECTION | OLD TESTAMENT - THE MINOR PROPHETS 89
Total Words | *1,320 (The 57th Biggest Book in The Bible)* *89*

| **MICAH** | 91
BIBLE SECTION | OLD TESTAMENT - THE MINOR PROPHETS 91
Total Words | *3,152 (The 39th Biggest Book in The Bible)* *91*

| **NAHUM** | 93
BIBLE SECTION | OLD TESTAMENT - THE MINOR PROPHETS 93
Total Words | *1,284 (The 58th Biggest Book in The Bible)* *93*

| **HABAKKUK** | 95
BIBLE SECTION | OLD TESTAMENT - THE MINOR PROPHETS 95
Total Words | *1,475 (The 56th Biggest Book in The Bible)* *95*

| **ZEPHANIAH** | 97
BIBLE SECTION | OLD TESTAMENT - THE MINOR PROPHETS 97

Total Words | *1,617 (The 54th Biggest Book in The Bible)* *97*

| HAGGAI | **99**

BIBLE SECTION | OLD TESTAMENT – THE MINOR PROPHETS ...99

Total Words | *1,130 (The 59th Biggest Book in The Bible)* *99*

| ZECHERIAH | **101**

BIBLE SECTION | OLD TESTAMENT - THE MINOR PROPHETS ..101

Total Words | *6,443 (The 32nd Biggest Book in The Bible)* *101*

| MALACHI | **103**

BIBLE SECTION | OLD TESTAMENT - THE MINOR PROPHETS ..103

Total Words | *1,781 (The 52nd Biggest Book in The Bible)* *103*

| MATTHEW | **105**

BIBLE SECTION | NEW TESTAMENT - THE GOSPELS 105

Total Words | *23, 684 (The 04th Biggest Book in The Bible)* *105*

| MARK | **107**

BIBLE SECTION | NEW TESTAMENT - THE GOSPELS 107

Total Words | *15,166 (The 23rd Biggest Book in The Bible)* *107*

| LUKE | **109**

BIBLE SECTION | NEW TESTAMENT - THE GOSPELS 109

Total Words | *25,939 (The 10th Biggest Book in The Bible)* *109*

| JOHN | **111**

BIBLE SECTION | NEW TESTAMENT - THE GOSPELS 111

Total Words | *19,094 (The 19th Biggest Book in The Bible)* *111*

| ACTS | **113**

BIBLE SECTION | NEW TESTAMENT – HISTORICAL BOOK 113

Total Words | *24,245 (The 14th Biggest Book in The Bible)* *113*

| ROMANS | **115**

BIBLE SECTION | NEW TESTAMENT – THE PAULINE EPISTLES115

Total Words | *9,422 (The 29th Biggest Book in The Bible)* *115*

1 CORINTHIANS..**117**

BIBLE SECTION | NEW TESTAMENT - THE PAULINE EPISTLES 117

Total Words | *9,462 (The 28th Biggest Book in The Bible)* *117*

| 2 CORINTHIANS |..**119**

BIBLE SECTION | NEW TESTAMENT - THE PAULINE EPISTLES 119

Total Words | *6,065 (The 33rd Biggest Book in The Bible)* *119*

| GALATIANS |..**121**

BIBLE SECTION | NEW TESTAMENT - THE PAULINE EPISTLES 121

Total Words | *3,084 (The 40th Biggest Book in The Bible)* *121*

| EPHESIANS |..**123**

BIBLE SECTION | NEW TESTAMENT - THE PAULINE EPISTLES 123

Total Words | *3,022 (The 41st Biggest Book in The Bible)* *123*

| PHILIPPIANS |..**125**

BIBLE SECTION | NEW TESTAMENT - THE PAULINE EPISTLES 125

Total Words | *2,183 (The 48th Biggest Book in The Bible)* *125*

| COLOSSIANS |..**127**

BIBLE SECTION | NEW TESTAMENT - THE PAULINE EPISTLES 127

Total Words | *1,979 (The 50th Biggest Book in The Bible)* *127*

| 1 THESSALONIANS |..**129**

BIBLE SECTION | NEW TESTAMENT - THE PAULINE EPISTLES 129

Total Words | *1,837 (The 52nd Biggest Book in The Bible)* *129*

| 2 THESSALONIANS |..**131**

BIBLE SECTION | NEW TESTAMENT - THE PAULINE EPISTLES 131

Total Words | *1,022 (The 60th Biggest Book in The Bible)* *131*

| 1 TIMOTHY |..**133**

BIBLE SECTION | NEW TESTAMENT - THE PAULINE EPISTLES 133

Total Words | *2,244 (The 47th Biggest Book in The Bible)* *133*

| 2 TIMOTHY |..**135**

BIBLE SECTION | NEW TESTAMENT - THE PAULINE EPISTLES 135

Total Words | *1,666 (The 53rd Biggest Book in The Bible)* *135*

| TITUS | **137**

BIBLE SECTION | NEW TESTAMENT - THE PAULINE EPISTLES 137

Total Words | *896 (The 61st Biggest Book in The Bible)*.............*137*

| PHILEMON | **139**

BIBLE SECTION | NEW TESTAMENT - THE PAULINE EPISTLES 139

Total Words | *430 (The 64th Biggest Book in The Bible)* *139*

| HEBREWS | **141**

BIBLE SECTION | NEW TESTAMENT - THE PENTATEUCH 141

Total Words | *6,897 (The 31st Biggest Book in The Bible)*............*141*

| JAMES | **143**

BIBLE SECTION | NEW TESTAMENT – GENERAL EPISTLES 143

Total Words | *2,304 (The 46th Biggest Book in The Bible)* *143*

| 1 PETER | **145**

BIBLE SECTION | NEW TESTAMENT – GENERAL EPISTLES 145

Total Words | *2,476 (The 45th Biggest Book in The Bible)* *145*

| 2 PETER | **147**

BIBLE SECTION | NEW TESTAMENT – GENERAL EPISTLES 147

Total Words | *1,553 (The 55th Biggest Book in The Bible)* *147*

| 1 JOHN | **149**

BIBLE SECTION | NEW TESTAMENT – GENERAL EPISTLES 149

Total Words | *2,516 (The 44th Biggest Book in The Bible)* *149*

| 2 JOHN | **151**

BIBLE SECTION | NEW TESTAMENT - GENERAL EPISTLES.......151

Total Words | *298 (The 65th Biggest Book in The Bible)* *151*

| 3 JOHN | **153**

BIBLE SECTION | NEW TESTAMENT – GENERAL EPISTLES 153

Total Words | *294 (This is the Smallest Book in The Bible)*..........*153*

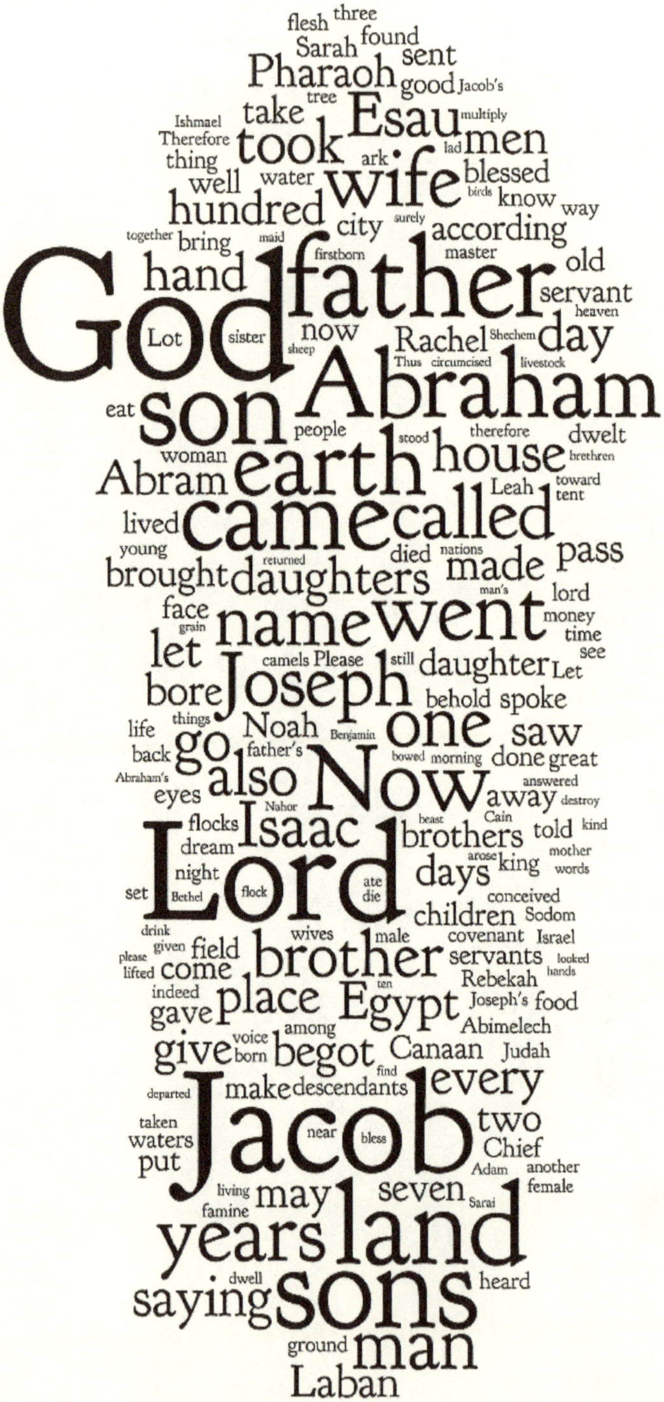

flesh three
Sarah found
sent
Pharaoh good Jacob's
tree
take
Esau
multiply
Ishmael
Therefore
took
lad
men
thing
ark
well water
wife
blessed
birds
know
hundred
way
city
surely
according
together bring
maid
firstborn
master
hand
old
God
father
servant
heaven
Lot
sister
now
sheep
Rachel
Shechem
day
Thus circumcised
livestock
Abraham
eat
son
people
stood
therefore
dwelt
woman
house
brethren
Abram
earth
Leah
toward
tent
lived
came
called
young
returned
died
nations
pass
brought
daughters
made
man's
lord
face
grain
name
went
money
time
let
camels Please
still
daughter
see
Let
bore
Joseph
behold
spoke
life
things
Noah
Benjamin
one
saw
back
go
father's
bowed morning
done
great
Abraham's
also
Now
answered
eyes
away
destroy
Nahor
flocks
Isaac
beast
Cain
told
kind
dream
brothers
arose
mother
night
Lord
days
king
words
set
Bethel
flock
ate
die
conceived
children
Sodom
drink
wives
male
covenant
Israel
given
field
servants
please
lifted
come
brother
looked
hands
Rebekah
ten
indeed
place
Egypt
Joseph's
food
gave
voice
among
Abimelech
give
born
begot
Canaan
Judah
find
departed
make
descendants
every
Jacob
taken
two
waters
near
bless
Chief
put
Adam
another
living
may
seven
female
famine
Sarai
years
land
dwell
heard
saying
sons
ground
man
Laban

| GENESIS |

Bible Section | OLD TESTAMENT - THE PENTATEUCH

Total Words | 38,265 (The 04th Biggest Book in The Bible)

Total Verses | 1,553

Total Chapters | 50

| This is the very **1st Book of the Bible..**

Genesis is the book of beginnings, of the creation of the universe, of the ground on which we stand, of men and women an uncovering, a revealing of the real stuff of which we are all made of, both the outside and the inside, and you know, your family is found here, 'cause it's a book of the early generations of mankind.

More than that though, Genesis a verbal photo album, it's a big book of biographies, and I tell you, no soap opera can compete with the characters in these fifty chapters my friends, I mean look at Jacob, a man so twisted, if he swallowed a nail he would spit out a screw!

But, most importantly, after the record of the fall of man, with the consequent introduction of the black poison of sin into humanity's center, couched in those early chapters of Genesis, is

THE PROMISE OF A COMING CHAMPION, A 'HEAD CRUSHER,' WHO WILL SQUASH THAT OLD DEVIL INTO THE DIRT AND MAKE EVERYTHING RIGHT, AFTER EVERYTHING WENT SO TERRIBLY WRONG!

| GENESIS | 01 of 66 |

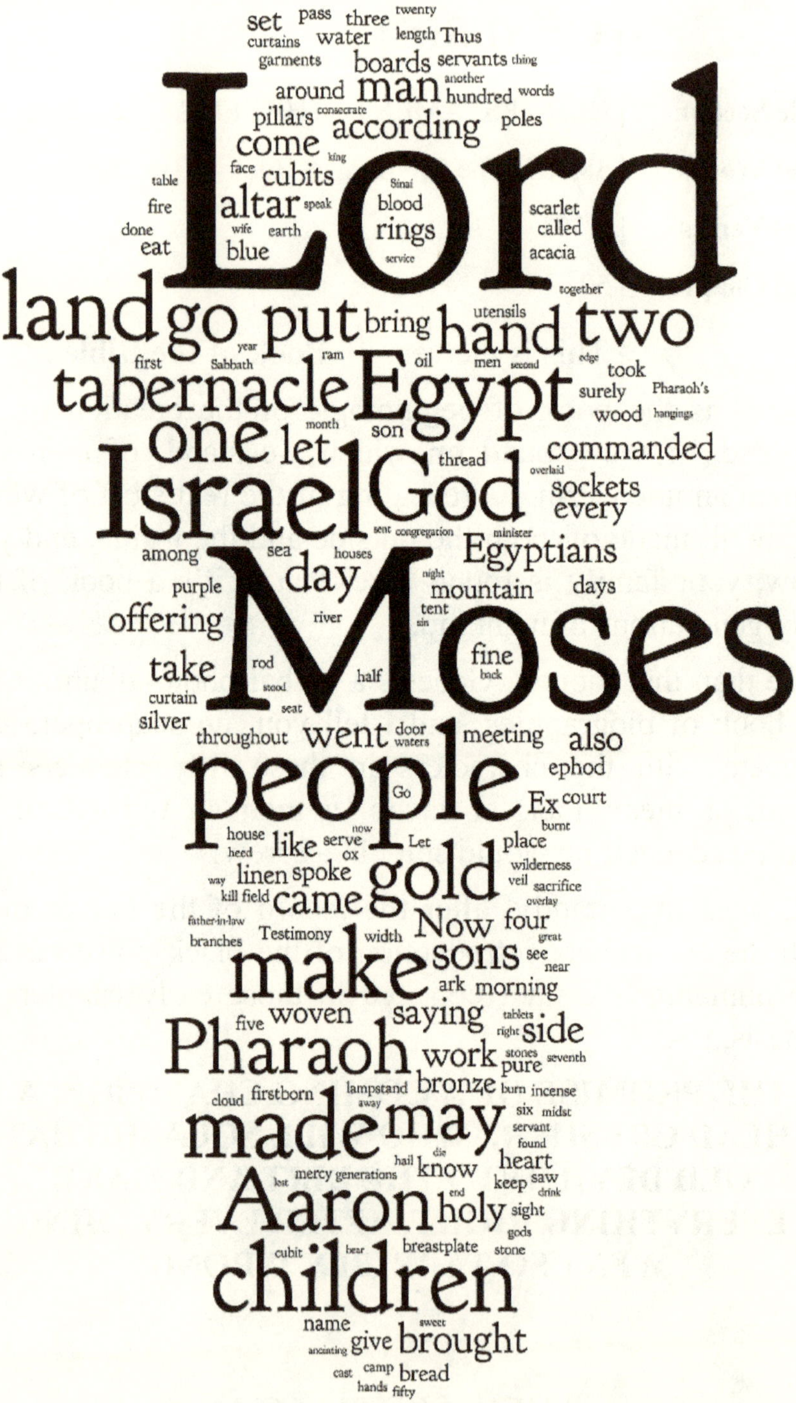
set
pass
three
twenty
curtains
water
length
Thus
garments
boards
servants
thing
another
around
man
hundred
words
pillars
consecrate
according
poles
come
king
Lord
face
cubits
table
Sinai
fire
altar
speak
blood
scarlet
done
wife
earth
rings
called
eat
blue
service
acacia
together
land
go
put
bring
utensils
hand
two
year
ram
oil
men
second
edge
first
Sabbath
took
tabernacle
Egypt
surely
Pharaoh's
wood
hangings
month
son
one
let
commanded
thread
Israel
God
overlaid
sockets
every
sent
congregation
minister
among
sea
houses
Egyptians
day
night
purple
mountain
days
tent
offering
river
sin
Moses
take
rod
fine
half
back
stood
curtain
seat
silver
throughout
went
door
waters
meeting
also
ephod
people
Go
Ex
court
burnt
house
now
heed
like
serve
Let
place
ox
way
linen
spoke
gold
wilderness
veil
sacrifice
kill
field
came
overlay
father-in-law
Now
four
Testimony
width
branches
great
see
make
sons
near
ark
morning
five
woven
saying
tablets
right
side
Pharaoh
work
stones
seventh
pure
firstborn
lampstand
bronze
burn
incense
cloud
away
six
midst
made
may
servant
found
die
hail
heart
know
mercy
generations
lost
keep
saw
end
drink
Aaron
holy
sight
gods
cubit
bear
breastplate
stone
children
name
sweet
anointing
give
brought
cast
camp
bread
hands
fifty

| EXODUS |

Bible Section	| OLD TESTAMENT - THE PENTATEUCH
Total Words	| 32,684 (The 07th Biggest Book in The Bible)
Total Verses	| 1,213
Total Chapters	| 40

| This is the **2nd Book of the Bible.**

Genesis left us with Jacob's small family tucked away in the land of Goshen, and over the centuries, from this family sprouted the twelve tribes of Israel, but now in Egypt, they are slaves longing for release and looking for a deliverer. Enter, stage left, "MOSES, THE LAWGIVER!"

Even so, it was God who really delivered the Israelites and He did it through blood, then led them, fed them, put up with them and eventually placed them in the Promised Land.

More though than the fiery blazing mountain of Horeb and the booming voice of God which filled the Israelites with a pant-filling fear, it is the sacrificial Lamb of the Passover and it is the blood painted on the lintel and door posts of exit ways that shows God's powerful protection and deliverance from all-pursuing justice.

YES, EXODUS IS THE 'BUY BACK' BOOK! IT'S THE STORY OF THE LOVE OF GOD – A LOVE OF A VERY JEALOUS KIND.

| EXODUS | 2 of 66 |

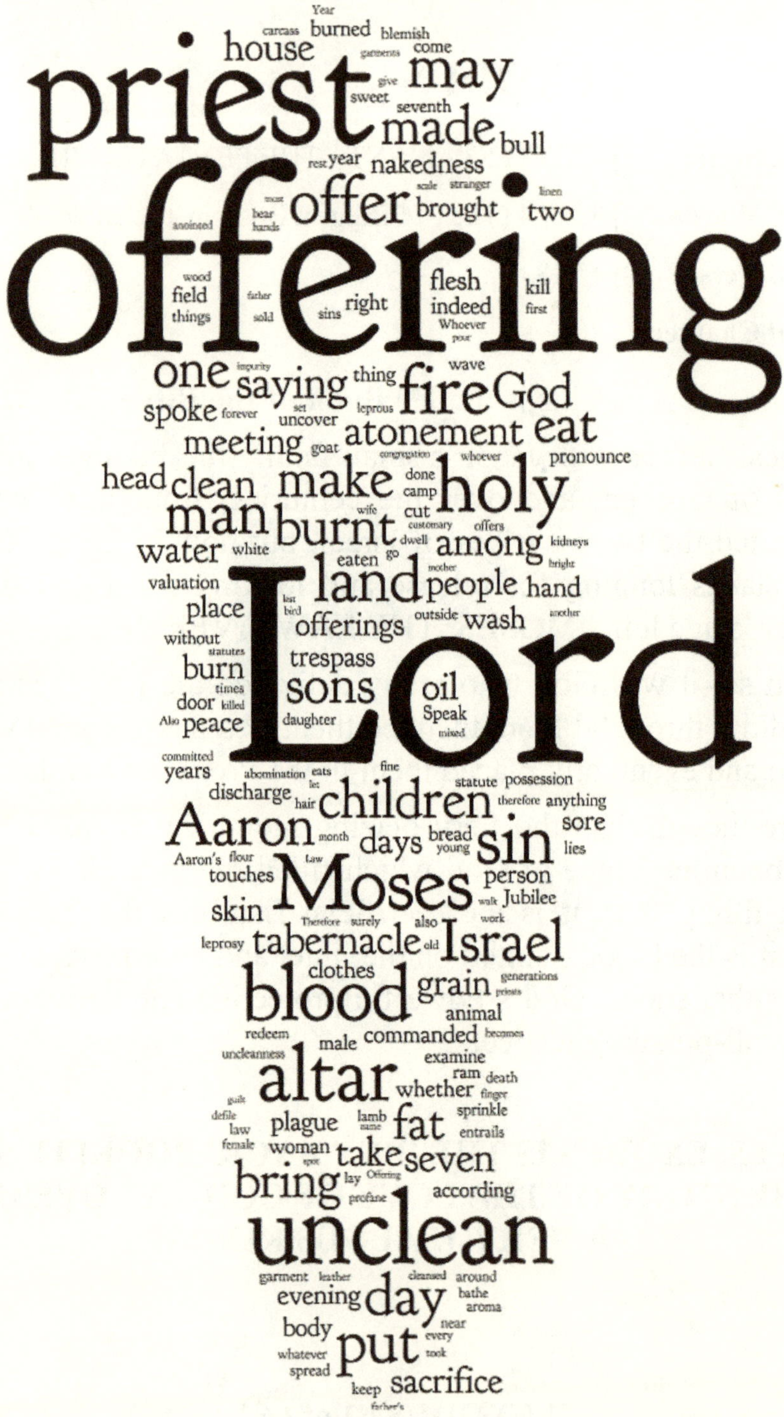

Year
carcass burned blemish
house come
priest may
give
sweet seventh
made bull
rest year nakedness
scale stranger
offer brought linen
bear two
anointed hands
offering
wood flesh kill
field father
things sold sins right indeed first
Whoever
pour
one impurity wave
saying thing fire God
spoke forever set leprous
uncover
meeting atonement eat
goat congregation whoever pronounce
head clean make done holy
camp
man wife cut
burnt customary offers
water white dwell among kidneys
eaten go bright
valuation mother
land people hand
place lest bird
outside wash another
without offerings
statutes
trespass
burn
Lord
times sons oil
door killed
Speak
Also peace daughter
mixed
committed
years fine
abomination eats statute possession
let
discharge hair children therefore anything
Aaron sore
month days bread sin
young lies
Aaron's flour law
touches Moses person
skin walk Jubilee
Therefore surely also work
leprosy tabernacle old Israel
clothes
blood grain generations
priests
animal
redeem
male commanded becomes
uncleanness examine
ram death
altar whether finger
guilt
defile lamb sprinkle
law plague fat
same entrails
female woman
take seven
spot
lay Offering
bring according
profane
unclean
garment leather cleansed around
evening day bathe
aroma
body near
every
put took
whatever
spread
keep sacrifice
father's

| LEVITICUS |

Bible Section	| OLD TESTAMENT - THE PENTATEUCH
Total Words	| 24,541 (The 12th Biggest Book in The Bible)
Total Verses	| 859
Total Chapters	| 27

| This is the **3rd Book of the Bible.**

When God, leading His people in the wilderness in the form of a pillar of smoke during the day, and a pillar of fire during the night, settled on a place to stop, that vast, moving and organized host of marching Israel, also halted with Him and put up their tents together. There in the very middle of those millions of folk, it was the Levites who also pitched the very tent of the Tabernacle of God, and once erected, God's tent received that same fiery pillar at its own center, even the touchdown of that terrific light-tornado coming to rest on the solid gold mercy seat, right there above the Ark of the Covenant!

Surrounding this glorious, pulsating and plutonium-like core, was but one group of people, even the primary people of service, even the bodyguards of God if you will! The Levites.

LEVITICUS IS THEIR OPERATIONS MANUAL.

IT'S THE BIG BOOK OF WORSHIP.

IT'S THE BIG BOOK OF BLOOD AND GUTS!

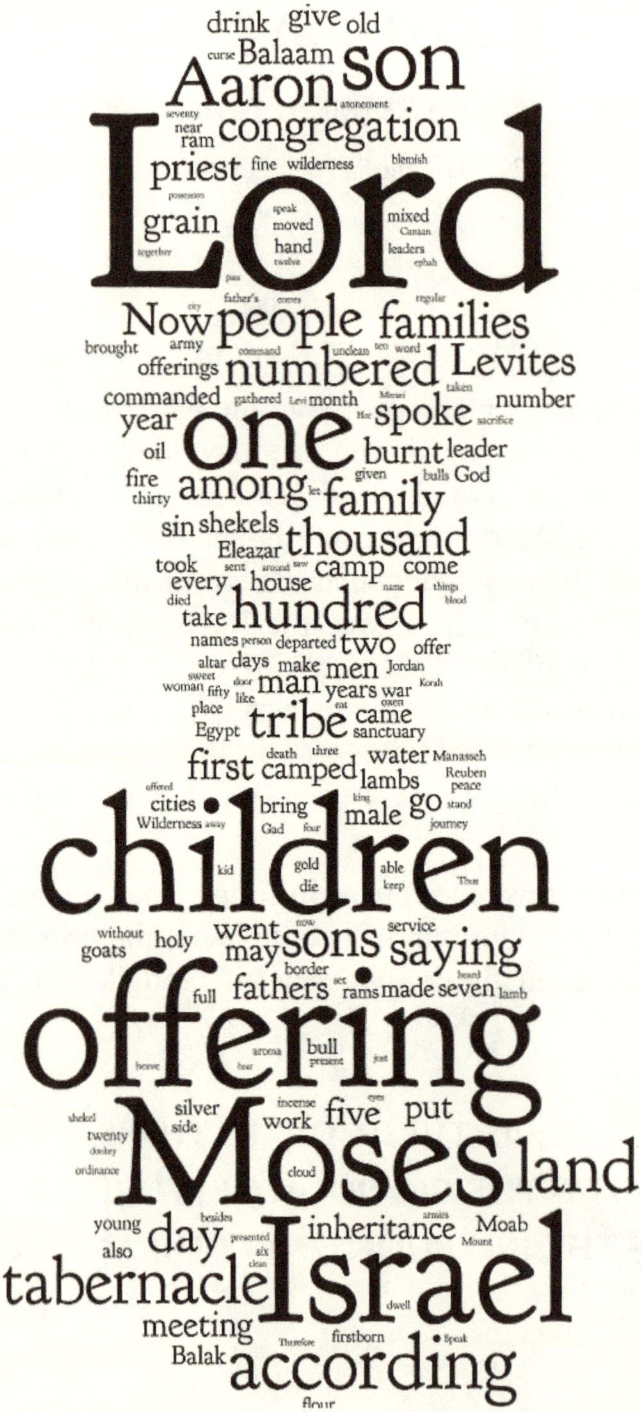
drink give old
curse Balaam son
Aaron
seventy atonement
near
ram congregation
Lord
priest fine wilderness blemish
grain speak moved hand mixed Canaan leaders
together twelve ephah
father's regular
Now people families
brought army command unclean word
offerings numbered Levites
commanded gathered Levi month taken number
year one spoke sacrifice
oil burnt leader
fire given bulls God
thirty among family
sin shekels
Eleazar thousand
took sent around camp come
every house name things
died blood
take hundred
names person departed two offer
altar days make men Jordan
sweet woman fifty door man years war Korah
place like eat oxen
Egypt tribe came sanctuary
death three water Manasseh
first camped lambs Reuben
offered peace
cities bring king go stand
Wilderness away Gad four male journey
children
kid gold able
die keep Thus
without went now service
goats holy may sons saying
border
full fathers set rams made seven lamb
offering
aroma bull
heave hear present
incense
silver
shekel side work five put
twenty
donkey
Moses land
ordinance cloud
young besides armies
day presented inheritance Moab
also six Mount
clean
tabernacle Israel
dwell
meeting
Therefore firstborn Speak
Balak according
flour

| NUMBERS |

Bible Section | OLD TESTAMENT - THE PENTATEUCH

Total Words | 32,893 (The 06th Biggest Book in The Bible)

Total Verses | 1,288

Total Chapters | 36

| This is the **Book of the Bible.**

Numbers is the book of murmurings and mumblings, and the double numberings of Israel, telling of how God trains His troops for war and then brings them to the swelling of the Jordan, just across from the mighty walls of Jericho.

Yes, this book is really the tale of two generations, tested in the wilderness for over forty years. The first generation failed to cross over Jordon because of unbelief, but the wilderness-birthed children of those condemned and black-hearted, unbelieving folk, fared much better. Though the wilderness would make that second generation winners at the last, the central and massive message of the book of Numbers, carried on the shockwave of that evil and rebellious explosion, right through to the New Testament and today, is quite frighteningly and simply this,

"BEWARE, BRETHREN, LEST THERE BE IN ANY OF YOU AN EVIL HEART OF UNBELIEF IN DEPARTING FROM THE LIVING GOD!"

THINK ON. YOU HAVE BEEN WARNED!

| NUMBERS | 4 of 66 |

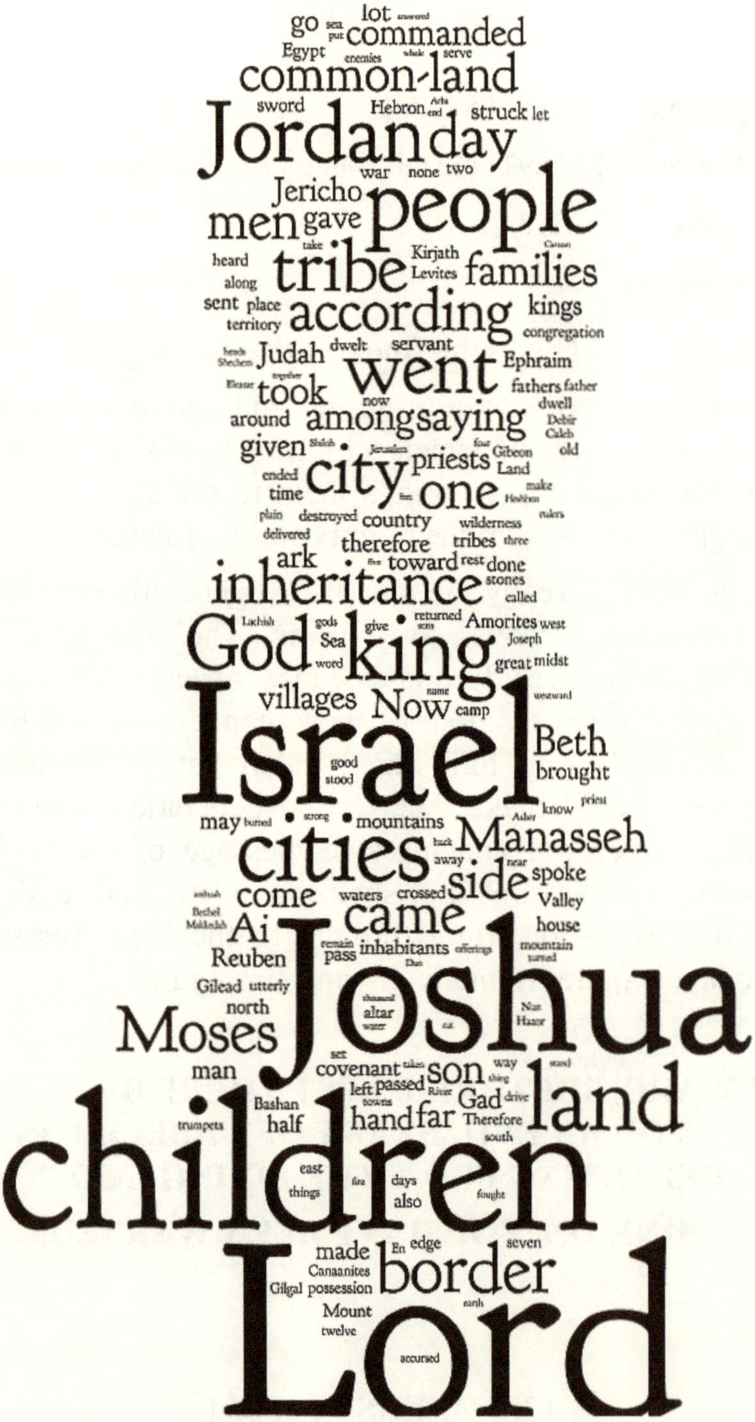
lot
go
sea
put
commanded
Egypt
enemies
whole
serve
common-land
sword
Hebron
end
struck
let
Jordan
day
war
none
two
Jericho
men
gave
people
take
heard
Kirjath
tribe
Levites
families
along
sent
place
territory
according
kings
congregation
Judah
dwelt
servant
Shechem
went
Ephraim
took
now
fathers
father
around
among
saying
dwell
Debir
Caleb
given
four
Gibeon
old
ended
city
priests
Land
time
one
make
plain
destroyed
country
wilderness
rulers
delivered
therefore
tribes
three
ark
toward
rest
done
inheritance
stones
called
Lachish
gods
give
returned
Amorites
west
God
Sea
king
Joseph
word
great
midst
villages
Now
name
camp
westward
Israel
Beth
good
stood
brought
priest
know
may
burned
strong
mountains
Asher
cities
back
Manasseh
away
near
spoke
come
waters
crossed
side
Valley
Bethel
Ai
came
house
remain
inhabitants
offerings
mountain
Reuben
pass
turned
Gilead
utterly
north
thousand
altar
Nun
Moses
Joshua
Hazor
water
set
man
covenant
taken
son
way
stand
left
passed
River
thing
Bashan
Gad
drive
towns
trumpets
half
hand
far
Therefore
land
south
east
things
fire
days
also
fought
children
made
En
edge
seven
Canaanites
border
Gilgal
possession
earth
Mount
twelve
accursed
Lord

| DEUTERONOMY |

Bible Section | OLD TESTAMENT - THE PENTATEUCH

Total Words | 28,351 (The 08th Biggest Book in The Bible)

Total Verses | 959

Total Chapters | 34

| This is the **5th Book of the Bible.**

Deuteronomy is a strong restating of the original law of God to this new, desert-born generation of God's people. Why this need for a restating of the law of God? 'Because those who do not remember the past, are most assuredly condemned to repeat it!'

Remember, because of Israel's previous unbelieving and hard-hearted rebellion, what should have been an eleven-day journey to the Promised Land, had now taken forty blinkin' years!

So, Deuteronomy is in fact the last Will and Testament if you like, of Moses the man of God and its focus is 'loving obedience. ' Deut 6:4-6 "Hear, O Israel: The Lord our God, the Lord is one! You shall love the Lord your God with all your heart, with all your soul, and with all your strength."

You see, only the treasured appreciation of God's love poured out upon them would energize Israel to keep His laws for good;,

ONLY THAT LOVE WOULD KEEP THEM TOGETHER.

| DEUTERONOMY| 5 of 66 |

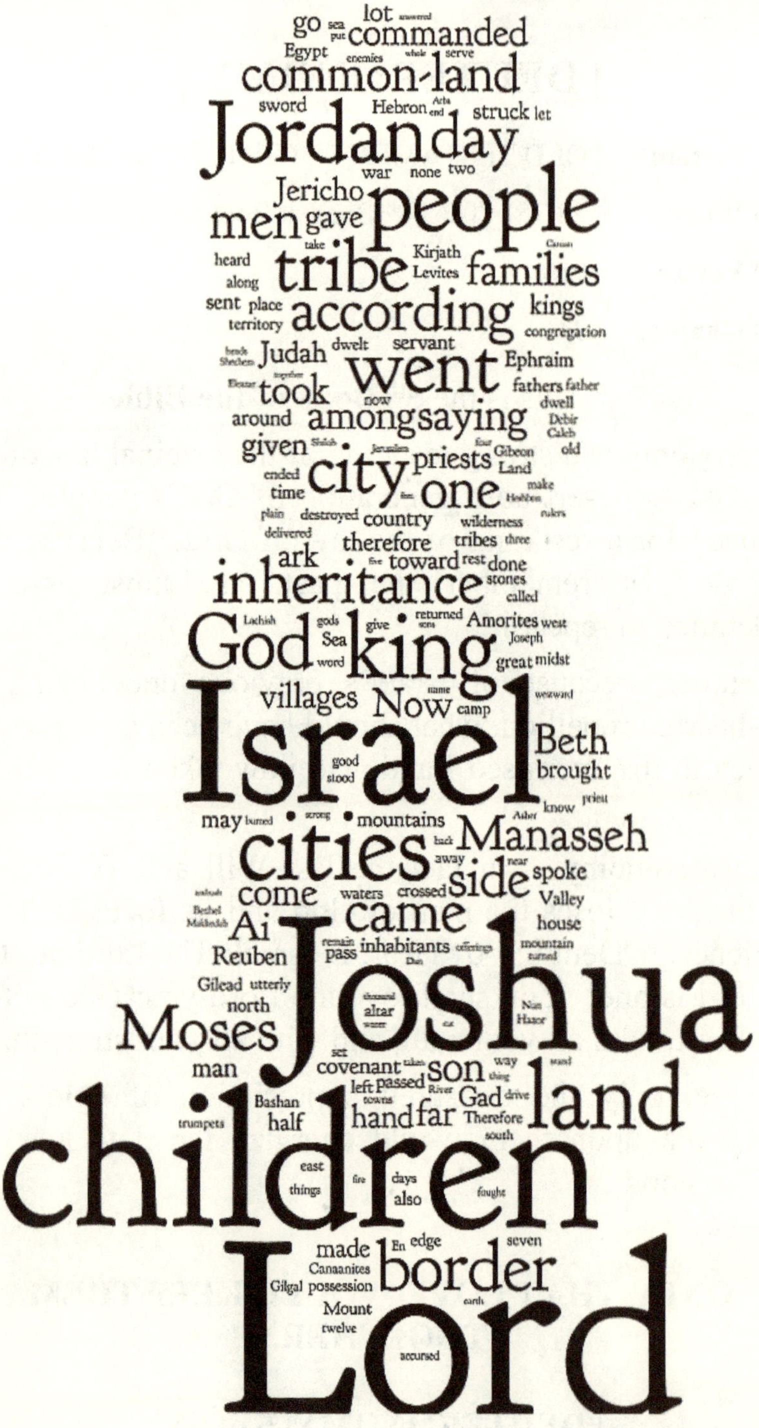

lot
go
commanded
Egypt
serve
common-land
sword
Hebron
struck
let
Jordan
day
war
none
two
Jericho
people
men
gave
heard
tribe
Kirjath
Levites
families
along
sent
place
territory
according
kings
congregation
Judah
dwelt
servant
went
Ephraim
took
fathers
father
now
dwell
around
among
saying
given
priests
Gibeon
old
city
Land
ended
time
one
make
plain
destroyed
country
wilderness
delivered
therefore
tribes
three
ark
toward
rest
done
inheritance
stones
called
returned
Amorites
west
God
give
Sea
king
Joseph
word
great
midst
villages
Now
camp
Israel
Beth
good
stood
brought
priest
may
mountains
know
cities
Manasseh
away
spoke
come
waters
crossed
side
Valley
Ai
came
house
inhabitants
mountain
Reuben
pass
Gilead
utterly
Joshua
north
altar
Moses
covenant
son
way
man
left
passed
River
Gad
drive
land
Bashan
half
hand
far
Therefore
trumpets
south
children
east
things
days
also
fought
made
edge
seven
Canaanites
border
Gilgal
possession
Mount
twelve
Lord
accursed

| JOSHUA |

Bible Section | OLD TESTAMENT - HISTORICAL BOOKS

Total Words | 18,853 (The 21st Biggest Book in The Bible)

Total Verses | 653

Total Chapters | 24

| This is the **6th Book of the Bible.**

If I might slightly alter Churchill's words to Parliament in 1940, I can almost hear General Joshua saying,

"You ask 'what is our policy?' I say, it is to wage war with all our might and with all the strength God has given us, and to wage war against a monstrous tyranny never surpassed in the dark and lamentable catalogue of human crime. That is our policy. .. You ask, 'what is our aim?' It is Victory! Victory in spite of all terrors, victory at all costs. Victory"

The book of Joshua is all about the 'God-war,' indeed Joshua is The Doomsday Book of the Canaanites, yes, Joshua is about genocide, and the commander of Heaven's armies is gripping His own sharp, two-edged sword for this one! For look now, Joshua 11:20 tells us "it was of the Lord to harden their hearts, that they should come against Israel in battle, that He might utterly destroy them, and

THAT THEY MIGHT RECEIVE NO MERCY ...."

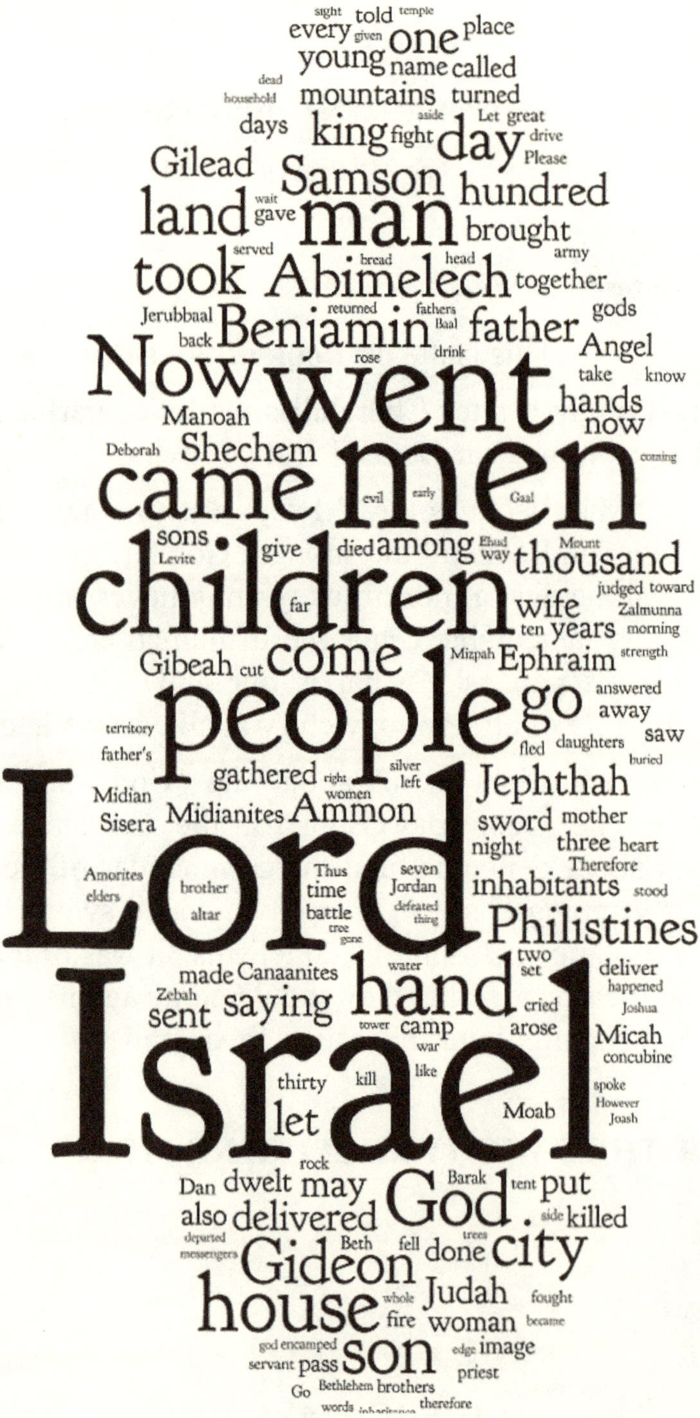
sight told temple
every given one place
young name called
dead
household mountains turned
aside Let great
days king fight day drive
Please
Gilead
Samson hundred
wait
land gave man
brought
served bread head army
took Abimelech together
Jerubbaal returned fathers gods
back Benjamin Baal father
Angel
rose drink
Now went
take know
hands
Manoah now
Deborah Shechem
coming
came men
evil early Gaal
sons
give died among Ehud Mount
Levite way thousand
children
judged toward
far wife Zalmunna
ten years morning
Mizpah
Gibeah cut come Ephraim strength
answered
people go
away
territory
saw
fled daughters
father's
buried
silver
gathered right left
Jephthah
women
Midian
Midianites Ammon
sword mother
Sisera
night three heart
Lord
Thus seven Therefore
Amorites
brother time Jordan inhabitants stood
elders
defeated
altar battle thing
Philistines
tree
gone
two
water set deliver
made Canaanites
happened
Zebah
hand
saying cried
Joshua
sent
tower camp arose
Micah
war
Israel
concubine
like
thirty kill
spoke
However
Moab Joash
let
rock
Barak
Dan dwelt may tent put
God
also delivered side killed
departed Beth fell trees
done city
messengers
Gideon
Judah
house whole fought
fire woman became
god encamped edge image
servant pass son
priest
Go Bethlehem brothers
words therefore

| JUDGES |

Bible Section | OLD TESTAMENT - HISTORICAL BOOKS

Total Words | 18,966 (The 20th Biggest Book in The Bible)

Total Verses | 618

Total Chapters | 21

| This is the **7th Book of the Bible.**

Welcome to weirdness! What with the delivery of twelve priestly, hacked-up, female body parts, sent to all the tribal leaders of Israel, all sliced from a chopped and sawn-up, gang-raped concubine, who had been quite literally sexually abused to death, make no mistake about it, the end of the book of Judges would be considered as maybe far too graphic even for a current day 'Slasher' movie.

How did Israel come to this?

How did yet another forgetful generation of drawing-back disobedience arise?

Well, the last verse in the book of Judges explains how, telling of this sorry state of the people of God, saying that, "In those days there was no king in Israel; everyone did what was right in his own eyes." (Judges 21:25 NKJV)

In answer to such apostate anarchy, God raised-up the Judges, who would become His very own law masters and this book is their own and very strange story!

WEIRD OR WHAT?

| JUDGES| 7 of 66 |

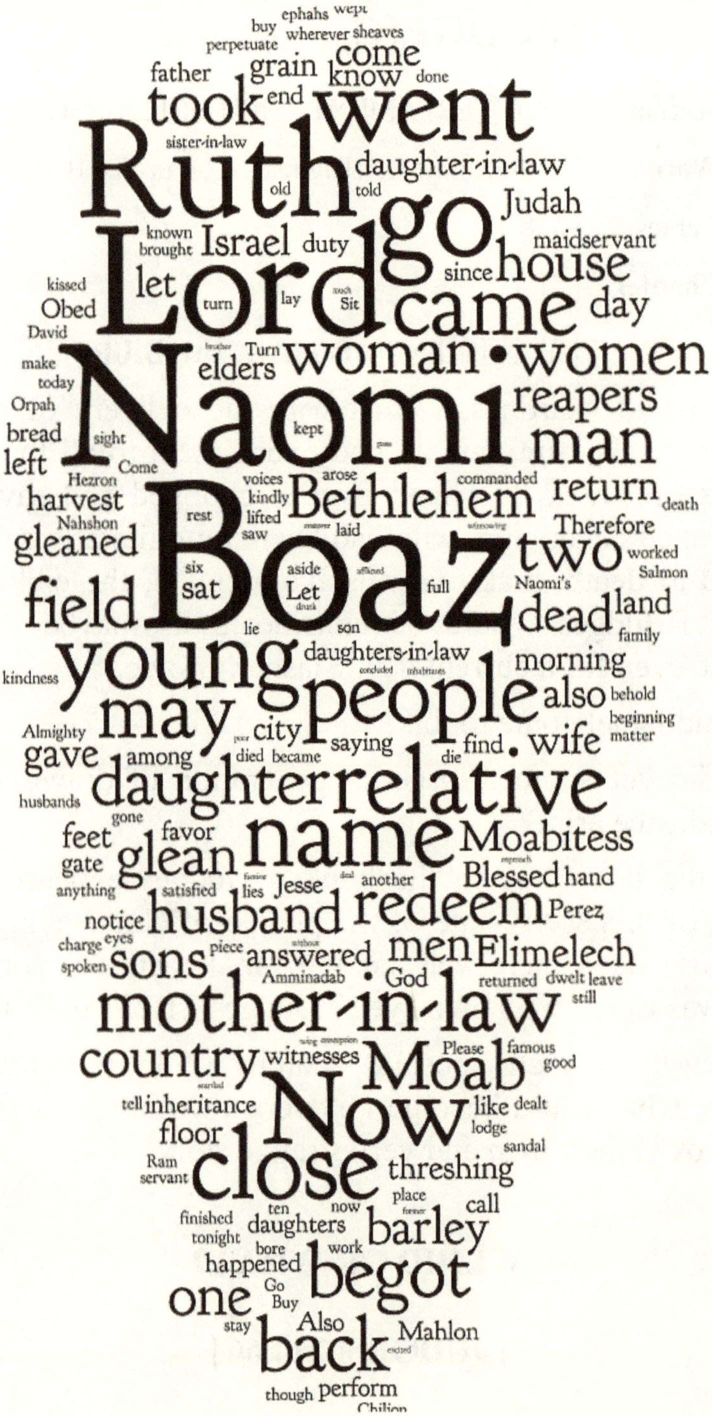

ephahs wept
buy wherever sheaves
perpetuate
come
father grain know done
took end went
sister-in-law
Ruth
daughter-in-law
old told
Judah
go
known brought Israel duty maidservant
let since house
kissed
Obed turn lay Sit
Lord came day
David
Turn
make elders woman • women
today
Naomi
Orpah reapers
bread sight kept man
left Come
Hezron voices arose commanded
harvest kindly Bethlehem return death
Nahshon rest lifted laid Therefore
saw
gleaned
Boaz two
six aside worked
sat Let Salmon
full Naomi's
field dead land
lie son family
young daughters-in-law
morning
kindness
people also behold
may
Almighty city beginning
saying find. wife matter
gave among died became die
daughter relative
husbands
gone
feet favor name Moabitess
gate glean
Blessed hand
anything satisfied lies Jesse another
redeem
notice husband Perez
charge eyes piece
spoken sons answered men Elimelech
Amminadab • God returned dwelt leave
still
mother-in-law
Please famous
country witnesses Moab good
tell inheritance like dealt
Now
lodge
floor sandal
Ram
servant close threshing
place call
ten now
finished daughters barley
tonight
bore work
happened begot
Go
one Buy
Also
stay Mahlon
back
though perform
Chilion

| RUTH |

Bible Section | OLD TESTAMENT - HISTORICAL BOOKS

Total Words | 2,574 (The 43rd Biggest Book in The Bible)

Total Verses | 85

Total Chapters | 4

| This is the **8th Book of the Bible.**

The Book of Ruth is better than any 'Heinz 57' fiction mix of Catherine Cookson, Jilly Cooper and a 'Mills & Boon' bodice- ripper, all laced together. It's about desire, you know, it's about people 'fancying the pants off one another', getting together over some popcorn. You see, the book of Ruth is a love story of metaphysical proportions!

Two of its mighty offspring will be a giant-slayer called David, and an almighty Messiah called Jesus!

What I love about this book is that it's about rawness in the presentation of real life and real people. At the beginning it's like looking at the loss of the Hindenburg, however, at the end it's like the raising of the Titanic and finding it better equipped and manned than when it sank.

Yes Ruth is about the redemption of real people, despite their wrong choices; it's about a wedding and a wonderful ending; it's about destiny and not damnation. Yes, it's about the Romance of Redemption, and it's about time you read it!

IT'S BLOOMIN' WONDERFUL!

| RUTH | 8 of 66 |

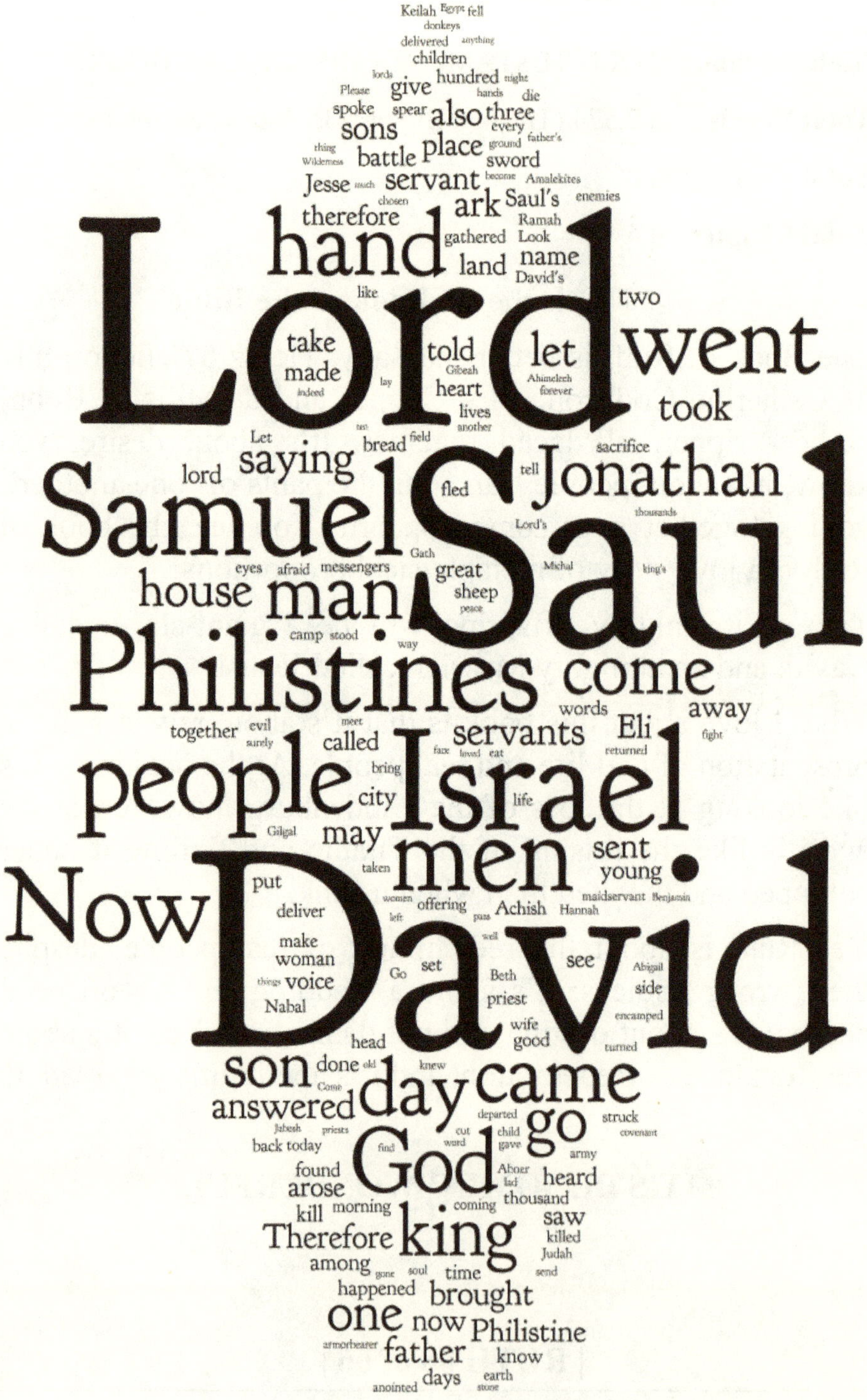

Keilah
Egypt
fell
donkeys
delivered
anything
children
lords
hundred
night
Please
give
hands
die
spoke
spear
also
three
sons
every
father's
thing
place
ground
Wilderness
battle
sword
Jesse
much
servant
become
Amalekites
chosen
ark
Saul's
enemies
therefore
Ramah
hand
gathered
Look
land
name
David's
like
two
Lord
take
told
let
went
made
Gibeah
lay
Ahimelech
indeed
heart
forever
took
lives
another
ten
Let
bread
field
saying
sacrifice
lord
tell
Jonathan
fled
Samuel
Saul
thousands
Lord's
Gath
eyes
afraid
messengers
great
Michal
king's
house
man
sheep
peace
camp
stood
way
Philistines
come
words
away
together
evil
meet
Eli
surely
servants
fight
called
face
loved
eat
returned
people
Israel
bring
city
life
Gilgal
may
sent
men
young
taken
put
Now
women
offering
maidservant
Benjamin
deliver
left
Achish
Hannah
pass
well
make
David
woman
set
see
Abigail
things
voice
Go
Beth
side
Nabal
priest
encamped
wife
head
good
turned
son
done
old
knew
Come
came
answered
day
departed
struck
Jabesh
priests
cut
child
go
covenant
back today
find
word
gave
army
God
found
Abner
lad
heard
arose
coming
thousand
kill
morning
saw
Therefore
king
killed
Judah
among
gone
soul
time
send
happened
brought
one
now
Philistine
armorbearer
father
know
anointed
days
earth
stone

| 1 SAMUEL |

Bible Section | OLD TESTAMENT - HISTORICAL BOOKS

Total Words | 25,048 (The 11th Biggest Book in The Bible)

Total Verses | 810

Total Chapters | 31

| This is the **9th Book of the Bible.**

Samuel, the last of the national judges and the first of the national prophets, rightly gives his name to one of the most dramatic books in the Bible where even today, the story of David and Goliath is known throughout the world.

David's defeat of Goliath summarizes the whole of First Samuel really, for as King Saul was "head and shoulders" above everyone else in Israel, he should have been the one to face Goliath. However, in his failure to meet the giant on the field of battle, King Saul showed his folly as a leader, and desperate lack of faith as a man, for it was there, whilst cowering in his tent, that Saul gave the keys of the Kingdom to David the Shepherd, who, full of faith and fantastic fortitude, took both Goliath's head and Saul's crown.

Yes, Samuel the seer was Israel's king-maker and First Samuel is the beginning of a tale of two kings, showing the foundation of the fledgling monarchy, which would eventually,

BRING FORTH THE PROMISED MESSIAH.

| 1 SAMUEL | 9 of 66 |

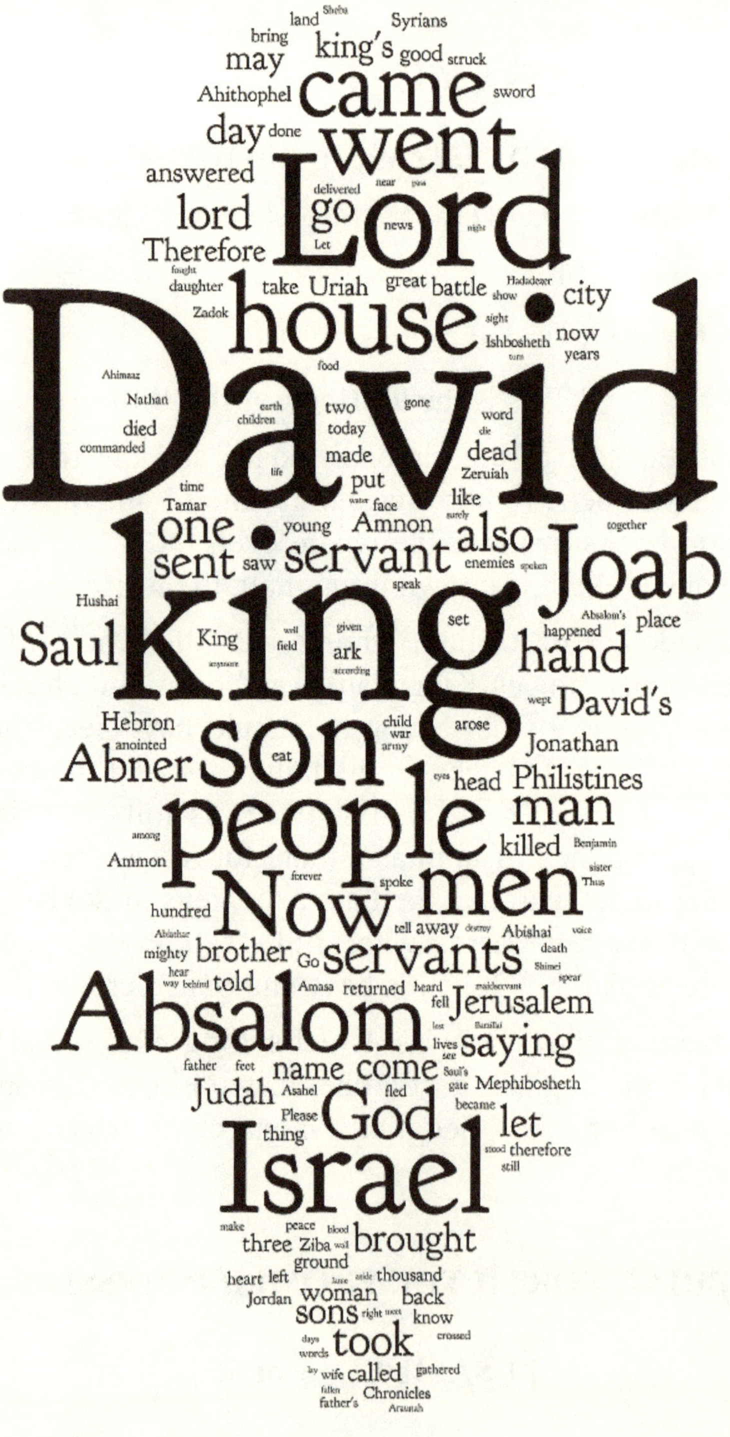
land
Sheba
Syrians
bring
king's
good
struck
may
came
Ahithophel
sword
day
done
went
answered
delivered
near
lord
go
Lord
news
Let
Therefore
fought
daughter
take
Uriah
great
battle
Hadadezer
show
city
Zadok
house
sight
Ishbosheth
now
food
years
David
Ahimaaz
Nathan
earth
children
two
gone
word
died
today
commanded
made
dead
life
put
Zeruiah
time
Tamar
water
face
like
surely
one
young
Amnon
together
also
sent
saw
servant
enemies
spoken
Joab
speak
Hushai
king
set
Absalom's
place
Saul
King
given
well
field
happened
ark
according
hand
wept
David's
Hebron
child
war
army
arose
anointed
Jonathan
Abner
son
eat
eyes
head
Philistines
people
man
among
killed
Benjamin
Ammon
sister
forever
spoke
Thus
Now
men
hundred
tell
away
destroy
Abishai
voice
Abiathar
mighty
brother
Go
servants
death
Shimei
hear
way
behind
told
Amasa
returned
heard
maidservant
spear
Absalom
fell
Jerusalem
lost
Barzillai
lives
see
saying
father
feet
name
come
Saul's
Judah
Asahel
fled
gate
Mephibosheth
became
God
Please
let
thing
Israel
stood
therefore
still
make
peace
blood
three
Ziba
wall
brought
ground
heart
left
aside
thousand
Jordan
woman
back
sons
right
went
know
days
words
took
crossed
wife
called
gathered
fallen
Chronicles
father's
Araunah

| 2 SAMUEL |

Bible Section | OLD TESTAMENT - HISTORICAL BOOKS

Total Words | 20,599 (The 17th Biggest Book in The Bible)

Total Verses | 695

Total Chapters | 24

| This is the **10th Book of the Bible.**

2nd Samuel is where all the many changes of color and flavor found in our lives are all so dirtily disclosed to us. It is, in effect, nothing short of ten Shakespearian epics, all soaked in petrol, wrapped up in a nail bomb, lit large, and then left to explode in our unsuspecting little laps.

2nd Samuel is where we see two great rebellions, both internal and external to King David's family; two great advisors in Ahithophel and Hushai, and two grand and clashing warlords in Joab and Abner.

Indeed, all these dualities of clashing-darkness and many more besides, shall constantly try to set the rising sun of David the King.

In the end though, David does reign over a united kingdom and, in death, leaves it to Solomon, that second-chance son, born of a sinful and sordid sexual relationship.

IT'S ALL ABOUT THE LIFE AND TIMES OF DAVID THE KING.

| 2 SAMUEL | 10 of 66 |

Omri
kings
took
around
found
hear
made
built
army
young
gave
evil
hundred
great
king's
David
turned
brought
Now
top
gone
way
Rehoboam
year
set
pillars
day
house
children
inner
Solomon
child
side
answered
toward
heaven
cast
Go
Jehoshaphat
priest
woman
spoke
word
happened
two
Nathan
Shimei
stones
work
reigned
went
cedar
altar
ten
prophet
come
Solomon's
three
Jezebel
Asa
God
book
rest
called
years
also
places
Let
Joab
good
stood
Israel
keep
given
blood
Ahijah
Jehoiada
five
sanctuary
Jeroboam
city
land
Ben-Hadad
may
away
statutes
killed
go
finished
back
place
sent
gods
put
Benaiah
walked
Hiram
sin
cut
days
month
one
left
dead
Naboth
Reigns
therefore
Also
written
Jerusalem
cherubim
know
told
time
water
eyes
war
earth
silver
bring
man
take
pass
gold
men
chariots
fathers
now
king
bread
heard
throne
Judah
make
Elijah
came
servant
build
acts
right
Adonijah
buried
King
saw
father
ark
Samaria
cities
let
twenty
four
offerings
Micaiah
life
son
high
Ahab
sight
kill
arose
chariot
wood
kingdom
wife
Egypt
hand
supplication
every
people
lord
prophets
bronze
cubits
seven
sons
name
walk
servants
according
commanded
Lord
eat
heart
spoken
Thus
give
wisdom
oxen
return
Baasha
became
peace
might
done
temple
saying
thousand
Chronicles
like
Therefore

| 1 KINGS |

Bible Section | OLD TESTAMENT - HISTORICAL BOOKS

Total Words | 24,512 (The 13th Biggest Book in The Bible)

Total Verses | 816

Total Chapters | 22

| This is the **11th Book of the Bible.**

1st Kings is the first book of the 'Annals of the Jewish kings.' Here is recorded the people of God's catastrophic descent into disobedience, and here is where God finally lets them go, sending them to be almost obliterated on the brick-hard boulevards of Babylon, hungry and open-mouthed below them, bellowing to be fed. Solomon's sex drive was to blame, for it was his multitude of foreign women who turned him into a sucker and wrecked the wisest man who ever lived, and in so doing, ruined the raiment of Jehovah's bride, tearing the twelve tribes asunder. Though disobedience had already sucked the milk and honey from Israel's breath, death took its time to gain power over her beauty.

IN THE MEANTIME, THE LIONS OF THE LORD, THOSE POWERFUL PROPHETS OF OLD, ARE ALWAYS TRYING TO MAKE THE BITTER WATERS SWEET AND THE BAD WAYS BETTER, BY PROCLAIMING BOTH THE LAW AND THE LETTER OF GOD.

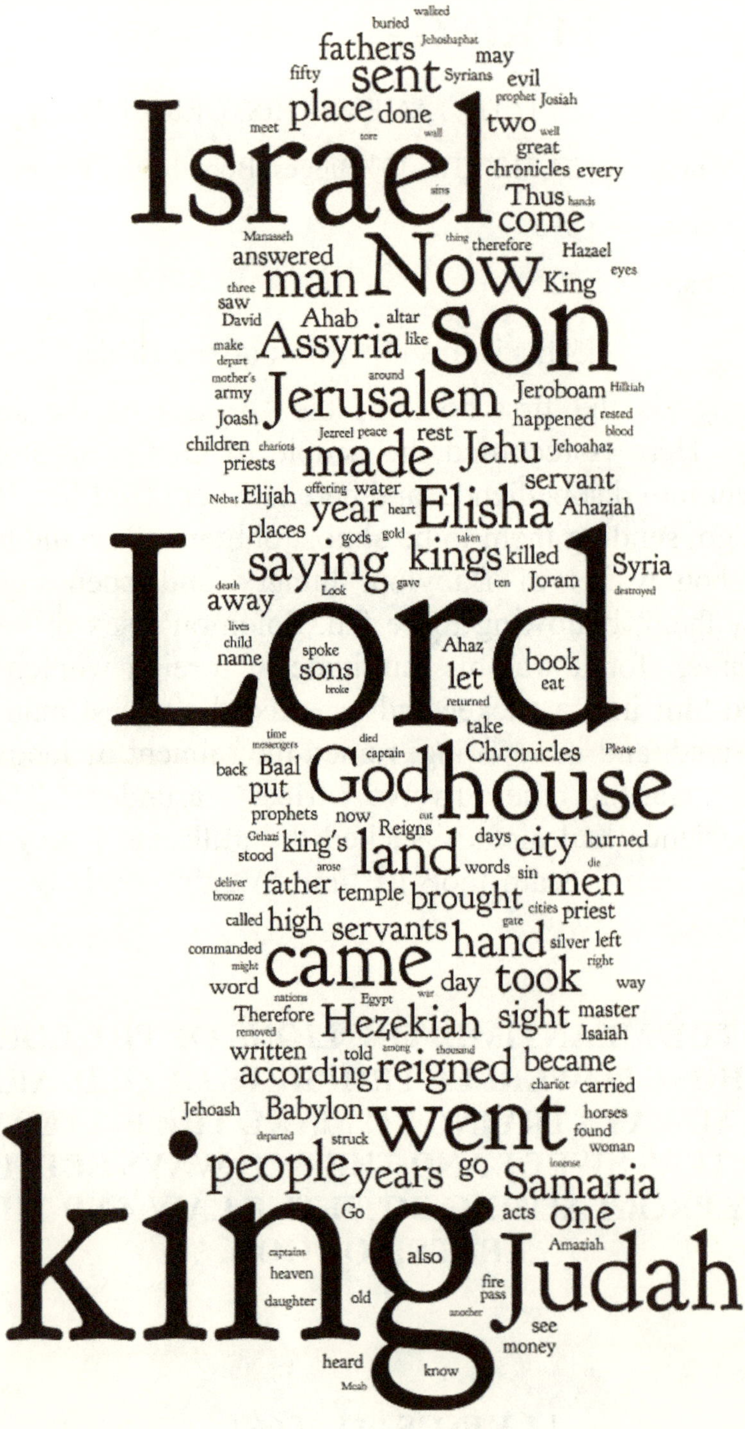
walked
buried
Jehoshaphat
fathers
may
fifty
sent
Syrians
evil
prophet
Josiah
place
done
two
meet
tore
wall
well
Israel
great
chronicles
every
sins
Thus
hands
come
Manasseh
thing
therefore
Hazael
answered
Now
eyes
three
man
King
saw
David
Ahab
altar
make
Assyria
like
son
depart
mother's
around
army
Jerusalem
Jeroboam
Hilkiah
Joash
happened
rested
blood
Jezreel
peace
rest
children
chariots
made
Jehu
Jehoahaz
priests
servant
Nebat
Elijah
offering
water
year
heart
Elisha
Ahaziah
places
gods
gold
taken
saying
kings
killed
Syria
death
Look
gave
ten
Joram
destroyed
away
Lord
lives
child
spoke
Ahaz
book
name
sons
let
eat
broke
returned
take
time
messengers
died
captain
Chronicles
Please
back
Baal
God
house
put
prophets
now
cut
Reigns
Gehazi
king's
days
city
burned
stood
land
arose
words
die
sin
deliver
father
men
bronze
temple
brought
cities
priest
called
high
gate
servants
hand
silver
left
commanded
might
came
right
word
day
took
way
nations
Egypt
war
Therefore
sight
master
removed
Hezekiah
Isaiah
written
told
among
thousand
according
reigned
became
chariot
carried
Jehoash
Babylon
went
horses
found
departed
struck
woman
people
years
go
incense
Samaria
Go
acts
one
king
Amaziah
captains
also
heaven
fire
Judah
daughter
old
pass
another
see
money
heard
know
Moab

| 2 KINGS |

Bible Section | OLD TESTAMENT - HISTORICAL BOOKS

Total Words | 23,519 (The 12th Biggest Book in The Bible)

Total Verses | 719

Total Chapters | 25

| This is the **16th Book of the Bible.**

2nd Kings is nothing short of the very picture of the second law of thermodynamics on amphetamines! It's like looking at the Lehman brothers on a spending spree. It is nothing but despairing madness. For here is the story of the disgraceful self-dismemberment and dastardly disemboweling of the children of God by their very own hand; that's right, 2nd Kings is disaster writ large, it's disaster on a stick! A bright, burning, neon stick with big, blood-red bells on it, the sound of which will make your ears tingle.

God's last attempt to turn His people around, is seen here in the usurping of these notorious kings, with the more powerful position of prophet. So, Elijah the great, is replaced by a 'slap head' called Elisha upon whose un-thatched 'bonce' was laid a double portion of the Spirit of God, which had rested upon his master, unfortunately, all to no avail,

FOR ISRAEL'S REBELLION WOULD LEAD TO GOD FINALLY FORSAKING THEM.

chief
called
according
went
captains
David
spear
offering
second
half-tribe
Saul
twenty
Gilead
throughout
therefore
Mahli
Moses
Elkanah
reigned
Benaiah
three
done
Shimei
heart
Merari
hand
defeated
every
Gershon
give
come
may
made
killed
came
father
make
Eleazar
Azariah
burnt
years
silver
twelve
time
fifth
Zadok
firstborn
Gad
Samuel
common-lands
day
days
instruments
music
son
David's
leaders
man
Eliel
great
Joab
Obed-Edom
took
daughter
Shemaiah
King
four
six
twenty-four
put
one
families
Ephraim
many
died
bronze
Solomon
forever
wife
people
treasuries
Jeduthun
house
given
heads
mighty
Caleb
Syrians
army
valor
place
houses
sister
Beth
gold
gave
Issachar
thousand
thirty
dwelt
born
Asaph
word
month
seven
let
far
Philistines
priests
bore
prepared
Levi
begot
Levites
men
towns
Hebron
captain
land
things
tabernacle
good
weight
set
Judah
like
away
sons
rest
name
tribe
work
Hezron
because
divisions
build
king
also
two
five
number
saw
built
Jerusalem
kingdom
Manasseh
Joel
children
covenant
service
Nathan
earth
God
Now
brought
sword
Oman
let
first
Heman
Ammon
battle
among
Lord
brethren
third
Also
sent
Therefore
Aaron
commanded
Benjamin
fell
brother
Zechariah
able
hundred
Israel
offerings
saying
servants
Genesis
war
gatekeepers
Kohath
fourth
bring
division
father's
altar
fathers
servant
Kish
cities
Shallum
Family
city
ark
Chief
king's

| 1 CHRONICLES |

Bible Section | OLD TESTAMENT - HISTORICAL BOOKS

Total Words | 20,365 (The 18th Biggest Book in The Bible)

Total Verses | 942

Total Chapters | 29

| This is the **13th Book of the Bible.**

The 50 million pages of Nazi information kept on the holocaust victims, are still stored in Germany on some 16 miles of shelving. This storage was important to the remnant of Jewish refugees who dared return to their European homeland, because displaced people need to know where they've come from and who and where their relatives are, for when they know this, they rediscover their anchor in space and time, and so can truly perceive their destiny in the oncoming years. Imagine then, another remnant returning to their homeland in Judah of old, not 6 years, but decades after their departure. Indeed, most of the returning exiles had been born in a foreign land and were coming back to a 'Heinz 57' variety of leftover Jews, who were now inter-married, multi-cultural, multi-faith and all messed up with it.

1ST CHRONICLES ADDRESSES THIS RESTORED AND MIXED UP REMNANT, AND BRINGS TO THE FORE, THE BLOODLINE OF JUDAH AND KING DAVID.

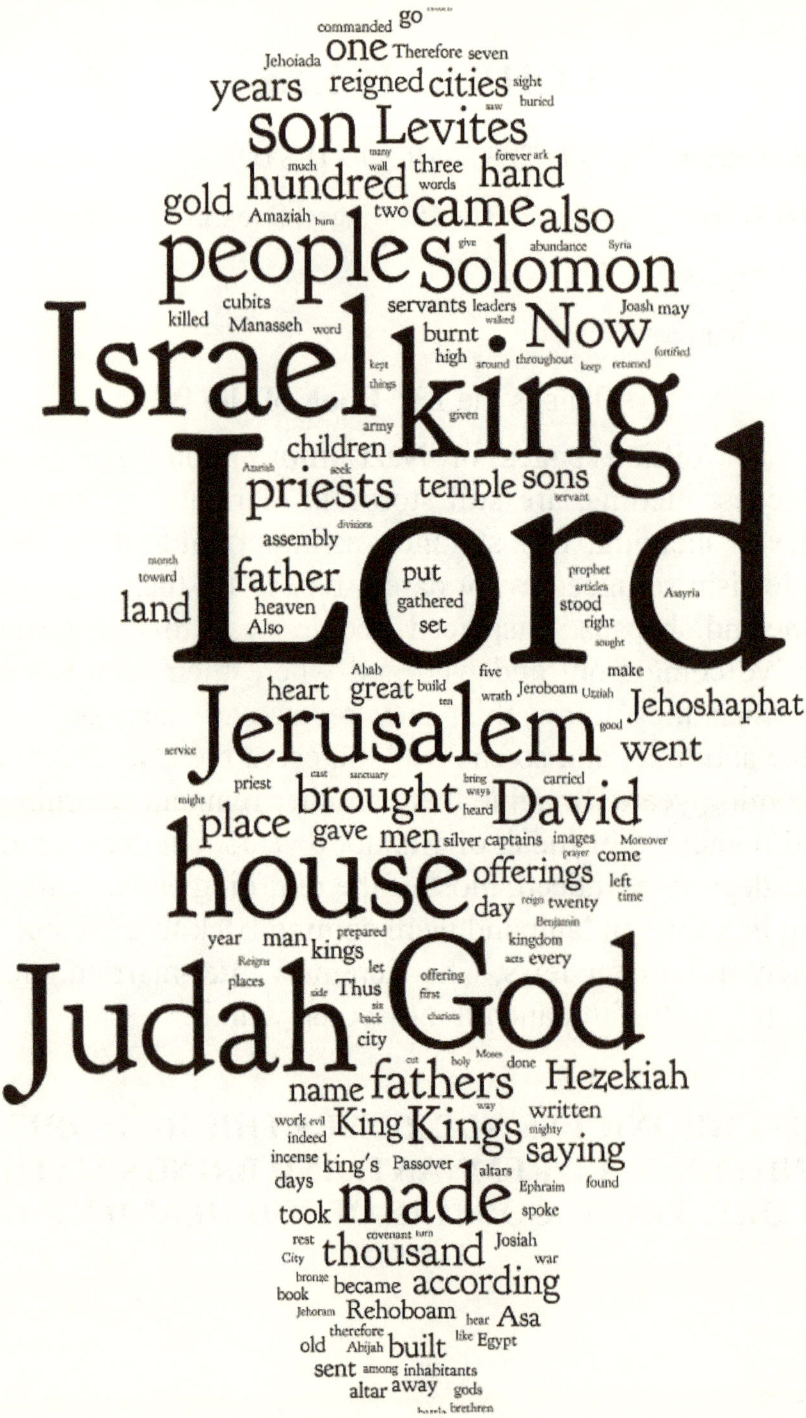

commanded
go
Jehoiada
one
Therefore
seven
years
reigned
cities
sight
saw
buried
son
Levites
many
much
wall
three
words
forever
ark
hand
gold
hundred
Amaziah
burn
two
came
also
people
give
abundance
Syria
Solomon
cubits
servants
leaders
walked
Joash
may
Israel
killed
Manasseh
word
burnt
Now
high
around
throughout
keep
returned
fortified
kept
things
king
given
army
children
Azariah
seek
priests
temple
sons
servant
divisions
assembly
Lord
month
toward
father
put
prophet
articles
Assyria
land
heaven
gathered
stood
Also
set
right
sought
Ahab
five
make
heart
great
build
ten
wrath
Jeroboam
Uzziah
Jehoshaphat
Jerusalem
good
service
went
cast
sanctuary
bring
ways
carried
priest
might
brought
heard
David
place
gave
men
silver
captains
images
Moreover
prayer
come
house
offerings
left
day
reign
twenty
time
Benjamin
year
man
prepared
kingdom
kings
acts
every
Reigns
let
offering
places
side
Thus
first
six
back
chariots
Judah
God
city
cut
holy
Moses
done
name
fathers
Hezekiah
way
work
evil
indeed
King
Kings
written
mighty
incense
king's
Passover
saying
days
altars
Ephraim
found
took
made
spoke
rest
covenant
turn
Josiah
City
thousand
war
bronze
book
became
according
Jehoram
Rehoboam
hear
Asa
therefore
old
Abijah
built
like
Egypt
sent
among
inhabitants
altar
away
gods
brethren

| 2 CHRONICLES |

Bible Section | OLD TESTAMENT - HISTORICAL BOOKS

Total Words | 26,069 (The 09th Biggest Book in The Bible)

Total Verses | 822

Total Chapters | 36

| This is the **14th Book of the Bible.**

2nd Chronicles is about Judah's history from Solomon's reign to the conclusion of the Babylonian exile. You see Jerusalem, that now broken down capital city, its trashed temple center, and its polluted people, must all be rebuilt to re-enable both proclamation and service to start again.

The sands of biblical instruction and the cement of warning are thoroughly combined in 2nd Chronicles to turn the returned remnant's toes into laying some solid concrete foundations for future generations. Ezra the scribe is the writer here, and he is recreating a nation, re-centering its people on its capital, its temple, its service, its privilege and its pride of place above all the nations of the earth.

To this end, Ezra spotlights all the great reformers of Judah's past, even the greatest and best kings. You see Ezra knew that

"THOSE WHO CANNOT REMEMBER THE PAST ARE CONDEMNED TO REPEAT IT." AND HE HAD NO INTENTION OF LETTING THAT HAPPEN AGAIN.

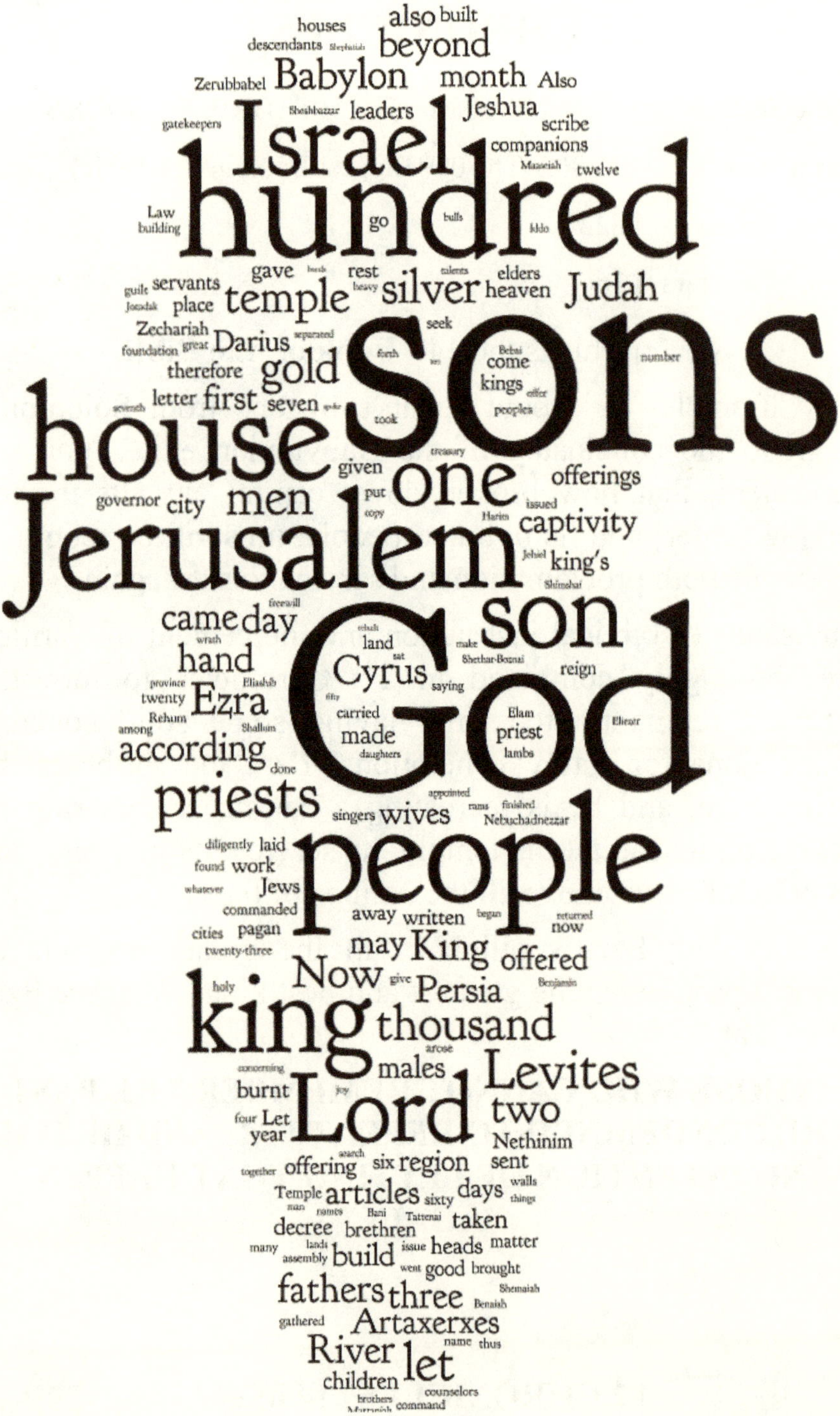

also built
houses
descendants
beyond
Zerubbabel
Babylon
month
Also
leaders
Jeshua
gatekeepers
Israel
scribe
companions
twelve
Law
building
hundred
go
gave
rest
elders
servants
temple
silver
heaven
Judah
place
Zechariah
seek
foundation
great
Darius
sons
number
therefore
gold
come
kings
letter
first
seven
peoples
house
took
given
one
offerings
governor
city
men
put
issued
captivity
Jerusalem
king's
came
day
son
hand
land
reign
Cyrus
God
province
twenty
Ezra
carried
Elam
Rehum
among
priest
according
made
lambs
done
priests
singers
wives
Nebuchadnezzar
diligently
laid
found
work
people
Jews
commanded
away
written
returned
now
cities
pagan
twenty-three
may
King
offered
holy
Now
Persia
king
thousand
males
Levites
burnt
Lord
two
four
Let
year
Nethinim
together
offering
six
region
sent
walls
Temple
articles
days
sixty
decree
brethren
taken
many
build
heads
matter
good
brought
fathers
three
Shemaiah
gathered
Artaxerxes
River
let
name
thus
children
counselors
brothers
command

| EZRA|

Bible Section | OLD TESTAMENT - HISTORICAL BOOKS

Total Words | 7,440 (The 30th Biggest Book in The Bible)

Total Verses | 280

Total Chapters | 10

| This is the **15th Book of the Bible.**

'Cometh the hour, cometh the man,' and so from the bowels of captivity in Babylon, activated, focused, determined, zealous, all studied up, prayed up and powerfully prepared, let me introduce you to 'Ezra The Scribe.' Even the very man who would both collect and collate all the Old Testament books.

Ezra, you see, having no temple in Babylon to serve, had set his heart on knowing the Word of God and living by it. AND THIS made Ezra look like, long for, and live, like no other man on earth. Indeed from Ezra we find the rise of the scribes, and today's wooden pulpit preachers, for Ezra is the first recorded man to set up a wooden pulpit and from that, to then give birth to the whole Jewish Synagogue system, from which framework, all our present day Christian churches hang their every structure.

EZRA'S 'RAISON D'ÊTRE' WAS TO REBUILD THE NATION'S SPIRITUAL FOUNDATIONS ON THE VERY WORD OF GOD, AND HE DID SO MOST DARINGLY.

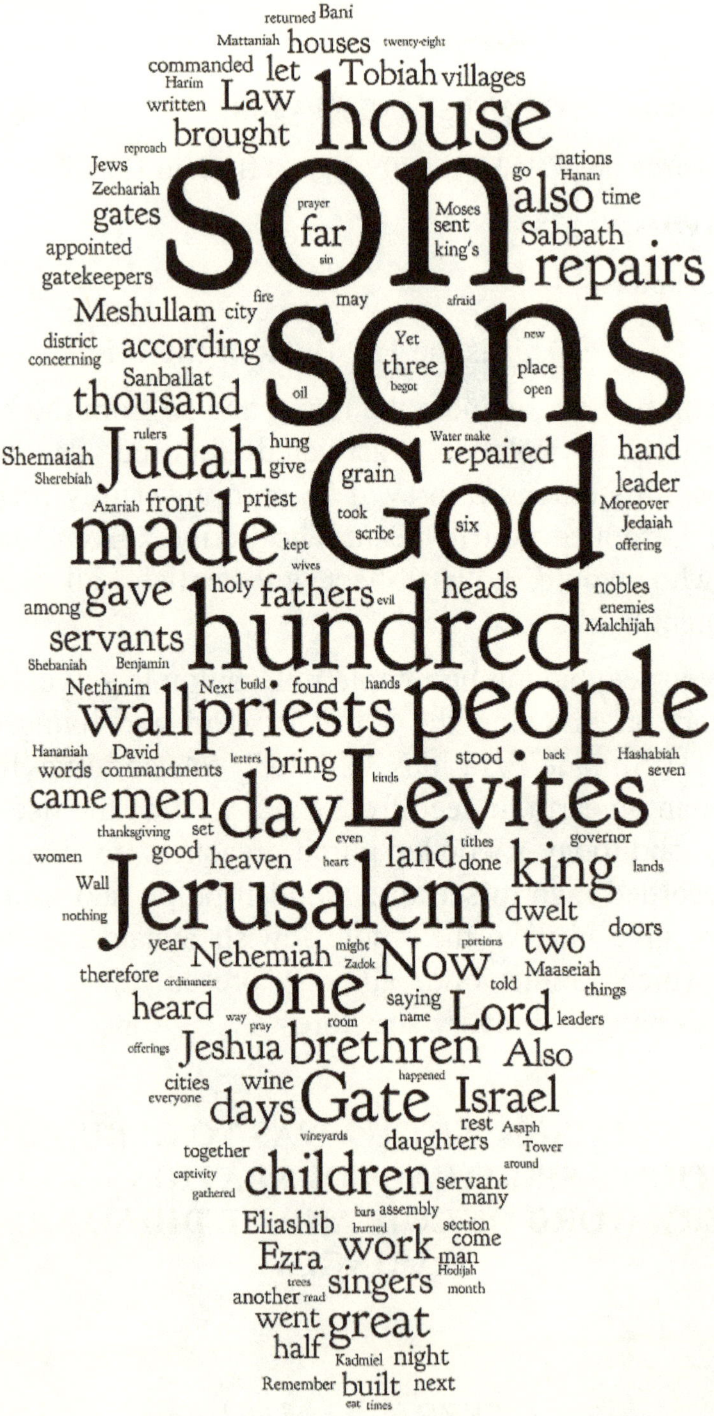
returned Bani
Mattaniah houses twenty-eight
commanded let Tobiah villages
Harim
written Law
house
brought
reproach
nations
Jews
son
go
Hanan
Zechariah
also time
prayer
Moses
gates
sent
far
Sabbath
appointed
king's
sin
repairs
gatekeepers
fire
may
afraid
Meshullam city
sons
district
Yet
new
concerning
according
Sanballat
three
place
begot
open
oil
thousand
rulers
Water make
Shemaiah
Judah
hung
repaired
hand
give
Sherebiah
grain
God
leader
Azariah front priest
Moreover
took
Jedaiah
made
six
scribe
kept
offering
wives
gave
holy
fathers
heads
nobles
among
evil
enemies
servants
hundred
Malchijah
Shebaniah
Benjamin
Nethinim
Next build found
hands
wall
priests
people
Hananiah David
stood
back
Hashabiah
words commandments
letters
bring
seven
kinds
came
men
day
Levites
thanksgiving set
even
tithes
governor
women
good
heaven
heart
land
done
king
lands
Wall
Jerusalem
nothing
dwelt
doors
year
might
portions
two
Nehemiah
Zadok
Now
Maaseiah
therefore
ordinances
one
told
things
heard
saying
Lord
way
pray
room
name
leaders
offerings
Jeshua
brethren
Also
cities
wine
happened
everyone
days
Gate
Israel
rest
Asaph
vineyards
together
daughters
Tower
around
captivity
children
servant
gathered
many
bars assembly
Eliashib
burned
section
come
Ezra
work
man
Hodijah
trees
singers
another
read
month
went
great
half
Kadmiel
night
Remember
built
next
eat times

| NEHEMIAH |

Bible Section | OLD TESTAMENT - HISTORICAL BOOKS

Total Words | 10,480 (The 27th Biggest Book in The Bible)

Total Verses | 406

Total Chapters | 13

| This is the **16th Book of the Bible.**

Nehemiah (meaning "comforted by Jehovah") was cup-bearer to King Artexerxes Longimanus, serving him in the Citadel of Shushan, but more than that, Nehemiah was a spiritual entrepreneur, packing a 'game-changing' mission plan out of which came the book of Nehemiah, which is the ultimate rebuilding reference manual.

As with Ezra, there is no record of a Divine visitation or direct call on Nehemiah's life which led him to do what he did, rather, Nehemiah presents himself in chapter one, simply as a man who was aware of the times and whose compassionate heart was moved for his countrymen to prayerfully and deeply consider both their and his position, and in the so doing, Nehemiah had in his heart and mind, constructed a plan of possible redemption. You must see this! For Nehemiah did not ask God for a plan, no, NEHEMIAH ALREADY HAD A PLAN and it was for one thing –

THE REBUILDING REDEMPTION OF JERUSALEM, WHICH GOD THROUGH NEHEMIAH ACCOMPLISHED, AGAINST ALL ODDS.

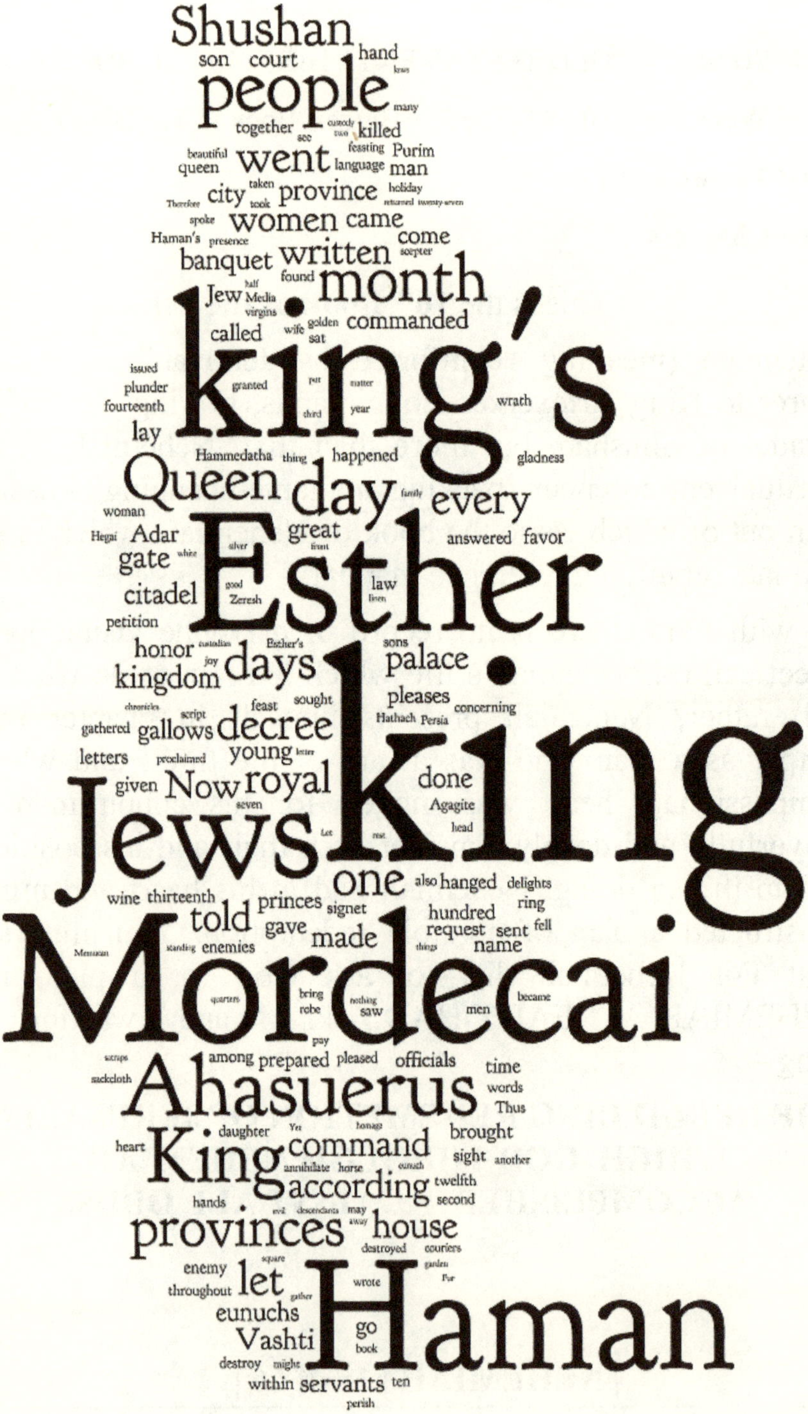
Shushan
hand
son
court
people
many
together
killed
see
feasting
Purim
beautiful
queen
went
language
man
city
taken
province
holiday
Therefore
took
returned
twenty-seven
spoke
women
came
Haman's
presence
come
scepter
banquet
written
half
found
month
Jew
Media
virgins
golden
commanded
called
wife
sat
king's
issued
plunder
granted
put
matter
fourteenth
third
year
wrath
lay
Hammedatha
thing
happened
gladness
Queen
day
family
every
woman
Esther
Hegai
Adar
great
answered
favor
gate
white
silver
front
good
law
citadel
Zeresh
listen
petition
honor
custodian
joy
Esther's
sons
palace
kingdom
days
king
chronicles
script
feast
sought
pleases
concerning
Hathach
Persia
gathered
gallows
decree
letters
proclaimed
young
letter
given
Now
royal
done
seven
Agagite
Jews
Let
head
one
also
hanged
delights
wine
thirteenth
princes
signet
ring
told
hundred
gave
request
sent
fell
standing
enemies
made
things
name
Mordecai
Memucan
quarters
bring
robe
nothing
saw
became
men
pay
scraps
among
prepared
pleased
officials
time
sackcloth
Ahasuerus
words
Thus
daughter
Yet
homage
brought
heart
King
command
sight
another
annihilate
horse
eunuch
according
twelfth
second
hands
evil
descendants
may
away
provinces
house
destroyed
couriers
square
garden
enemy
let
throughout
wrote
Pur
gather
Haman
eunuchs
go
Vashti
book
destroy
might
within
servants
ten
perish

| ESTHER |

Bible Section	| OLD TESTAMENT – HISTORICAL BOOKS
Total Words	| 5,633 (The 34th Biggest Book in The Bible)
Total Verses	| 167
Total Chapters	| 10

| This is the **17th Book of the Bible.**

Esther is where the hand of God is seen in all the gloves of human circumstance; yes, this is the book where the name of God is never mentioned but where He is seen to be working: in the bedroom; in the battle plans; in the bottles of wine and even in the mouth of that royal buffoon, Xerxes.

Yes, God is seen in the book of Esther, bending history to His divine purposes, so that He might fulfil His promises to His forgetful people, who, while sailing on the stormy seas of His permissive will, see up close that the providences of God make great doors to swing on even the smallest of hinges. Nothing and no one, you see, is outside of the Sovereign influence of God, and this we call 'Providence,' and **that** is the core of what Esther is all about, even

TO SHOW US THE CONCENTRATED ATTENTION OF GOD BROUGHT TO BEAR IN EVERY DETAIL OF OUR LIVES.

| ESTHER |17 of 66 |

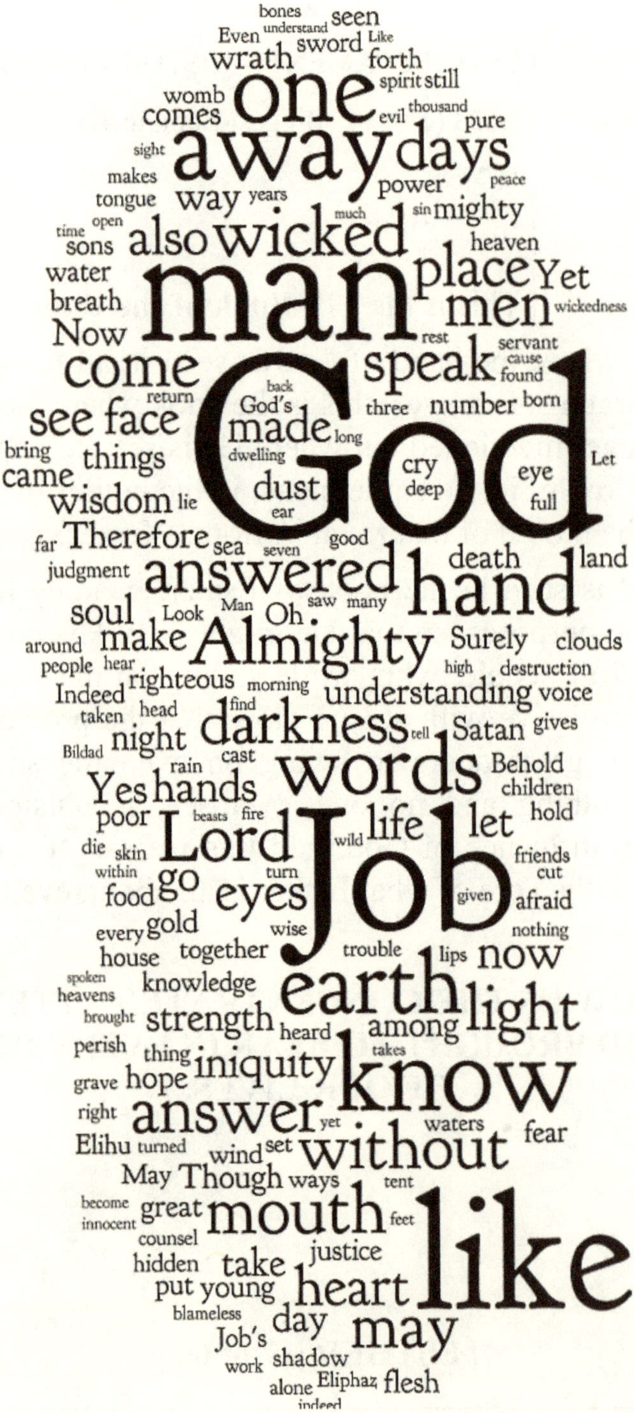

bones
understand seen
Even sword Like
wrath forth
womb one spirit still
comes evil thousand pure
sight away days
makes power peace
tongue way years
time open much sin mighty
sons also wicked heaven
water man place Yet
breath men wickedness
Now rest servant
come speak cause found
back
return God's three number born
see face made long
bring things dwelling God Let
came cry eye
dust deep
wisdom lie ear full
far Therefore sea seven good
judgment answered death land hand
soul Look Man Oh saw many
around make Almighty Surely clouds
people hear high destruction
Indeed righteous morning understanding voice
taken head find
Bildad night darkness tell Satan gives
rain cast
Yes hands words Behold children
poor beasts fire life let hold
die skin Lord wild Job friends
within turn cut
food go eyes given afraid
every gold wise nothing
house together trouble lips now
spoken heavens knowledge earth
brought strength light
heard among
perish thing takes
grave hope iniquity know
right answer yet waters fear
Elihu turned wind set without
May Though ways tent
become innocent great mouth feet like
counsel justice
hidden take
put young heart
blameless day may
Job's shadow
work
alone Eliphaz flesh
indeed

| JOB |

Bible Section | OLD TESTAMENT - POETRY

Total Words | 18,098 (22nd Biggest Book in The Bible)

Total Verses | 1070

Total Chapters | 42

| This is the **18th** Book in the Bible.

IT'S WHERE the spiritual veil is drawn aside to reveal Satan regularly appearing before God to give an account of his earthly actions. How strange is that? In addition to this, God seems to incite a vicious trial upon his most favored servant, Job, in which Satan seeks to prove three things: That people do and say the right thing only when it's worth it;

That there is no such thing as an unselfish following of God, and therefore,

God is only worth worshipping if He keeps coming up with the goods of provision and protection, in other words they only follow Him for what they can get … not because of who He is.

It's a hell of an accusation for sure and it's made before all the watching hosts of the spiritual realm; make no mistake about it, job might be the whipping boy here – but the attack is made by Satan on the worthiness of the very essence of god himself.

THIS IS THE SCARIEST BOOK OF THEM ALL!

| JOB |18 of 66 |

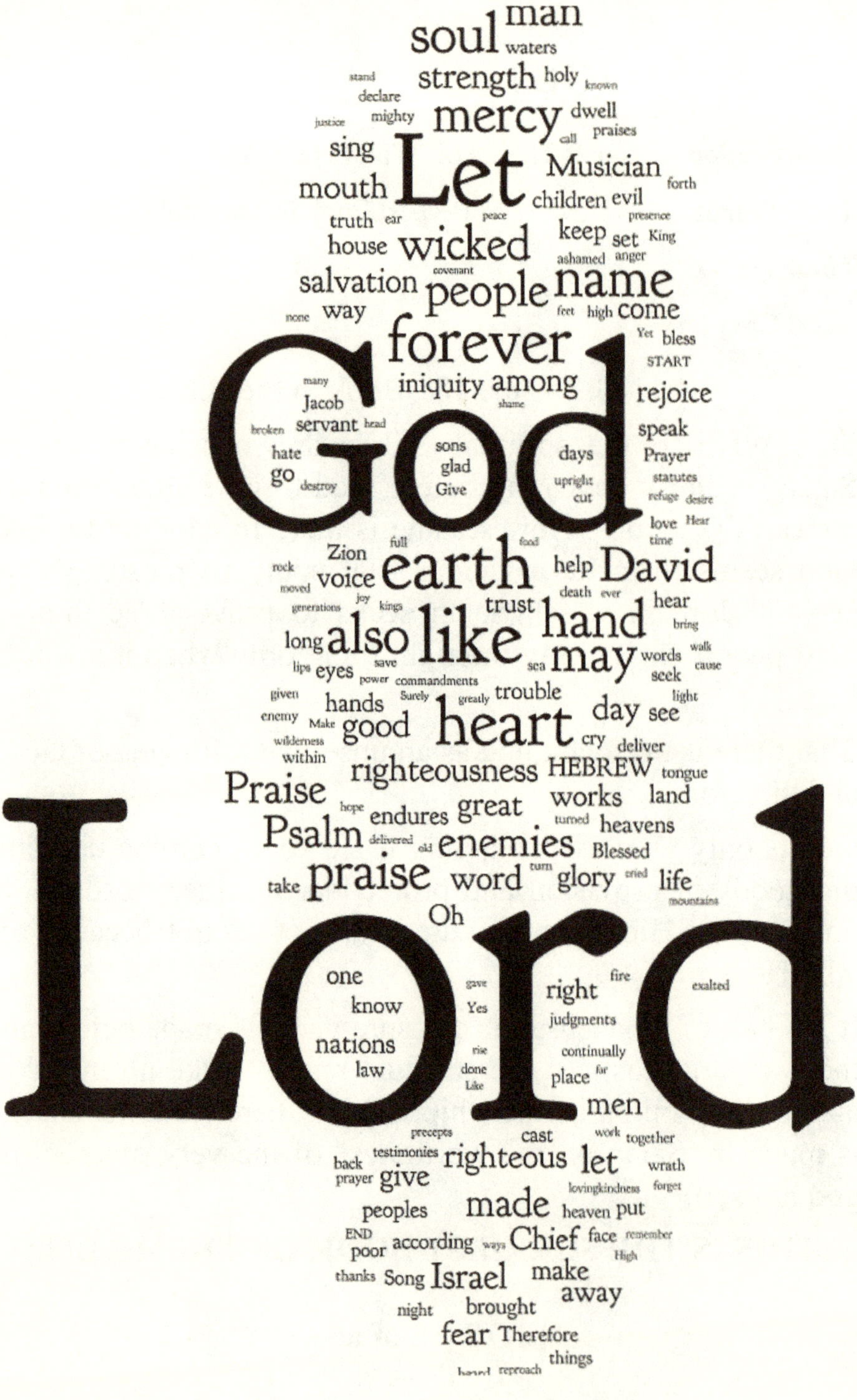

man
soul
waters
stand
strength
holy
known
declare
justice
mighty
mercy
dwell
call
praises
sing
Let
Musician
mouth
forth
children
evil
truth
ear
peace
presence
keep
set
King
house
wicked
ashamed
anger
covenant
salvation
people
name
none
way
feet
high
come
forever
Yet
bless
START
God
many
iniquity
among
rejoice
Jacob
shame
broken
servant
head
speak
sons
days
hate
Prayer
glad
go
destroy
upright
statutes
Give
cut
refuge
desire
love
Hear
full
food
time
Zion
rock
help
David
earth
voice
moved
death
ever
joy
hear
generations
kings
trust
hand
bring
long
also
like
may
walk
sea
words
lips
save
eyes
cause
power
commandments
seek
given
Surely
greatly
trouble
light
hands
day
see
enemy
Make
good
heart
cry
wilderness
deliver
within
righteousness
HEBREW
tongue
Praise
works
land
hope
endures
great
turned
heavens
Psalm
delivered
old
enemies
Blessed
turn
take
praise
word
glory
cried
life
mountains
Oh
Lord
one
fire
gave
right
exalted
know
Yes
judgments
nations
rise
continually
law
done
for
place
Like
men
precepts
cast
work
together
testimonies
back
righteous
let
wrath
prayer
give
lovingkindness
forget
peoples
made
heaven
put
END
according
ways
Chief
face
remember
poor
High
thanks
Song
Israel
make
away
night
brought
fear
Therefore
things
hand
reproach

| PSALMS |

Bible Section | OLD TESTAMENT - POETRY

Total Words | 42,685 (This is the Biggest Book in The Bible!)

Total Verses | 2,461

Total Chapters | 150

| This is the **19th Book of the Bible.**

Although two thirds of these 150 Psalms might be ascribed to King David himself, that so-called 'sweet-singer of Israel,' we know that he was far from sweet and find many of his Psalms are very sour indeed!

The other one third are from various inspired poets and bards up to and including Ezra the scribe and I can tell you therefore, that every shade of human emotion is found in this book the lyrics of which can be said, sung or shouted, whichever way the inclination takes you. That's right, the Psalms are the most versatile of vehicles that you will ever find to express just how you really feel.

So, whether it's in Kings College or 'Costa Coffee,' whether it's in the boardroom, bathroom or the bedroom; in the storm or in the shower, we are commanded to sing "to one another in Psalms" even teaching and telling one another off with them. (Eph 5:19 & Col 3:16 NKJV). You know, I think we are singing the wrong songs!

PSALMS, A TUNE AND A LYRIC FOR EVERY CIRCUMSTANCE OF YOUR LIFE.

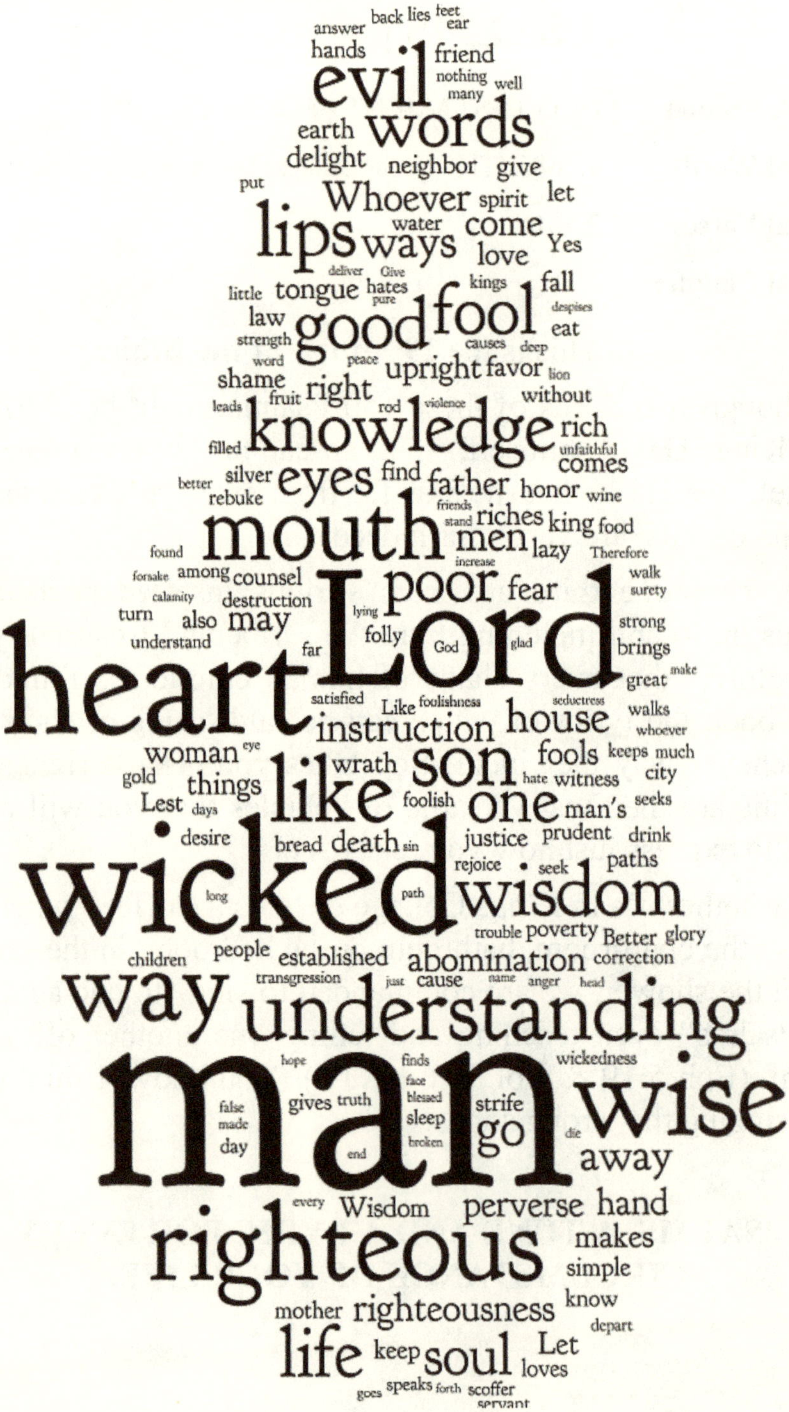
answer back lies feet ear
hands evil friend nothing well many
earth words
delight neighbor give
put Whoever spirit let
lips water come ways Yes love
deliver Give
little tongue hates kings fall
law pure good fool despises eat
strength causes deep
word peace upright favor lion
shame fruit right without
leads rod violence
knowledge rich
filled unfaithful comes
silver eyes find father honor wine
better rebuke
friends riches
mouth stand king food men
found lazy Therefore increase
forsake among counsel poor walk
calamity destruction fear surety
turn also may lying strong
understand Lord brings
far folly God glad
heart make great
satisfied Like foolishness seductress walks
instruction house whoever
woman eye fools keeps much
gold things wrath son hate witness city
Lest days like foolish one man's seeks
desire bread death sin justice prudent drink
rejoice seek paths
wicked long path wisdom
trouble poverty Better glory
children people established abomination correction
way transgression just cause name anger head
understanding
hope finds wickedness
man face
false gives truth blessed strife wise
made sleep go die
day broken end away
every Wisdom perverse hand
righteous makes
simple
know
mother righteousness depart
life keep soul Let loves
goes speaks forth scoffer
servant

| PROVERBS |

Bible Section | OLD TESTAMENT - POETRY

Total Words | 15,038 (The 24th Biggest Book in The Bible)

Total Verses | 915

Total Chapters | 31

| This is the **20th Book of the Bible.**

Here's a good proverb: "A boy with no brains is as reliable as a chocolate teapot!" Now, that's one of my sayings and it might be shallow, but it's a Proverb never the less, because the saying itself is: Self-evident, Self-illustrative, Instructive and Memorable and so are these thirty one chapters of Proverbs, all spoken, collected and collated by Solomon and other wise men.

These proverbs are dehydrated fruit, if you will, all waiting to have the water of investigation added; they are dark sayings, waiting for discourse to draw out the meaning; they are wisdom encapsulated, that is, they are applied knowledge given from God's perspective and in so being, they are: The very keys to a good life, they are a lady ready to be wed, and a bed on which to lay your thick head and wake up wise. They are rich saying, never to be despised and if you do, you will be like a fat, little leprechaun that gets into bed with a hungry crocodile!

THEY ARE APPLES OF GOLD IN FRAMES OF SILVER. DO YOU GET THE PICTURE?

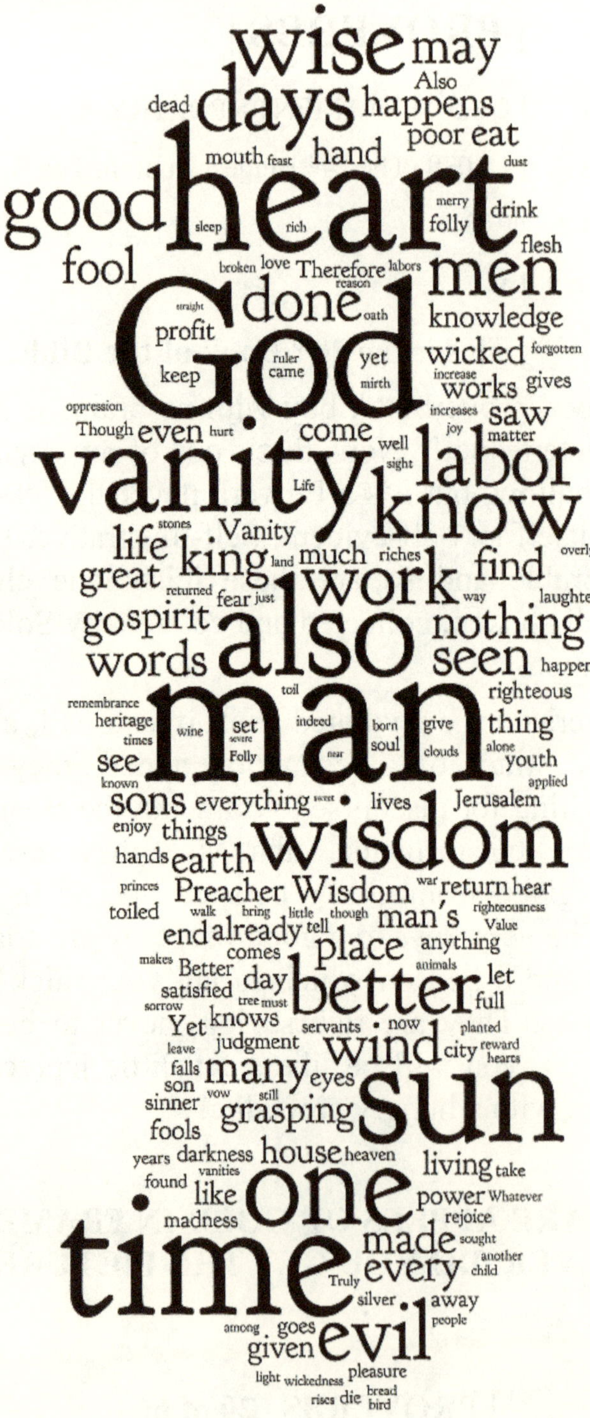
wise
may
Also
dead
days
happens
poor
eat
mouth
feast
hand
dust
good
heart
merry
drink
sleep
rich
folly
flesh
fool
broken
love
Therefore
labors
reason
men
straight
done
oath
knowledge
profit
God
ruler
came
yet
wicked
forgotten
keep
mirth
increase
works
gives
oppression
increases
saw
Though
even
hurt
come
joy
matter
well
sight
vanity
labor
Life
know
stones
Vanity
life
overly
king
land
much
riches
find
great
work
returned
fear
just
way
laughter
go
spirit
also
nothing
words
seen
happen
toil
remembrance
man
righteous
heritage
wine
set
indeed
born
give
thing
times
severe
soul
alone
see
Folly
near
clouds
youth
known
applied
sons
everything
sweet
lives
Jerusalem
enjoy
things
wisdom
hands
earth
princes
Preacher
Wisdom
war
return
hear
toiled
walk
bring
little
though
man's
righteousness
end
already
tell
Value
place
anything
makes
comes
Better
animals
day
let
satisfied
better
sorrow
tree
must
full
Yet
knows
servants
now
planted
leave
judgment
wind
city
reward
hearts
falls
many
son
eyes
vow
still
sinner
grasping
sun
fools
years
darkness
house
heaven
living
take
found
vanities
one
like
power
Whatever
madness
rejoice
time
made
sought
another
every
child
Truly
silver
away
among
goes
people
given
evil
light
wickedness
pleasure
rises
die
bread
bird

| ECCLESIASTES |

Bible Section	| OLD TESTAMENT - POETRY
Total Words	| 5,580 (The 35th Biggest Book in The Bible)
Total Verses	| 222
Total Chapters	| 12

| This is the **21st Book of the Bible.**

Written by a preacher, even King Solomon himself, the wisest man who ever lived, who, never the less, found sin to be stronger than the wisest of hearts and whose foreign wives and harem of 'plenty pleasure' turned his heart on a journey away from God.

Yes, Solomon became a rolling stone and being the richest and the most powerful man who had ever lived, tried everything under this present sun to satiate his Godless thirst, and, like Mick Jagger, though Solomon "tried and tried", he could in-fact "get no satisfaction."

Ecclesiastes is the no-holds-barred journal of a man on the move away from God, trying 'sex, drugs and rock and roll' and a whole lot more besides to try and ease his mind, only to find that, the best a man can do is to enjoy the simple things in life each day to the full, remembering that in the end, he shall all go on to Judgement.

FIND A CORPSE AND SIT WITH IT. THAT'LL BE YOU ONE DAY AND DON'T YOU FORGET IT. ALL THINGS END IN JUDGEMENT.

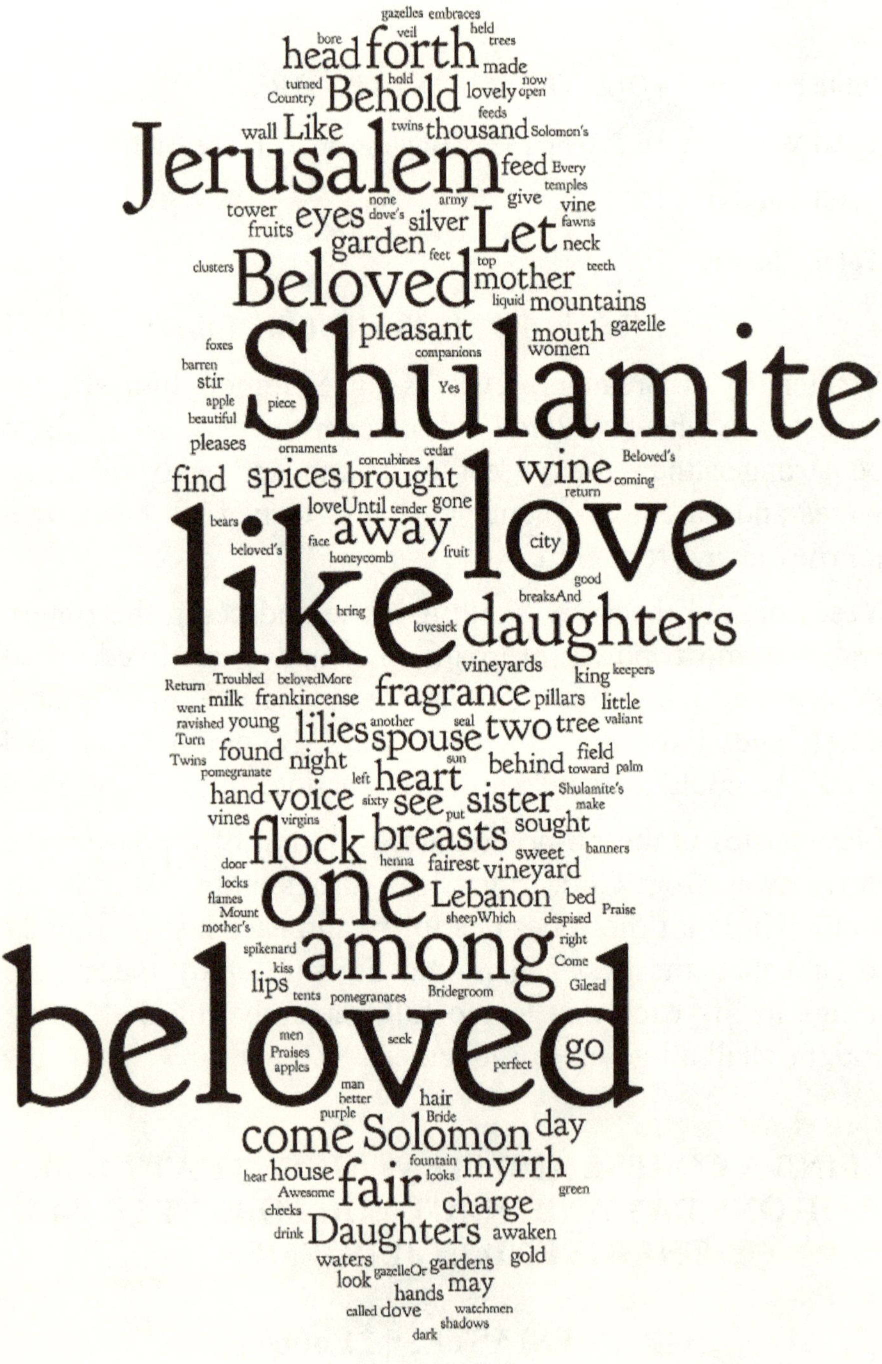
gazelles
embraces
veil
held
bore
trees
head
forth
made
turned
hold
now
Country
Behold
lovely
open
feeds
wall
Like
twins
thousand
Solomon's
Jerusalem
feed
Every
temples
none
army
give
tower
eyes
dove's
vine
fruits
silver
Let
fawns
garden
neck
feet
clusters
top
teeth
Beloved
mother
liquid
mountains
pleasant
mouth
gazelle
foxes
companions
women
barren
Shulamite
stir
Yes
apple
piece
beautiful
pleases
ornaments
cedar
concubines
Beloved's
find
spices
brought
wine
coming
return
loveUntil
tender
gone
bears
away
love
face
city
beloved's
fruit
honeycomb
like
good
breaksAnd
bring
lovesick
daughters
vineyards
Troubled
belovedMore
king
keepers
Return
milk
frankincense
fragrance
pillars
went
little
ravished
young
another
seal
two
tree
valiant
lilies
spouse
Turn
found
field
Twins
night
sun
behind
toward
palm
pomegranate
left
heart
hand
Shulamite's
voice
sixty
see
sister
make
put
vines
virgins
sought
flock
breasts
banners
sweet
door
henna
fairest
vineyard
locks
one
Lebanon
bed
flames
Mount
Praise
sheepWhich
mother's
despised
among
right
spikenard
kiss
Come
lips
Gilead
tents
pomegranates
Bridegroom
beloved
men
seek
go
Praises
apples
perfect
man
better
hair
purple
Bride
day
come
Solomon
fountain
myrrh
hear
house
looks
fair
Awesome
green
charge
cheeks
drink
Daughters
awaken
gold
waters
gardens
look
gazelleOr
may
hands
called
dove
watchmen
shadows
dark

| THE SONG OF SOLOMON |

Bible Section | OLD TESTAMENT - POETRY

Total Words | 2,658 (The 42nd Biggest Book in The Bible)

Total Verses | 117

Total Chapters | 8

| This is the **22nd Book of the Bible.**

Canticles, the Song of Songs, is it sexy or what! Yes, before we sometimes rightly spiritualize many of the things in this book, let's not forget that, at its center, without being obscene in any sense of that word, it is a most erotic love poem. Yes, the Song of Solomon is a song of sensuous imagery you see, of intimate love between a bride; bedded by her husband. But the Song of Songs also overlays its very literal self, with layer upon layer of spiritual imagery, all representing the passionate relationship between God and the people He loves.

It is all about all-consuming love, all-reaching and all-knowing love, even that the love of a very jealous kind.

IT IS ABOUT A LOVE THAT TATTOOS THE HEART; LOVE LIKE A BLAZING FIRE; LOVE WHICH IS "AS STRONG AS DEATH AND AS CRUEL AS THE GRAVE" (SONG OF SONGS 8:6 NKJV); LOVE THAT WOULD SEND HIS SON TO DIE AND TO SAVE, HIS OWN BEAUTIFUL AND BELOVED BRIDE.

| SONG OF SOLOMON | 22 of 66 |

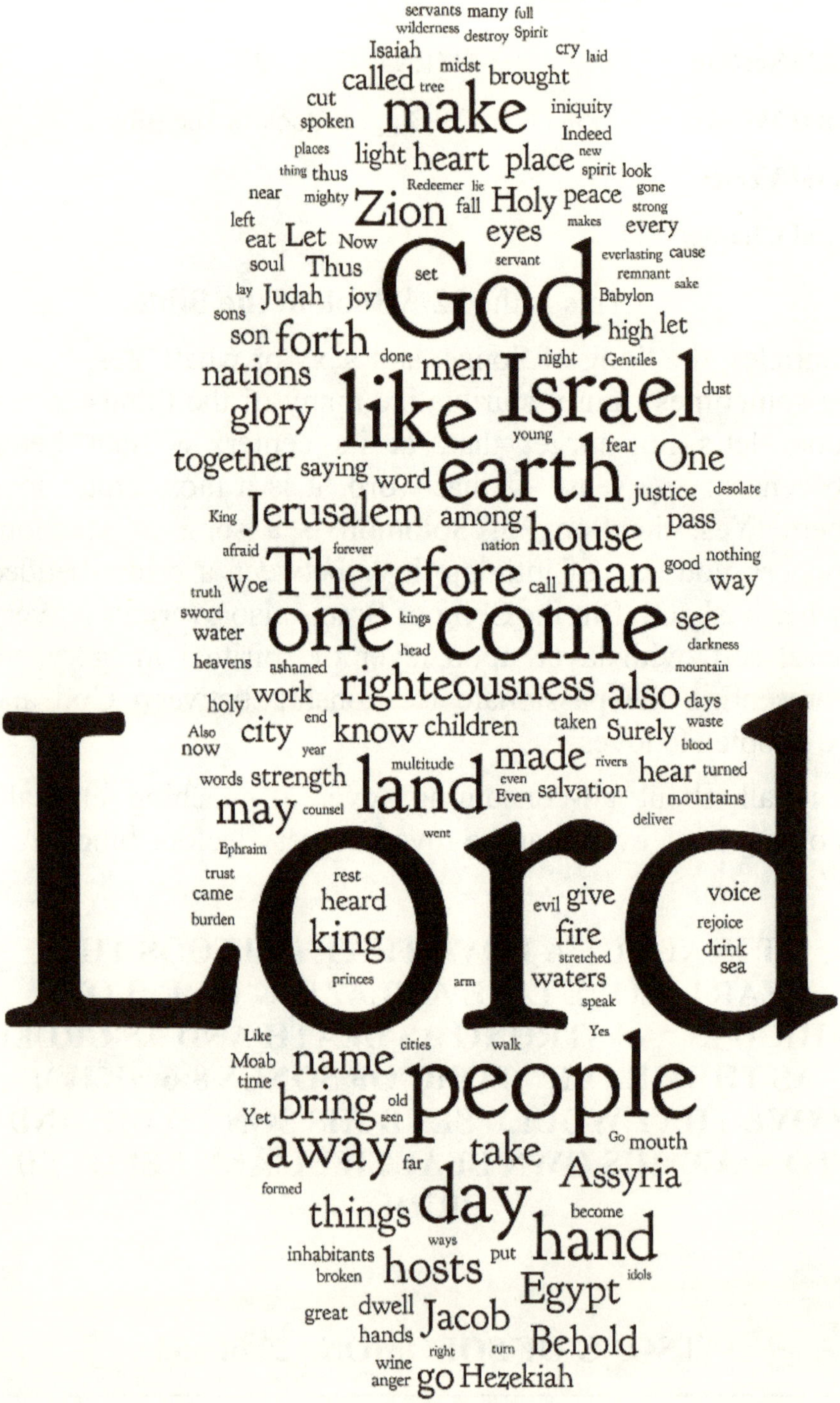
servants many full
wilderness destroy Spirit
Isaiah cry laid
midst
called tree brought
cut
spoken make iniquity
Indeed
places light heart place new
thing thus spirit look
Redeemer lie gone
near mighty Zion fall Holy peace strong
left makes every
eat Let Now eyes
soul Thus servant everlasting cause
set remnant
lay Judah joy God sake
Babylon
sons high let
son forth
done night Gentiles
nations men
Israel dust
glory like
young
fear
together saying One
word earth justice desolate
King Jerusalem among pass
house
afraid forever nation nothing
good
Woe Therefore call man way
truth
sword kings see
water one come
head darkness
heavens ashamed mountain
righteousness also
holy work days
end taken Surely waste
Also city know children
now year blood
made
multitude rivers hear turned
words strength
even
land Even salvation
may counsel mountains
deliver
went
Ephraim
trust rest
came voice
heard evil give
burden rejoice
king fire
drink
stretched sea
princes arm waters
speak
Lord
Like Yes
cities walk
Moab name
time
people
old
Yet bring seen
Go mouth
away take
far
Assyria
formed
day
things become
hand
ways
inhabitants put
hosts
broken idols
Egypt
great dwell
Jacob
hands Behold
right turn
wine
anger go Hezekiah

| ISAIAH |

Bible Section | OLD TESTAMENT – THE MAJOR PROPHETS

Total Words | 37,040 (The 05th Biggest Book in The Bible)

Total Verses | 1,292

Total Chapters | 66

| This is the **23rd Book of the Bible.**

Written by that prophet "of unclean lips," who saw the Lord high and lifted up, and out of this majestic vision of God, was led to prophesy and write with such exalted and majestic grandeur, that no other prophet competes with what is widely regarded as a masterpiece of Hebrew literature.

More than an academic though, Isaiah was the man commanded by God to go naked and barefoot around Jerusalem for three years as a prophetic sign! And he did, for Isaiah was sold out to his calling which especially touched his family, so much so, that his wife is known as 'the prophetess, ' and his two sons even possess prophetic names, one of which is, Maher-shalal-hash-baz or "hasten booty, speed and spoil," which frankly, I don't think even the Beckham's, could compete with!

THIS BOOK IS A HEADY 'RUMTOPF' OF CHRISTMAS DELIGHT AND JAM-PACKED FULL OF MESSIANIC HOPE. "FOR UNTO US A CHILD IS BORN; UNTO US A SON IS GIVEN."

(Isaiah 9:6 NKJV)

| ISAIAH | 23 of 66 |

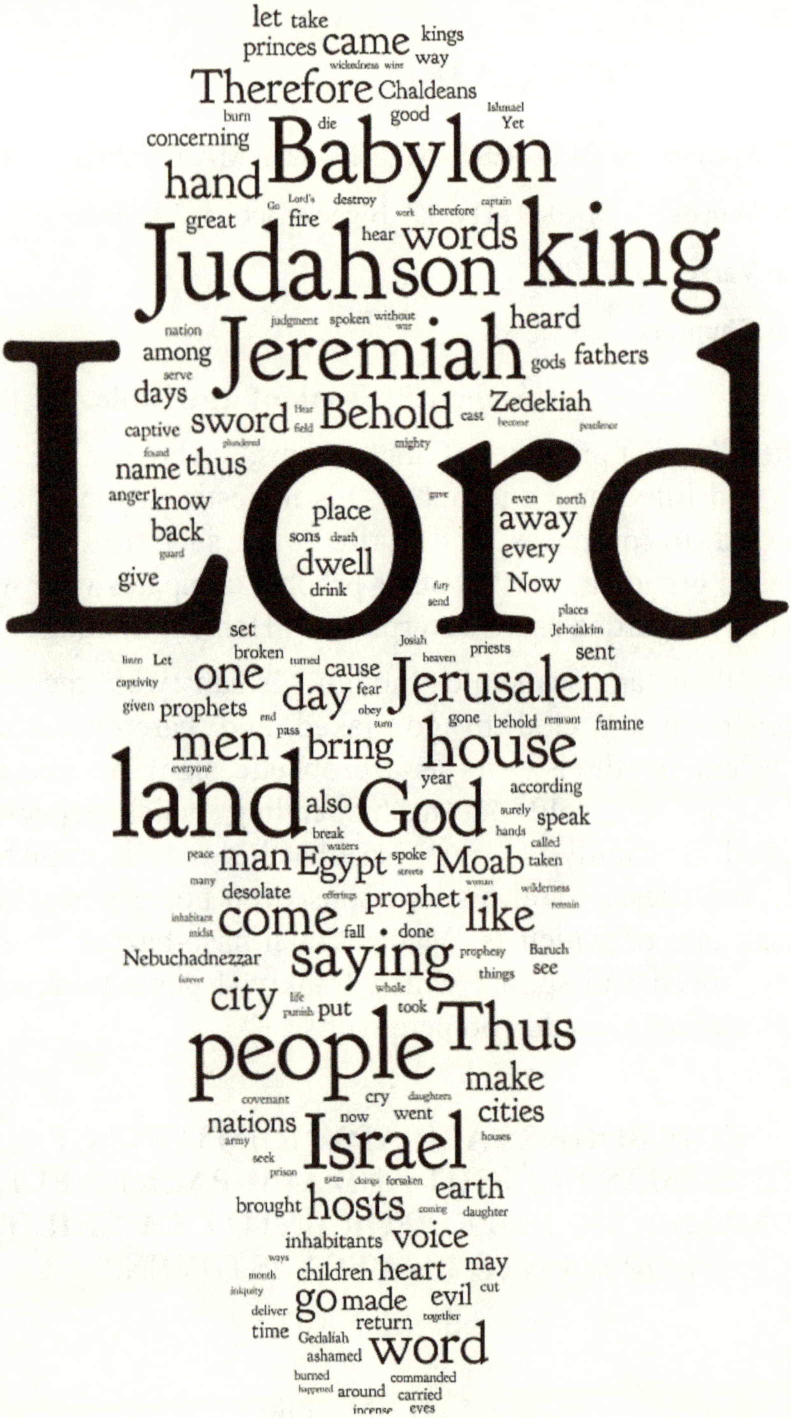

let take
princes came kings way
wickedness wine
Therefore Chaldeans
burn good Ishmael
die Yet
concerning
Babylon
hand
Go Lord's destroy work therefore captain
great fire
hear words
Judah son king
judgment spoken without war
heard
nation
Jeremiah
among
gods fathers
serve
days
Lord
sword Behold Zedekiah
Hear field
cast become pestilence
captive
plundered mighty
found
name thus
anger know
gave even north
place
away
back
sons death
every
guard
dwell
give
drink
fury Now
send
places
set
Jehoiakim
Josiah
broken
priests
listen Let turned heaven sent
one cause
captivity
day fear
Jerusalem
obey
given prophets
end
gone behold remnant famine
pass turn
men bring house
everyone
year
according
land also God
surely speak
break hands
called
peace waters
man Egypt spoke Moab taken
streets
many woman
desolate wilderness
offerings prophet
remain
inhabitant like
come
midst fall done
saying
Nebuchadnezzar prophesy Baruch
things see
forever whole
city
life
punish put took
Thus
people
make
covenant cry daughters
now went cities
nations
Israel
army houses
seek
prison
gates doings forsaken earth
brought hosts
coming daughter
inhabitants voice
ways
may
month children heart
iniquity cut
go made evil
deliver together
time return
Gedaliah
word
ashamed
burned commanded
happened around carried
incense eyes

| JEREMIAH |

Bible Section | OLD TESTAMENT – THE MAJOR PROPHETS

Total Words | 42,654 (The 02nd Biggest Book in The Bible)

Total Verses | 1,364

Total Chapters | 52

| This is the **24th Book of the Bible.**

Jeremiah, the bachelor prophet had no easy ministry, for not only was his commission to be '***destructively constructive,***' but his personality led him to take things very personally indeed.

On top of all this, this seer saw the unspeakable horrors which would happen to rebellious Israel and it became a burden which baptized him into broken-heartedness, while his honesty pushed him into violent hostility from those that did not wish to hear his message. All these physical and spiritual crises led him into continual argument with God regarding his calling, in which he wanted vindication, but out of which, he felt only betrayed and let down by an overpowering and uncaring Deity. Jeremiah was a weeping depressive who spent most of his ministry in emotional mud right up to his neck, yet in the greatest act of faith, he can still cry out to God most high saying "*Heal me, O Lord, and I shall be healed; Save me, and I shall be saved, For You are my praise.*" (Jeremiah 17:14 NKJV)

"WHERE IS THE WORD OF LORD? – LET IT COME NOW!"

| JEREMIAH | 24 of 66 |

restore
elders pitied sigh
destroyed adversaries
food young sinned bear done
eyes
feast mercies
cloud bones
prayer like wandered people
virgin life
gold forgotten women
blood fury bitterness
reproach fierce commanded dwell head
sins
longer full daughter
street schemes
faint strength wilderness
cry streets
adversary
bring near become things
tears desolate caused
anger virgins come enter together called woe
priest turn heart dust
pleasant brought day beauty
God
exalted punishment Look
may roaming earth
ways every
generation set
affliction
bread hand
slain enemy Young
without
end face Lord
keep mothers good fire
opened turned
comfort Edom
captivity spread help water
go afflicted
comforter king
behold broken crush aside cried
ground children hands
also Even
Therefore among Judah seen
gone consider heaven iniquity
fulfilled
show nations Jerusalem wood enemy.He
ceased man swallowed
men mouth
sorrow sanctuary Zion away wall
joy hope priests city thrown
far
fallen poured enemies right sword
given herBecause Give dim
bent made Let Go heard
glad spurned one Like
midst night days Surely case
touch transgressions skin
fine comes mourning cast peoples find
drink rest forever assembly menHave
gates back Israel unclean
wait covered trampled song
within destruction See
cut around time
fail soul eye
princes pass

| LAMENTATIONS |

Bible Section	| OLD TESTAMENT – THE MAJOR PROPHETS
Total Words	| 3,411 (The 04th Biggest Book in The Bible)
Total Verses	| 154
Total Chapters	| 5

| This is the **25th Book of the Bible.**

Each of the five chapters of Lamentations is a poem, which in turn comes together as a whole to form one single '**Song of Lament,'** even a 'Song of Waiting,' written by the poet/prophet Jeremiah, the original 'man of constant sorrow.'

It's an amazing piece of work, poetically crafted to string the heart with such a tone of longing sorrow, that it will arrest its hearers with a spirit of heart-breaking repentance.

However, the original hearers neither repented nor believed that God would judge Jerusalem in the way Jeremiah proclaimed it, so much so, that in answer to the mocking abuse he so constantly received he cries out, "Is it nothing to you, all you who pass by? Behold and see if there is any sorrow like my sorrow" (Lamentations 1:12NKJV).

I suppose only one thing sustained Jeremiah in his desperate slough of despondency and that was his ultimate hope in the unfailing compassion of a merciful God.

"GREAT IS THY FAITHFULNESS."

| LAMENTATIONS | 25 of 66 |

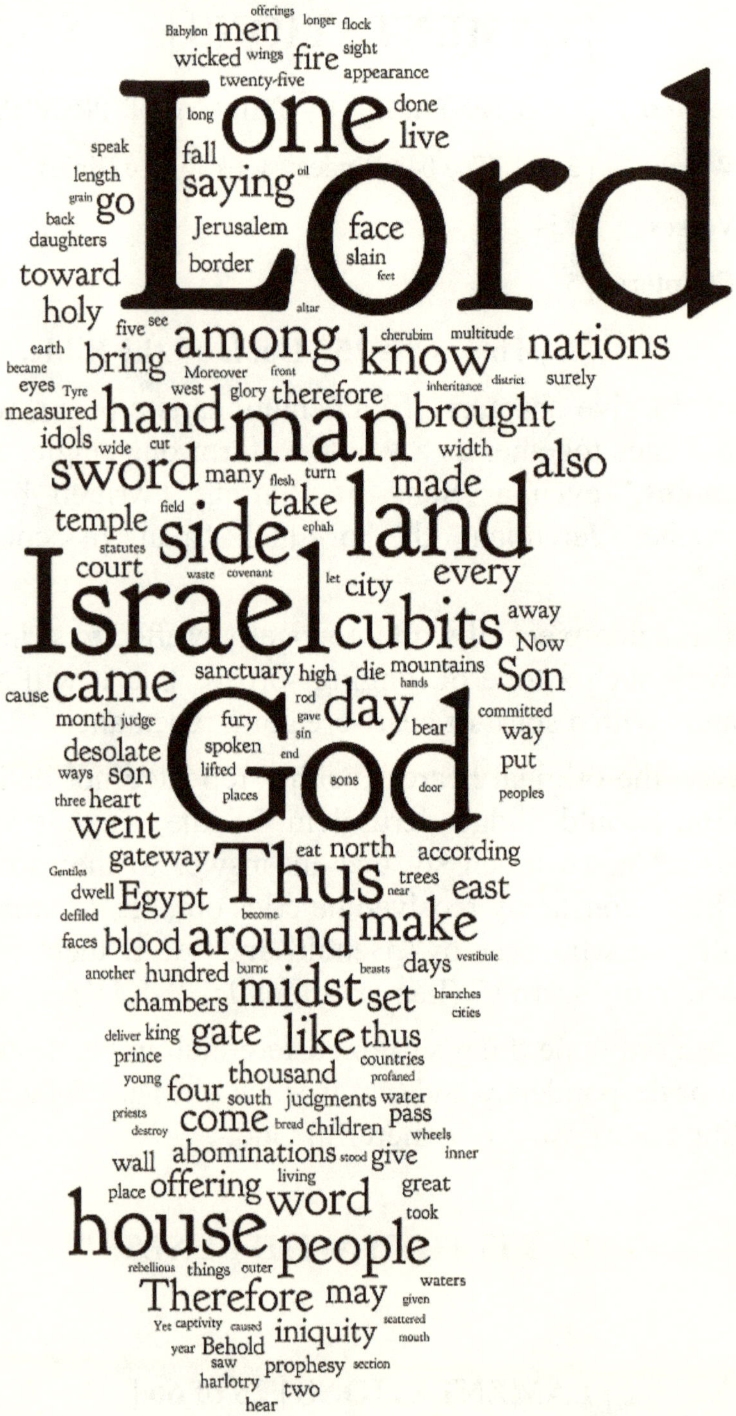

offerings
Babylon
men
longer
flock
wicked
wings
fire
sight
twenty-five
appearance
Lord
one
long
done
live
speak
fall
length
oil
saying
grain
go
back
Jerusalem
face
daughters
toward
border
slain
feet
holy
altar
five
see
among
know
nations
earth
cherubim
multitude
became
bring
Moreover
front
surely
eyes
Tyre
west
glory
therefore
inheritance
district
measured
hand
man
brought
idols
wide
cut
width
sword
many
flesh
turn
also
made
take
land
field
temple
side
ephah
statutes
court
waste
covenant
let
city
every
Israel
cubits
away
Now
sanctuary
high
die
mountains
hands
Son
cause
came
rod
day
committed
month
judge
fury
gave
sin
bear
way
desolate
spoken
end
God
put
ways
son
lifted
sons
door
three
heart
places
peoples
went
gateway
eat
north
according
Gentiles
Thus
trees
east
dwell
Egypt
near
defiled
become
make
faces
blood
around
vestibule
another
hundred
burnt
beasts
days
chambers
midst
set
branches
cities
deliver
king
gate
like
thus
prince
countries
young
thousand
profaned
four
south
judgments
water
priests
come
bread
children
pass
destroy
wheels
wall
abominations
stood
give
inner
place
offering
living
great
word
took
house
people
rebellious
things
outer
waters
Therefore
may
given
Yet
captivity
caused
iniquity
scattered
year
Behold
mouth
saw
prophesy
section
harlotry
two
hear

| EZEKIEL |

Bible Section | OLD TESTAMENT – THE MAJOR PROPHETS

Total Words | 39,402 (The 03rd Biggest Book in The Bible)

Total Verses | 1,273

Total Chapters | 48

| This is the **26th Book of the Bible.**

Written by a captive 'priest-cum-prophet' speaking to the remnant of Israel, over the top of the voices of false prophets, all giving false hope, Ezekiel uses exasperated language to get his point across; even language that was not fitting for God to use!

Unfortunately it was God who said this 'stuff' and it is surprisingly shocking and deeply offensive even to modern ears. You see, God is desperate to get His true message across and He uses desperate language from the lips and life of one of the most dramatic prophets to have ever walked the earth.

Even so, Ezekiel is the prophet of the Spirit and the Glory of God, and though his imagery is sometimes so shallow that a little lamb could wade through them, it is often so deep that an elephant can barely swim in them.

He's Marcel Marceau, Jackson Pollock, Damien Hurst, Von Daniken and Shakespeare, all rolled into one. Ezekiel is God's attention-getter!

NOW HEAR THE WORD OF THE LORD.

| EZEKIEL| 26 of 66 |

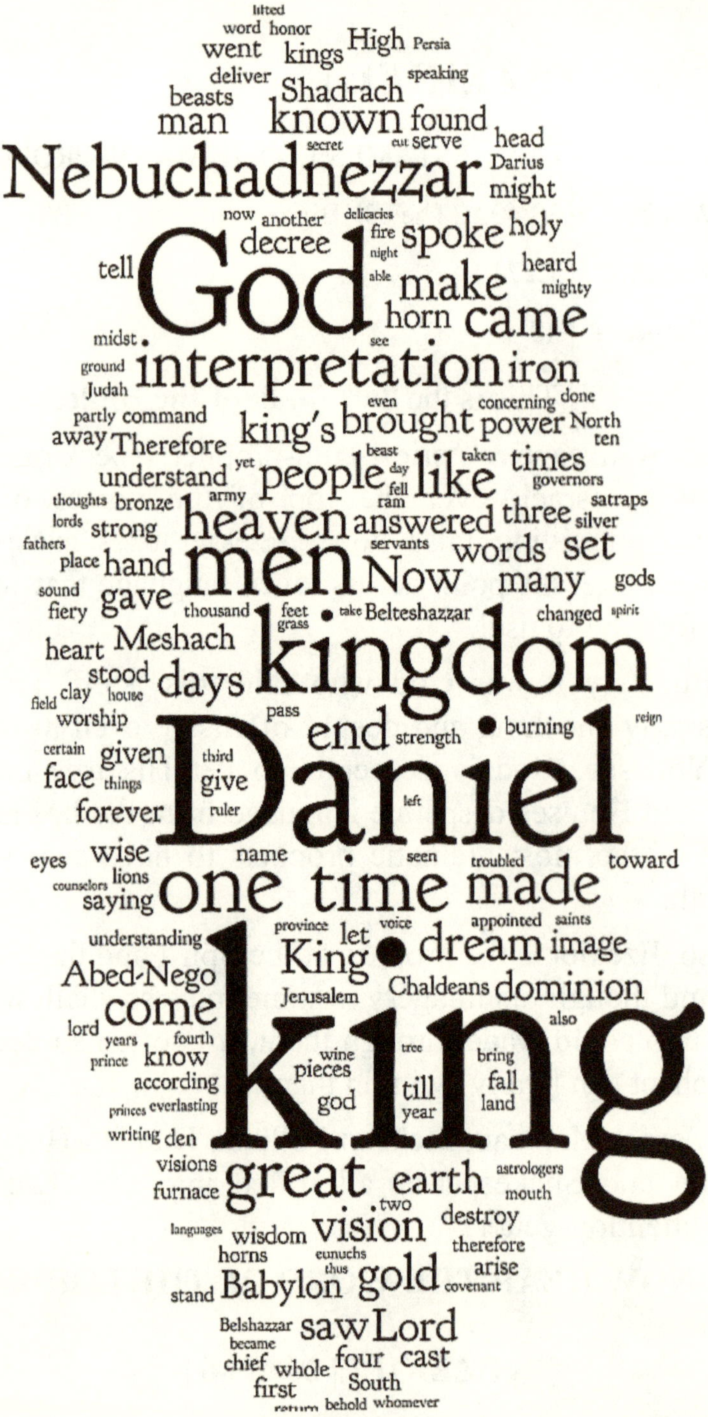
lifted
word honor
went kings High Persia
deliver speaking
beasts Shadrach
man known found
secret cut serve head
Nebuchadnezzar Darius
might
now another delicacies
decree fire spoke holy
night
tell God heard
able make mighty
horn came
midst see
ground interpretation iron
Judah even concerning done
partly command
away Therefore king's brought power North
ten
beast taken
yet day times
understand people like
fell governors
thoughts bronze army ram satraps
lords strong heaven answered three silver
fathers servants words set
place hand men
sound Now many gods
fiery gave thousand feet take Belteshazzar changed spirit
grass
Meshach
heart
stood kingdom
clay house days
field
worship pass reign
end burning
strength
certain given
third
face things give Daniel
forever ruler left
eyes wise name seen troubled toward
lions
counselors one time made
saying
understanding province voice appointed saints
let
King dream image
Abed-Nego
Jerusalem Chaldeans dominion
come
lord also
years fourth
prince know wine tree bring
pieces king fall
according
princes everlasting god till land
year
writing den
visions astrologers
furnace great earth mouth
two
languages wisdom vision destroy
horns eunuchs therefore
thus arise
stand Babylon gold covenant
Belshazzar saw Lord
became
chief whole four cast
first South
return behold whomever

| DANIEL |

Bible Section | OLD TESTAMENT – THE MAJOR PROPHETS

Total Words | 11,602 (26th Biggest Book in The Bible)

Total Verses | 357

Total Chapters | 12

| This is the **27th Book of the Bible.**

Daniel was not only the historian, but also THE prophet of Babylonian Captivity, who is referred to as being "*greatly beloved IN HEAVEN*" (Daniel 9:23; 10:11 & 19 NKJV).

Daniel is a man of purpose and prayer, so much so, that he was the only man who knew what the handwriting on the wall was all about. Jesus simply calls Him – "Daniel the Prophet" (Matt 24:15 NKJV).

Indeed, Daniel is later delivered from the lion's den to become the prophet of the Sovereignty of God over every person, nation and empire on the planet, for Daniel is at his core, not just the prophet of passing empires, but the prophet of the coming Kingdom of God! So much so, that Daniel's twelve chapters provide the skeletal structure upon which fixes all the sinews and muscles of every other prophecy; it is even the hub of all past, present and future prophetic investigation, showing that the Sovereign God can save even from the hottest of fiery flames.

Daniel, HE'S THAT IMPORTANT.

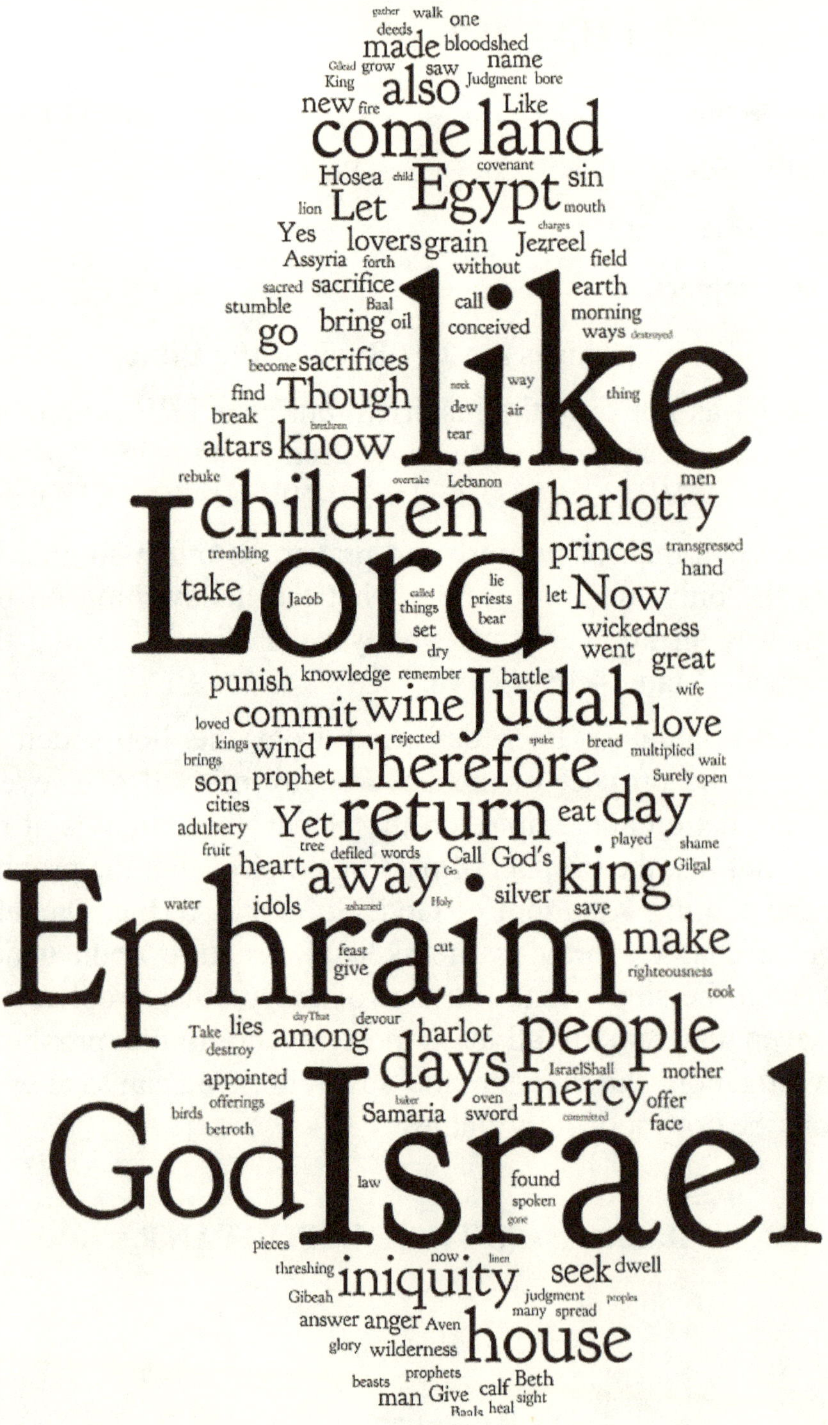

walk
one
deeds
made
bloodshed
name
grow
saw
King
Judgment
bore
new
fire
also
Like
come
land
Hosea
child
covenant
sin
Egypt
lion
Let
mouth
Yes
lovers
grain
Jezreel
Assyria
forth
without
field
sacred
sacrifice
earth
stumble
Baal
call
morning
go
bring
oil
conceived
ways
become
sacrifices
like
way
find
Though
thing
break
dew
air
tear
altars
know
rebuke
Lebanon
men
children
harlotry
Lord
trembling
princes
transgressed
hand
take
lie
Jacob
called
priests
let
Now
things
bear
set
wickedness
went
dry
great
punish
knowledge
remember
battle
wife
loved
commit
wine
Judah
love
kings
wind
rejected
spoke
bread
multiplied
brings
Therefore
wait
son
prophet
Surely
open
cities
day
eat
adultery
Yet
return
fruit
tree
defiled
words
played
shame
heart
Call
God's
away
king
Gilgal
water
idols
silver
save
Ephraim
make
feast
cut
give
righteousness
took
Take
lies
devour
harlot
among
people
destroy
days
IsraelShall
mother
appointed
mercy
offerings
oven
offer
birds
Samaria
sword
face
betroth
God
Israel
law
found
spoken
gone
pieces
now
threshing
iniquity
seek
dwell
Gibeah
judgment
answer
anger
many
spread
Aven
glory
wilderness
house
beasts
prophets
Beth
man
Give
calf
sight
heal

| HOSEA |

Bible Section | OLD TESTAMENT - THE MINOR PROPHETS

Total Words | 5,174 (The 36th Biggest Book in The Bible)

Total Verses | 197

Total Chapters | 14

| This is the **28th Book of the Bible.**

Hosea is the second scariest book of them all, for God always shapes his prophets to fit the message, and Hosea, this GIANT of the first of the Minor Prophets is shaped by God like no other prophet, for Hosea is called to prophesy to an adulterous nation. You see God commanded this man to break the Mosaic Law and go and marry a prostitute. Her name was Gomer and Hosea loved her, and, after marriage, he fell in love with her even more and you know, they seemed happy and had children. However, Hosea eventually finds out:

Firstly, that Gomer was back on the game and secondly, that a couple of the kids weren't his anyway! In this, HOSEA KNEW EXACTLY how God felt toward deceitful Israel and thus was able to deliver God's message from a broken home and a broken heart of love, his theme being nothing short of 'total redemption.' Amazing, or what?

"COME, AND LET US RETURN TO THE LORD; FOR HE HAS TORN, BUT HE WILL HEAL US; HE HAS STRICKEN, BUT HE WILL BIND US UP."

(Hosea 6:1 NKJV)

| HOSEA | 28 of 66 |

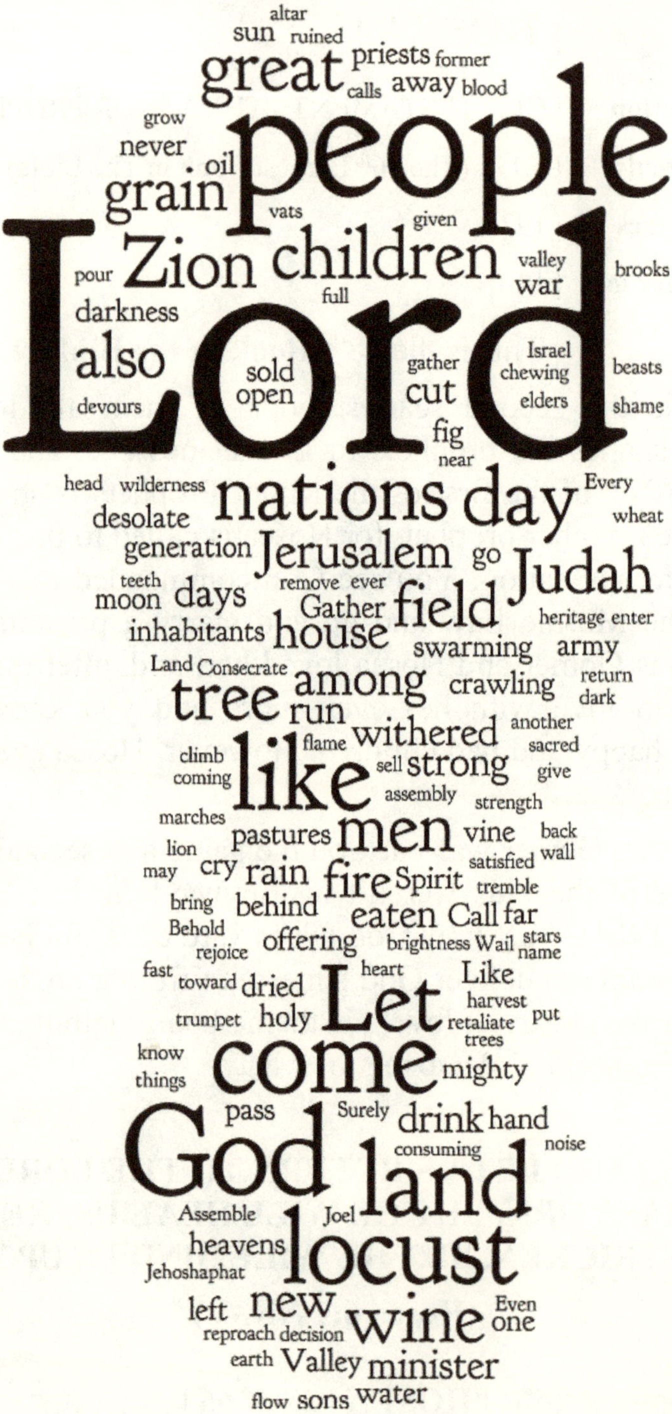
altar
sun ruined
great priests former
calls away blood
grow
never
oil
people
grain
vats given
Lord
Zion children
valley
brooks
pour
war
full
darkness
Israel
also
sold
gather
chewing
beasts
open
cut
elders
devours
shame
fig
near
head wilderness
Every
nations day
desolate
wheat
generation
Jerusalem
go
Judah
teeth
remove ever
moon days
Gather
field
heritage enter
inhabitants
house
swarming
army
Land Consecrate
among
crawling
return
dark
tree
run
another
withered
flame
sacred
climb
like
sell strong
coming
give
assembly
strength
marches
men
pastures
vine
back
lion
wall
satisfied
may
cry
rain
fire
Spirit
tremble
bring
behind
eaten Call far
Behold
offering
brightness Wail
stars
rejoice
name
fast
heart
Like
toward dried
Let
harvest
trumpet
holy
retaliate
put
trees
know
come
mighty
things
pass
Surely
drink hand
God
consuming
noise
land
Assemble
Joel
heavens
locust
Jehoshaphat
left
new
Even
one
reproach decision
wine
earth
Valley
minister
flow sons water

| JOEL |

Bible Section | OLD TESTAMENT – THE MINOR PROPHETS

Total Words | 2,033 (The 49th Biggest Book in The Bible)

Total Verses | 73

Total Chapters | 3

| This is the **29th Book of the Bible.**

Joel the prophet sees farther than anyone else into the future, for he sees both the church age and the day of the Lord, even extending right into the millennial age to come.

The first part of these just three chapters of the book, deals with one of the most poetic and pictorially accurate descriptions of a plague of locusts, found anywhere in literature, and it is most definitely presented as a '***shod from the Shaddai'*** or a 'destruction from the Almighty.' The answer to such a catastrophic calamity in the Southern Kingdom of Judah must be both a change of heart and ways all seen chiefly in their returning to God. Now, although Joel is one of the best examples of prophecy, having both an immediate and still to come future fulfilment, yet, whether present or future, Joel's message is the same,

'DON'T RIP YOUR CLOTHES APART, BUT RIP YOUR HEARTS APART IN REPENTANCE, AND RETURN TO GOD; LET HIM RESTORE, RENEW AND REVIVE YOU.'

| JOEL| 29 of 66 |

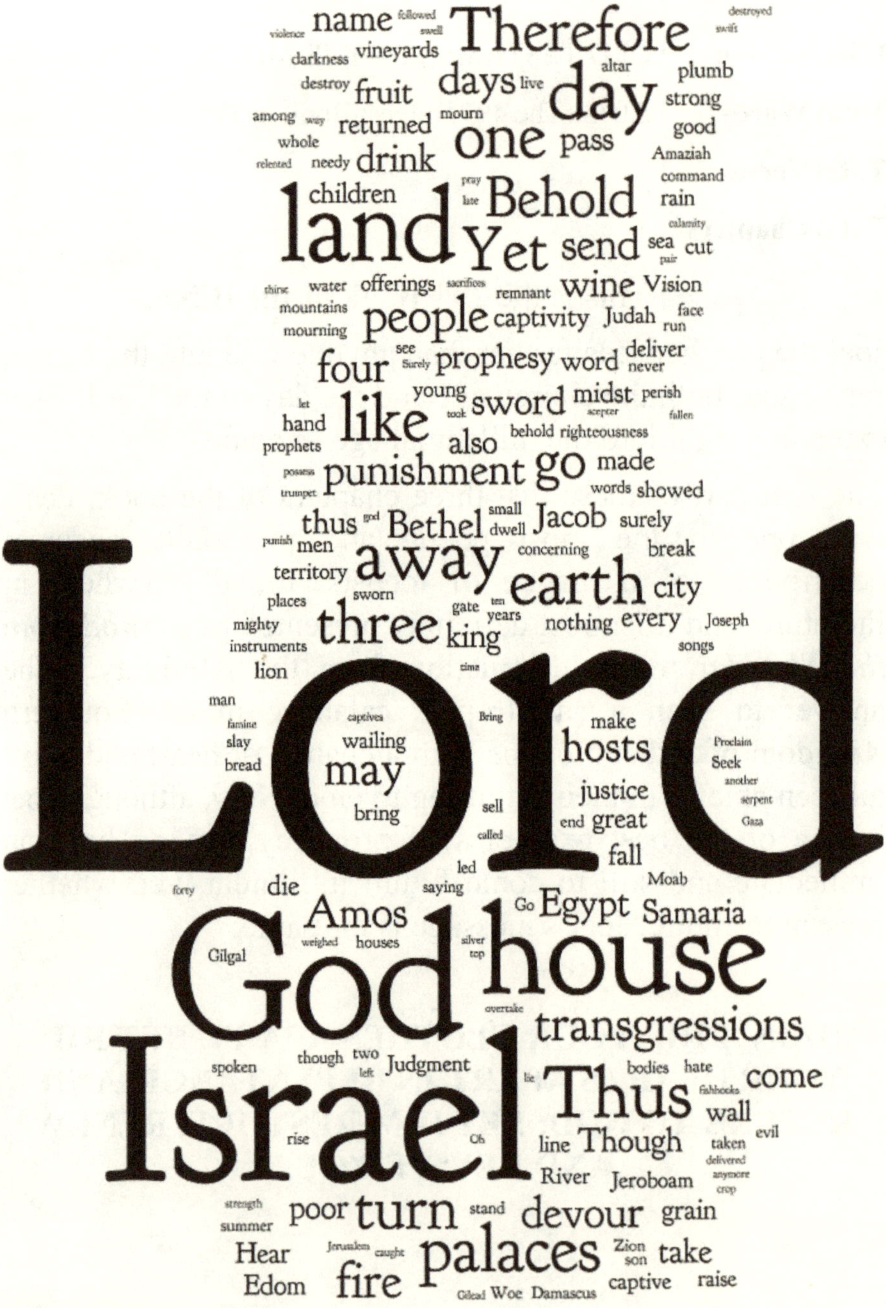
Lord
Israel
God
house
land
Therefore
day
one
Behold
Yet
send
people
like
away
earth
three
Amos
Thus
palaces
turn
fire
transgressions
punishment
go
name
vineyards
darkness
days
fruit
returned
drink
children
plumb
strong
good
Amaziah
command
rain
pass
wine
Vision
offerings
captivity
Judah
prophesy
word
four
sword
midst
deliver
perish
young
also
righteousness
behold
made
showed
words
Jacob
surely
Bethel
thus
small
dwell
break
concerning
territory
men
city
nothing
every
Joseph
king
years
gate
places
mighty
instruments
songs
lion
man
hosts
may
wailing
make
justice
great
end
bring
sell
fall
Moab
die
Egypt
Samaria
Gilgal
houses
Judgment
spoken
though
two
come
wall
bodies
hate
line
Though
River
Jeroboam
evil
taken
poor
devour
grain
summer
Hear
Edom
take
Zion
son
captive
raise
Woe
Damascus

| AMOS |

Bible Section | OLD TESTAMENT - THE MINOR PROPHETS

Total Words | 4,216 (The 37th Biggest Book in The Bible)

Total Verses | 146

Total Chapters | 9

| This is the **30th Book of the Bible.**

Amos, this simple seasonal laborer and herdsmen, born in the Southern Kingdom, was called by God to preach and prophesy to the Royalty of the Northern Kingdom.

So, Amos marches into the Royal Court and cries out "The Lord roars from Zion, and utters His voice from Jerusalem; the pastures of the shepherds mourn, and the top of Carmel withers." (Amos 1:2 NKJV)

Thus getting their attention, Amos then pronounces judgement on each and every one of Israel's surrounding enemies…using the same refrain of, ***"for three transgressions and for four I will judge…..***Syria, Tyre, Edom, Damascus Gaza, etc, etc" (Amos 1:3 NKJV) and oh they loved that, for these nations deserved judgement in rejecting God;

Now then, once Amos gets their mental ascent to the rightness of it all, he then turns his big guns on them. And God Himself, not only now owns up to being the cause of all their current calamites, but says that He is now going to personally come and take them out!

PREPARE TO MEET THY GOD!

| AMOS| 30 of 66 |

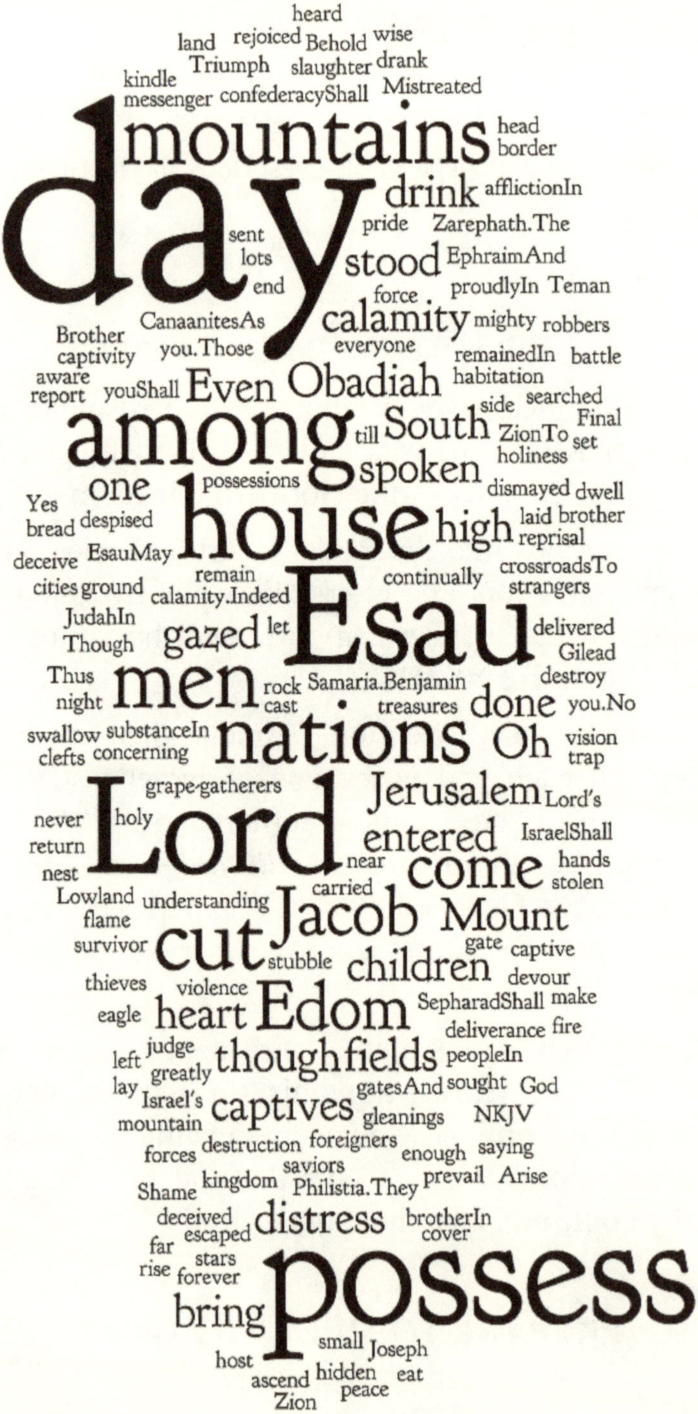

heard
land rejoiced Behold wise
Triumph slaughter drank
kindle
messenger confederacyShall Mistreated
day
mountains head border
drink afflictionIn
sent pride Zarephath.The
lots stood EphraimAnd
end force proudlyIn Teman
CanaanitesAs calamity mighty robbers
Brother captivity you.Those everyone remainedIn battle
aware report youShall Even Obadiah habitation
among South side searched
till ZionTo Final set holiness
one possessions spoken dismayed dwell
Yes bread despised house high laid brother reprisal
deceive EsauMay
remain continually crossroadsTo strangers
cities ground calamity.Indeed
Esau
JudahIn Though gazed let delivered Gilead
Thus night men rock cast Samaria.Benjamin destroy
treasures done you.No
swallow substanceIn clefts concerning nations Oh vision trap
grape-gatherers Jerusalem Lord's
never holy
Lord
return entered IsraelShall
nest near come hands stolen
carried
Lowland understanding flame Jacob Mount
survivor cut gate captive
stubble children
thieves violence devour
eagle heart Edom SepharadShall make
deliverance fire
left judge greatly though fields peopleIn
lay gatesAnd sought God
Israel's mountain captives gleanings NKJV
forces destruction foreigners enough saying
Shame kingdom saviors Philistia.They prevail Arise
deceived escaped distress brotherIn cover
far rise stars forever
possess
bring
small Joseph
host hidden eat
ascend peace
Zion

| OBADIAH |

Bible Section | OLD TESTAMENT - THE MINOR PROPHETS

Total Words | 669 (The 62nd Biggest Book in The Bible)

Total Verses | 21

Total Chapters | 1

| This is the **31st Book of the Bible.**

Abraham had Isaac, that 'child of promise', and he had twin boys, Jacob, from whom sprang the twelve tribes of Israel, and Esau, from whom sprang the Edomites. This shortest book of the Old Testament of just 27 verses is a prophecy of Judgement against these Edomites.

Rediscovered by the West in 1812, the ancient city of Petra was the seemingly impregnable fortress seat of this particular people, so much so, that in 1917 Lawrence of Arabia recruited Bedouin women fighters living in the vicinity of Petra, who were able to completely decimate the advancing German and Turkish forces there.

I suppose the heart problem with Esau, the man who would rather have a bowl of soup than serve God, became magnified, multiplied and manifest in the Edomite nation, and that problem was very simply 'pride.' This pride set Edom up to oppose the people of God and accuse and abuse them. Just like the devil and just like the devil,

"I WILL BRING YOU DOWN"

| OBADIAH | 31 of 66 |

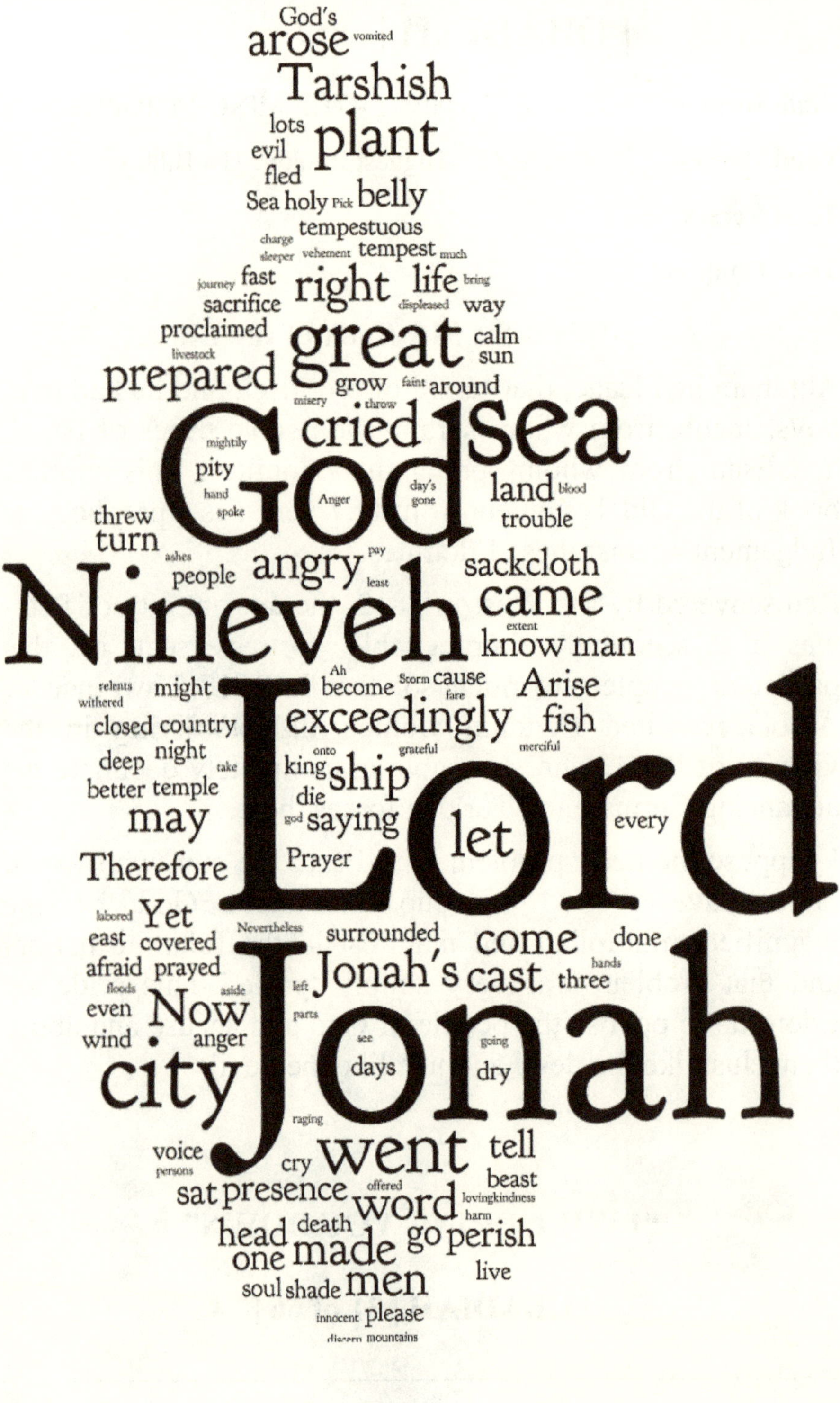
God's
arose
vomited
Tarshish
lots
plant
evil
fled
Sea
holy
Pick
belly
tempestuous
charge
sleeper
vehement
tempest
much
journey
fast
right
life
bring
sacrifice
displeased
way
proclaimed
great
calm
livestock
sun
prepared
grow
faint
around
misery
throw
cried
sea
God
mightily
pity
day's
land
blood
hand
Anger
gone
spoke
threw
trouble
turn
ashes
pay
people
angry
sackcloth
least
Nineveh
came
extent
know
man
Ah
relents
might
become
Storm
cause
Arise
withered
fare
exceedingly
closed
country
fish
onto
grateful
merciful
night
deep
take
king
ship
better
temple
die
Lord
may
god
saying
let
every
Therefore
Prayer
labored
Yet
Nevertheless
east
covered
surrounded
come
done
afraid
prayed
hands
Jonah's
cast
three
floods
aside
left
even
Now
parts
wind
anger
see
going
Jonah
city
days
dry
raging
voice
went
tell
persons
cry
beast
sat
presence
offered
lovingkindness
word
harm
head
death
go
perish
one
made
live
soul
shade
men
innocent
please
mountains

| JONAH |

Bible Section | OLD TESTAMENT - THE MINOR PROPHETS

Total Words | 1,320 (The 57th Biggest Book in The Bible)

Total Verses | 48

Total Chapters | 4

| This is the **32nd Book of the Bible.**

Jonah records the biggest single turning to God in recorded history, through words delivered from probably the most reluctant preacher that ever lived! So, it appears that the very naughty Ninevites are ready to turn to God and God is determined to get the message of repentance to this same people whose hearts are ready to hear it.

Unfortunately, Jonah did not want to know that his God was also the God of the non-Jews, especially as the Ninevites had acted like Nazis towards Israel. So, angry & ornery Jonah, 'legs it' in the opposite direction to which God had commanded him to go.

A great storm sees frightened sailors throwing Jonah into the mouth of a great fish, prepared by God as Jonah's new method of transport, which eventually vomits the stomach acid, bleached-white, resurrected-from-the-dead Jonah into the streets of that great city.

After the turning to God, Jonah 'the petulant', receives a chastising question from the patient heart of God.

"SHOULD I NOT PITY?"

(Jonah 4:11 NKJV)

| JONAH | 32 of 66 |

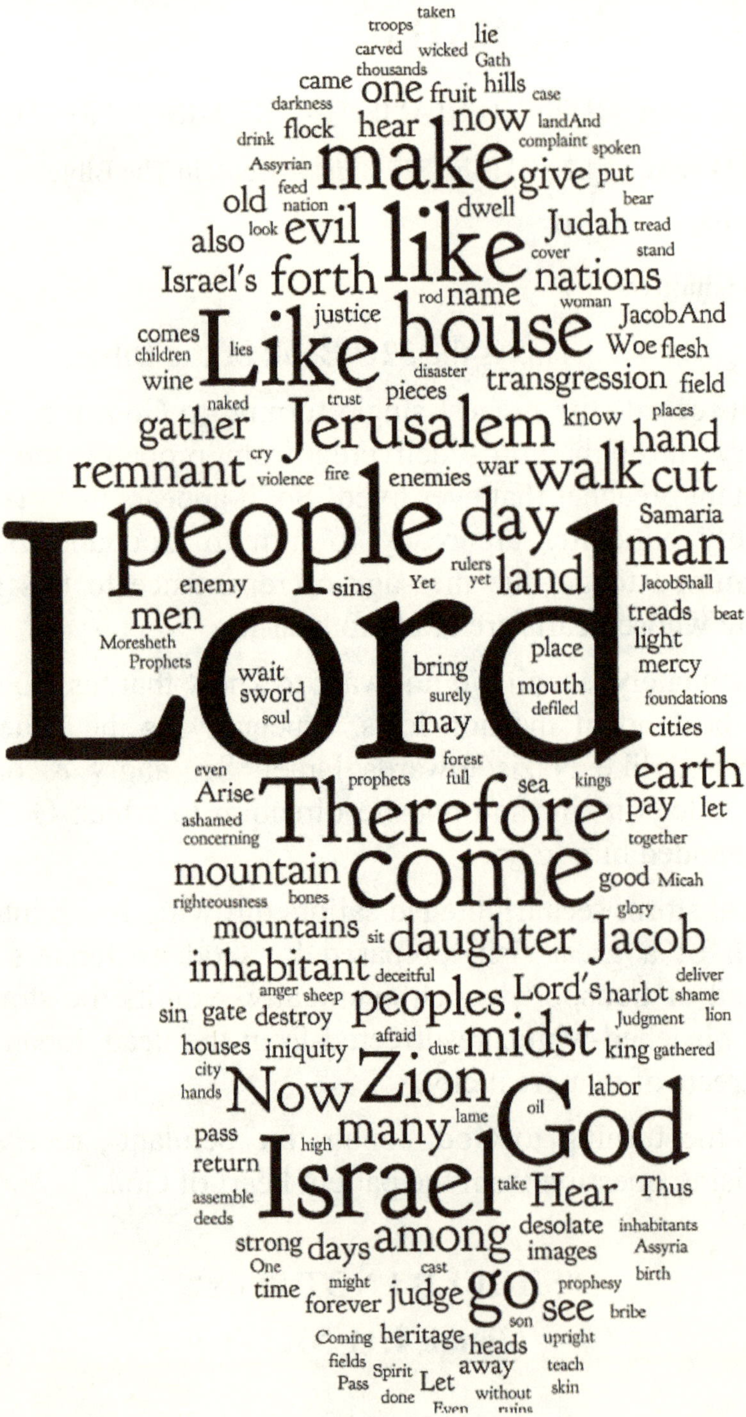
taken
troops
lie
carved
wicked
Gath
thousands
came
one
fruit
hills
case
darkness
drink
flock
hear
now
landAnd
complaint
Assyrian
make
spoken
give
put
feed
old
nation
dwell
bear
also
look
evil
like
Judah
tread
cover
stand
Israel's
forth
nations
rod
name
woman
justice
JacobAnd
comes
Like
house
children
lies
Woe
flesh
wine
disaster
transgression
field
naked
trust
pieces
know
places
gather
Jerusalem
hand
cry
remnant
violence
fire
enemies
war
walk
cut
people
day
Samaria
Lord
man
rulers
enemy
sins
Yet
yet
land
JacobShall
men
treads
beat
Moresheth
light
Prophets
place
wait
bring
mercy
sword
mouth
surely
foundations
soul
defiled
may
cities
forest
even
prophets
full
kings
earth
Arise
sea
Therefore
pay
let
ashamed
concerning
together
mountain
come
good
Micah
righteousness
bones
glory
mountains
sit
daughter
Jacob
inhabitant
deceitful
deliver
anger
sheep
Lord's
harlot
shame
sin
gate
destroy
peoples
Judgment
lion
houses
iniquity
afraid
dust
midst
king
gathered
city
hands
Now
Zion
labor
oil
lame
God
pass
many
high
return
Israel
assemble
take
Hear
Thus
deeds
desolate
inhabitants
strong
days
among
images
Assyria
One
cast
might
prophesy
birth
time
judge
go
forever
see
bribe
son
Coming
heritage
heads
upright
fields
away
teach
Spirit
Let
Pass
done
without
skin
Even
ruins

| MICAH |

Bible Section | OLD TESTAMENT - THE MINOR PROPHETS

Total Words | 3,152 (The 39th Biggest Book in The Bible)

Total Verses | 105

Total Chapters | 7

| This is the **33rd Book of the Bible.**

Micah's name means, 'Who is Like Jehovah?' And most certainly Micah is a book of judgement on the whole of Israel. However, the announcement of impending judgement is tempered by a touching tenderness, for he says consistently, "Who is like God in proclaiming truth, pronouncing mercy, pleading with people; in pardoning sin, in passing by our offences and in plunging our sins into the depth of the sea?" For through the black battle-smoke of impending doom, Micah catches sight of the mercies of God bringing future glory and redemption to Israel. Indeed, it is again Micah who sees and says, "Out of you shall come forth to Me the One to be Ruler in Israel, Whose goings forth are from of old, from everlasting." (Micah 5:2 NKJV)

You see, even in pronouncing judgement, Micah cannot stop speaking about the magnificence of God's goodness. Why?

BECAUSE GOD DELIGHTS IN MERCY

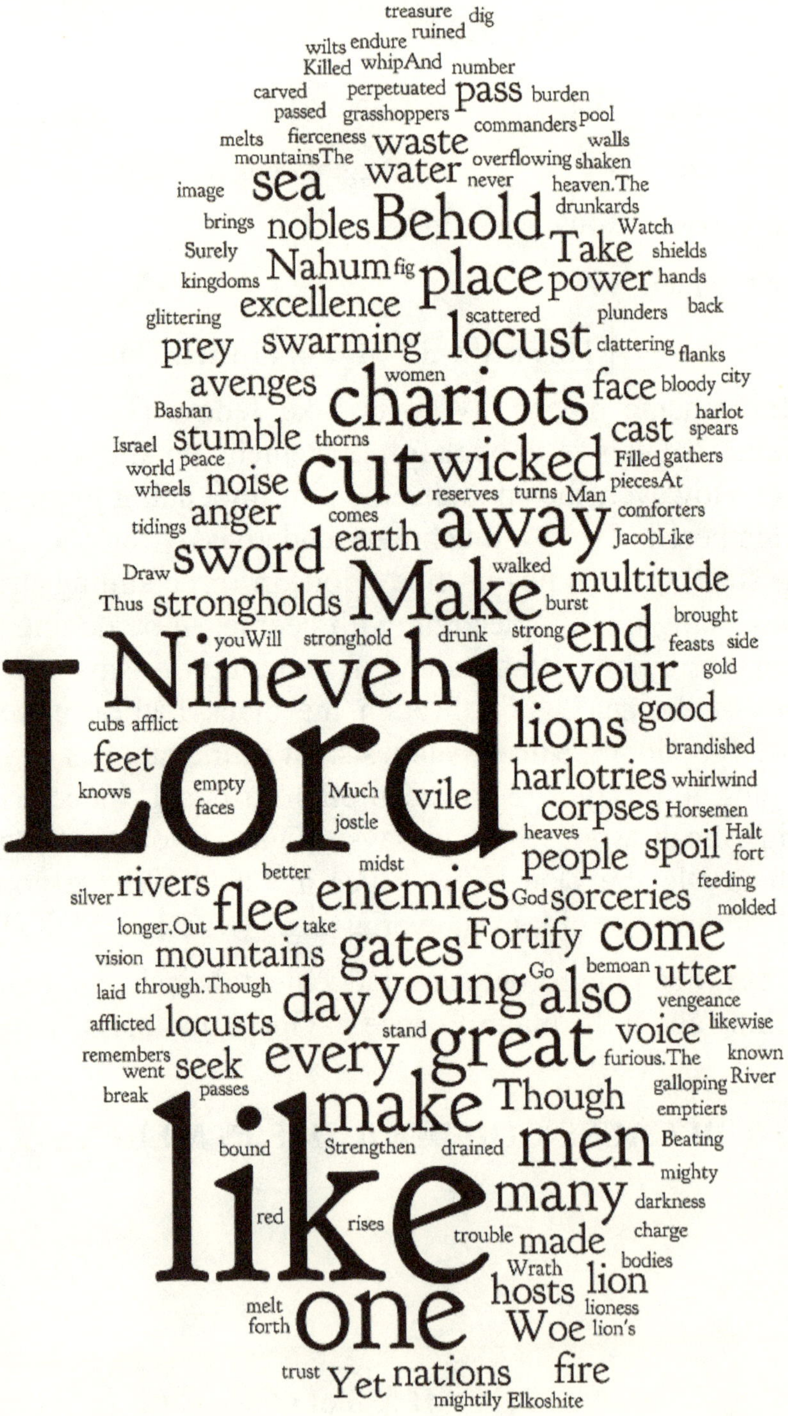
treasure dig
ruined
wilts endure
Killed whipAnd number
carved perpetuated pass burden
passed grasshoppers commanders pool
melts fierceness waste walls
mountainsThe overflowing shaken
image sea water never heaven.The
brings nobles Behold drunkards
Watch
Surely Take shields
Nahum fig
kingdoms place power hands
glittering excellence scattered plunders back
prey swarming locust clattering flanks
avenges women face bloody city
Bashan chariots harlot
Israel stumble thorns cast spears
world peace wicked Filled gathers
wheels noise cut reserves turns Man piecesAt
tidings anger comes comforters
away
sword earth JacobLike
Draw walked multitude
Thus strongholds Make burst brought
youWill stronghold drunk strong end feasts side
Nineveh devour gold
good
cubs afflict lions
feet brandished
Lord
harlotries whirlwind
knows empty Much vile
faces jostle corpses Horsemen
heaves Halt
people spoil fort
better midst feeding
silver rivers enemies God sorceries
flee molded
longer.Out take
vision mountains gates Fortify come
Go bemoan utter
laid through.Though young also
day vengeance
afflicted locusts stand voice likewise
remembers great known
went seek every furious.The River
break passes galloping
make Though emptiers
bound Strengthen drained men Beating
mighty
like many darkness
red rises trouble made charge
Wrath bodies
hosts lion
melt lioness
forth one Woe lion's
trust Yet nations fire
mightily Elkoshite

| NAHUM |

Bible Section | OLD TESTAMENT - THE MINOR PROPHETS

Total Words | 1,284 (The 58th Biggest Book in The Bible)

Total Verses | 47

Total Chapters | 3

| This is the **34th Book of the Bible.**

The only theme concerning this small book of just three chapters is the judgement of the capital city of Assyria, Ninevah!

Nahum prophesied 100 years after Jonah, and that repentant generation had long since passed. However, God even gave Ninevah a further 100 years to repent after this message had been delivered.

It's true you know what Jonny Cash sang, "You can run on for a long time but sooner or later God'll cut you down." Know this as well, that no matter how large the empire, no matter how powerful the godless nation, if it is godless, it will be cut down and made to disappear.

Judah is encouraged to know that God is aware of their heart-quaking fear towards Assyria and that they were no longer to worry, because God is going to make Nineveh empty, desolate and wasted.

WHERE THE LORD HAS HIS WAY IN THE WHIRLWIND AND THE STORM

| NAHUM | 34 of 66 |

molded Cushan entered
stronghold flashing
men's anger
heard
heap fig many evil
leopards
uttered
earth God high
Violence
cover drunk Lord's glory offense
violence
walked slay feet
empty arrows The delivered
stone live Though
hold set may
horses covets
net whirlwind vines Selah maker
proverb went Therefore soul
hills days Which comes marches take Rottenness
sin
forth.For sea Habakkuk plentiful
possess
forth become
displeased blood And shame hand beasts
never
drink silence righteous light food
startled eyes
stood Musician
also judgment
perverse
hook mountains
nations.And deal fly wrath breadth ahead
poor
therefore gather Woe made
answer waters
look
labor revive shameful
told power everlasting hands
god cry Just
gold watch wickedness.Why come
wine
riddle see make people fierce
praise passed sand sworn
midst image them.They
deride proceed earthen carve temple.Let
burden proud salvation Even arises
hastens
Question
perpetual Prophet's trouble.When
Anointed.You
exposed rivers dwell charge lips appointed trouble
deep increases What
Behold transgresses
glittering years
came divided house
like
vision just trust saw
Paran.Selah wicked without
Yet right struck plunder
mind Holy knowledge
head astounded
nations feasting
work land
faces Live bottle iniquity
marched trembled long
end
city voice
Lord arrows
holy silver fold
overflowing
vain neighbor
satisfied
plundered
rejoice peoples
One prophet
afraid

| HABAKKUK |

Bible Section | OLD TESTAMENT - THE MINOR PROPHETS

Total Words | 1,475 (The 56th Biggest Book in The Bible)

Total Verses | 56

Total Chapters | 3

| This is the **25th Book in the Bible.**

Habakkuk is where the prophet says "there, there, there." Yes, Luther declares that Habakkuk means 'love's embrace' and he comforts Israel, holding them close, even as one might embrace a weeping child, to quiet it with the assurance that, "if God wills, it shall soon be better." However, the prophet did not have it 'all together' even in his own heart, and it's McGee that says Habakkuk is, "the doubting Thomas of the Old Testament and the prophet that has a question mark for a brain!" And he did! He had two big questions:

Firstly WHY DOES GOD PERMIT EVIL? And

Secondly, WHY DOES GOD USE EVIL NATIONS TO PUNISH NATIONS NOT AS EVIL AS THEM?

Habakkuk got his answer when God told him that, contrary to Him not doing anything, He was actively at work now in judging the nations of the earth. This scared Habakkuk, but he responds in faith, in effect saying, "I know that I can make it; I know that I can stand, no matter what may come my way, my life is in Your hands."

"IN YOUR WRATH O LORD – REMEMBER MERCY"

| HABBAKUK | 35 of 66 |

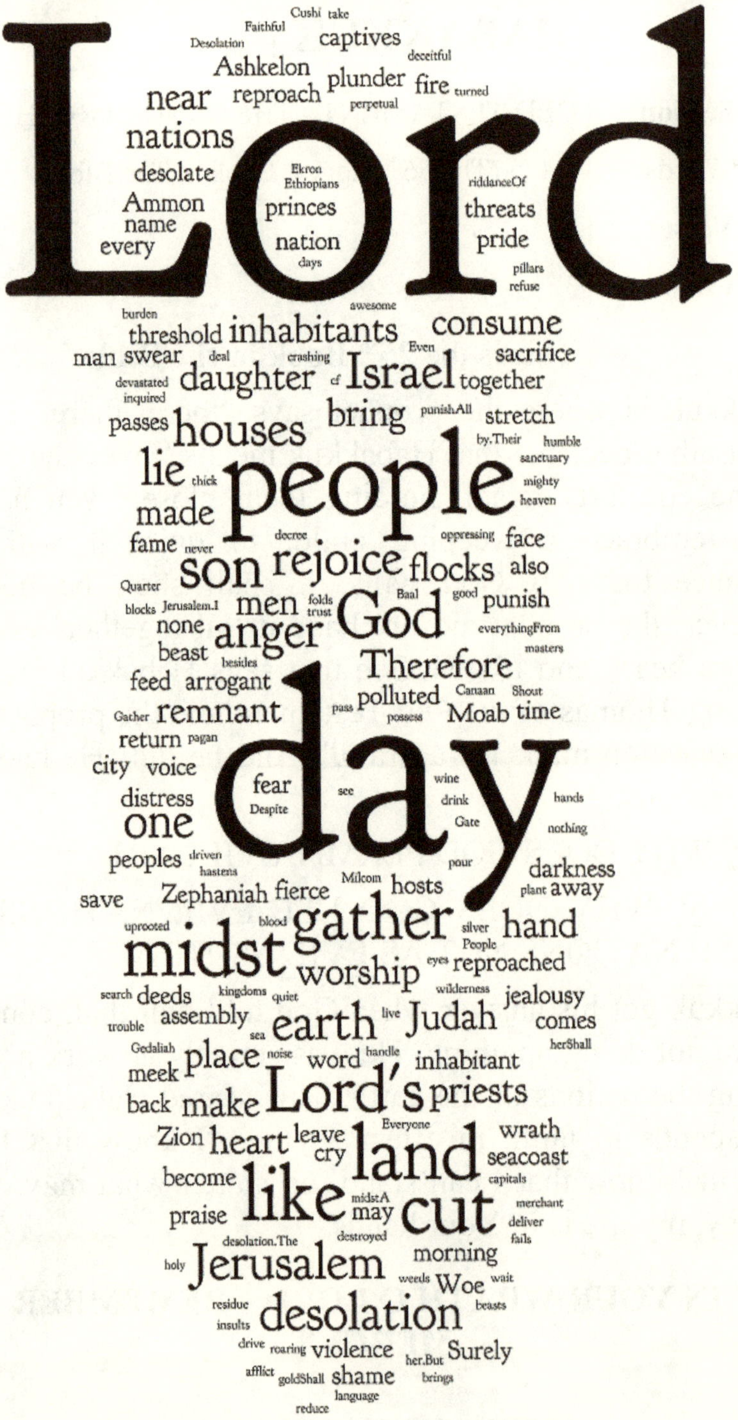

Lord
Cushi take
Faithful
Desolation
captives
deceitful
Ashkelon
plunder
fire
turned
near
reproach
perpetual
nations
desolate
Ekron
Ethiopians
riddanceOf
Ammon
princes
threats
name
every
nation
pride
days
pillars
refuse
burden
awesome
threshold
inhabitants
consume
man
swear
deal
crashing
Even
sacrifice
devastated
daughter
cf
Israel
together
inquired
bring
punishAll
stretch
passes
houses
by.Their
humble
sanctuary
lie
thick
people
mighty
heaven
made
decree
oppressing
face
fame
never
son
rejoice
flocks
also
Quarter
Baal
good
blocks
Jerusalem.I
men
folds
trust
God
punish
none
anger
everythingFrom
beast
masters
besides
Therefore
feed
arrogant
day
Canaan
Shout
polluted
Gather
remnant
pass
possess
Moab
time
return
pagan
city
voice
wine
fear
see
drink
hands
distress
Despite
Gate
one
nothing
peoples
driven
hastens
pour
darkness
save
Zephaniah
fierce
Milcom
hosts
plant
away
uprooted
blood
gather
silver
hand
People
midst
eyes
reproached
worship
search
deeds
kingdoms
quiet
wilderness
jealousy
trouble
assembly
earth
live
Judah
comes
Gedaliah
sea
herShall
meek
place
noise
word
handle
inhabitant
back
make
Lord's
priests
Everyone
Zion
heart
leave
cry
land
wrath
seacoast
become
capitals
like
midstA
may
cut
merchant
praise
deliver
desolation.The
destroyed
fails
holy
Jerusalem
morning
weeds
Woe
wait
residue
beasts
insults
desolation
drive
roaring
violence
her.But
Surely
afflict
goldShall
shame
brings
language
reduce

| ZEPHANIAH |

Bible Section | OLD TESTAMENT - THE MINOR PROPHETS

Total Words | 1,617 (The 54th Biggest Book in The Bible)

Total Verses | 53

Total Chapters | 3

| This is the **36th Book of the Bible.**

Zephaniah is the prophet of Royal blood, descended from Hezekiah. He was born out of 'the killing-time' of mad Manasseh, who filled Jerusalem with blood from one end to the other. The prophecy gives you the sense that, the water has boiled away from around the un-pierced can in the now empty pan on the hot stove and the internal pressure of God's avenging justice is about to explode all over the planet's kitchen, and that there is no way to turn the heat down anymore before it happens!

Yes, the whole planet is going to be judges, for apart from predicting the eventual and utter desolation of Judah, and her surrounding enemies, this prophecy is chiefly about 'the Day Of The Lord,' which appears 23 times in this short book, and refers to an apocalyptic end-of--the-world judgement on all nations after which, those committed and remaining remnant people will then worship God freely and He will become their mighty King and defender, only then singing them into settledness.

VERY DISTURBING

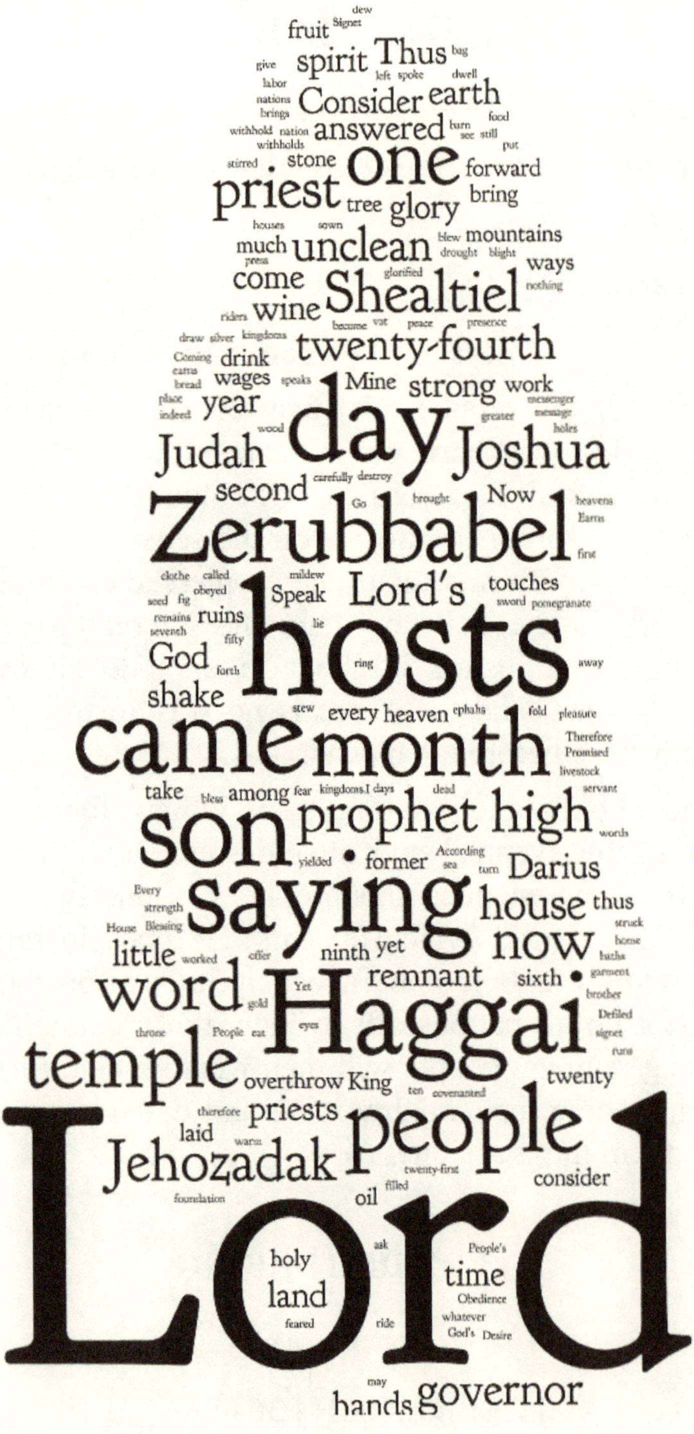
dew
fruit
Signet
spirit
Thus
bag
give
left
spoke
dwell
labor
nations
Consider
earth
brings
food
withhold
nation
answered
burn
see
still
withholds
put
stirred
stone
one
forward
priest
bring
tree
glory
houses
sown
much
unclean
blew
mountains
press
drought
blight
come
glorified
ways
Shealtiel
nothing
riders
wine
become
vat
peace
presence
draw
silver
kingdoms
twenty-fourth
Coming
drink
earns
bread
wages
speaks
Mine
strong
work
place
year
messenger
indeed
message
greater
wood
holes
day
Judah
Joshua
carefully
destroy
second
Now
Go
brought
heavens
Zerubbabel
Earns
first
clothe
called
mildew
touches
seed
fig
obeyed
Speak
Lord's
sword
pomegranate
remains
ruins
seventh
lie
fifty
God
hosts
forth
ring
away
shake
stew
every
heaven
ephahs
fold
pleasure
came
month
Therefore
Promised
livestock
take
bless
among
fear
kingdoms.I
days
dead
servant
son
prophet
high
words
yielded
former
According
sea
turn
Darius
Every
saying
strength
house
thus
House
Blessing
struck
little
worked
offer
ninth
yet
now
home
baths
word
remnant
sixth
garment
Yet
gold
Haggai
brother
Defiled
throne
People
eat
eyes
signet
runs
temple
overthrow
King
ten
covenanted
twenty
therefore
priests
laid
warm
people
Jehozadak
twenty-first
consider
foundation
filled
oil
Lord
holy
ask
People's
time
land
Obedience
whatever
feared
ride
God's
Desire
may
hands
governor

| HAGGAI |

Bible Section | OLD TESTAMENT – THE MINOR PROPHETS

Total Words | 1,130 (The 59th Biggest Book in The Bible)

Total Verses | 38

Total Chapters | 2

| This is the **37th Book of the Bible.**

Haggai is the prophet to and for the Temple. He spoke the word of the Lord to the returned remnant, to those Jews who came back from Babylon and to those Jews who, because of the difficulties they had faced from their enemies without and within, had laid the foundation of the temple, but had now stopped the building of it.

Haggai was God's cattle prod to get these 'tools down' folks moving again, and so God zapped them, asking, "How come your houses are fantastic and mine's like a Grecian peasant's, not even half built and rusty along with it?"

It was enough to shock them into action and God encouraged them by saying in effect "Fear Not I am With You, so be strong, be strong, be strong and keep on working, and don't worry about the glories of the past temple the glories of the future will be even better". And He means here the far off millennial future. God is very long sighted- His people needed to be as well.

COME TO THE DESIRE OF ALL NATIONS.

| HAGGAI | 37 of 66 |

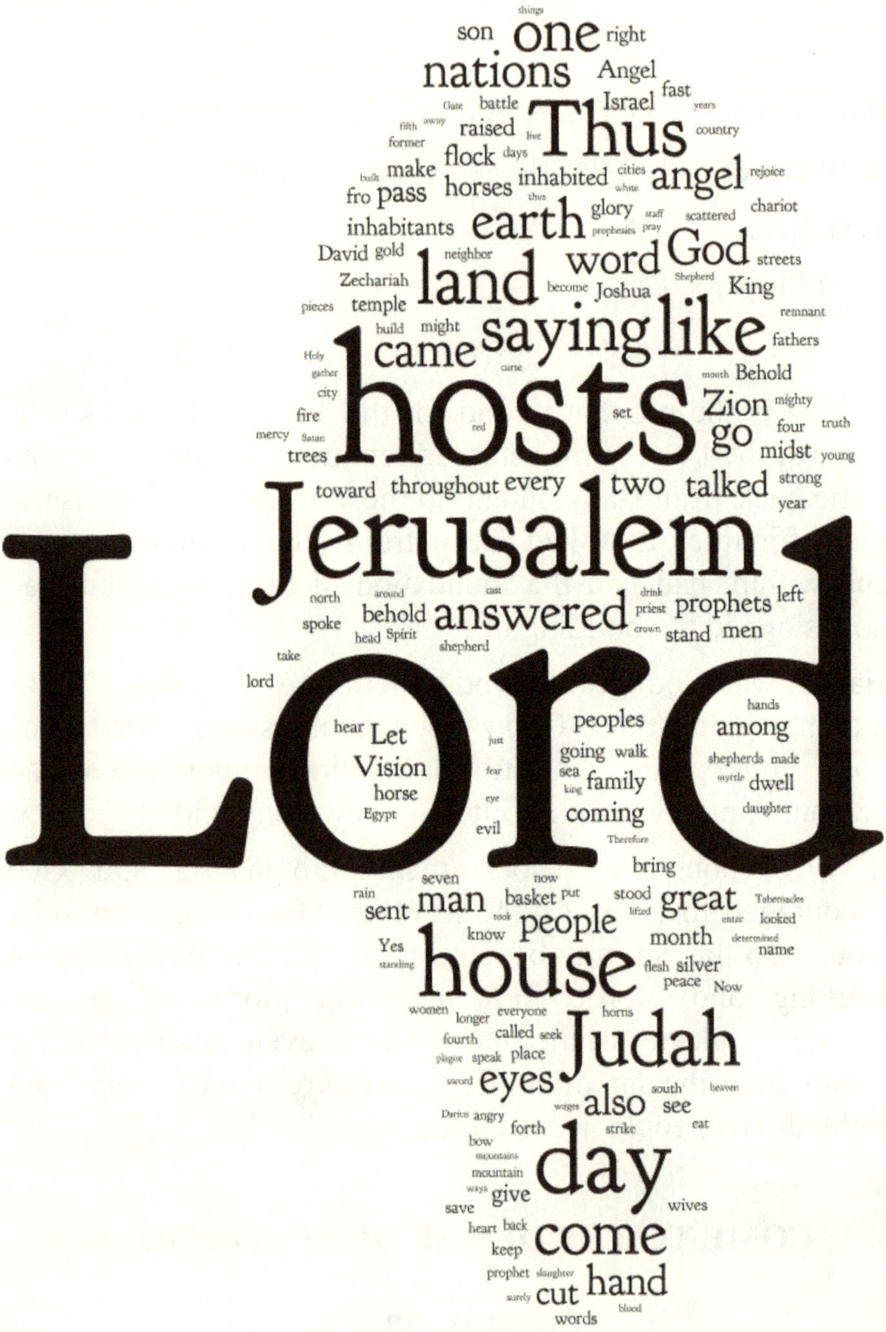
Lord
hosts
Jerusalem
Thus
house
Judah
day
come
saying
like
land
earth
God
word
angel
nations
one
answered
came
talked
two
every
throughout
toward
man
people
great
hand
cut
eyes
also
son
right
Angel
Israel
fast
battle
raised
flock
make
pass
horses
inhabited
inhabitants
glory
scattered
chariot
country
rejoice
cities
David
gold
neighbor
Zecharian
temple
pieces
Joshua
King
streets
remnant
fathers
build
might
Behold
Zion
go
set
mighty
four
truth
midst
young
fire
mercy
trees
strong
year
city
gather
Holy
north
behold
spoke
head
Spirit
shepherd
priest
prophets
left
stand
men
take
lord
hear
Let
Vision
horse
Egypt
peoples
going
walk
sea
family
coming
evil
among
hands
shepherds
made
dwell
daughter
bring
seven
now
rain
sent
basket
put
stood
looked
know
month
name
Yes
silver
peace
Now
flesh
women
longer
everyone
horns
fourth
called
seek
speak
place
south
see
angry
forth
strike
eat
bow
mountain
give
save
wives
heart
back
keep
prophet
words
former
fro
days
years
red
Satan
just
fear
eye
king
crown
drink
cast
around

| ZECHERIAH |

Bible Section	| OLD TESTAMENT - THE MINOR PROPHETS
Total Words	| 6,443 (The 32nd Biggest Book in The Bible)
Total Verses	| 211
Total Chapters	| 14

| This is the **38th Book of the Bible.**

Zechariah is the martyr who, according to Jesus, was slain between the temple and the altar. He is the son of Berechiah, the son of Iddo, and this encouraging cluster of three names can be constructed to mean, 'God remembers and blesses in the appointed time'.

Zechariah contains more Messianic prophecies than any of the other Minor Prophets, even ten visions in all, and they were all given in one night! Chapter 14, the last chapter of this book, is one of the most magnificent millennial montages ever constructed; speaking of the outcome of Armageddon, the physical return of Christ, all resulting in massive topographical, elemental and spiritual changes upon the surface of the earth. Especially in that area of Israel and Jerusalem, and indeed, even in the whole earth and everything in it. Such that, even the pots and pans in the kitchen shall also bear an internal and an external testimony to the change, even a mark as to its true intention. Oh, and here is the millennial mark Zecheriah speaks of,

"HOLINESS TO THE LORD!"

(Zech 14:20 NKJV)

| ZECHERIAH | 38 of 66 |

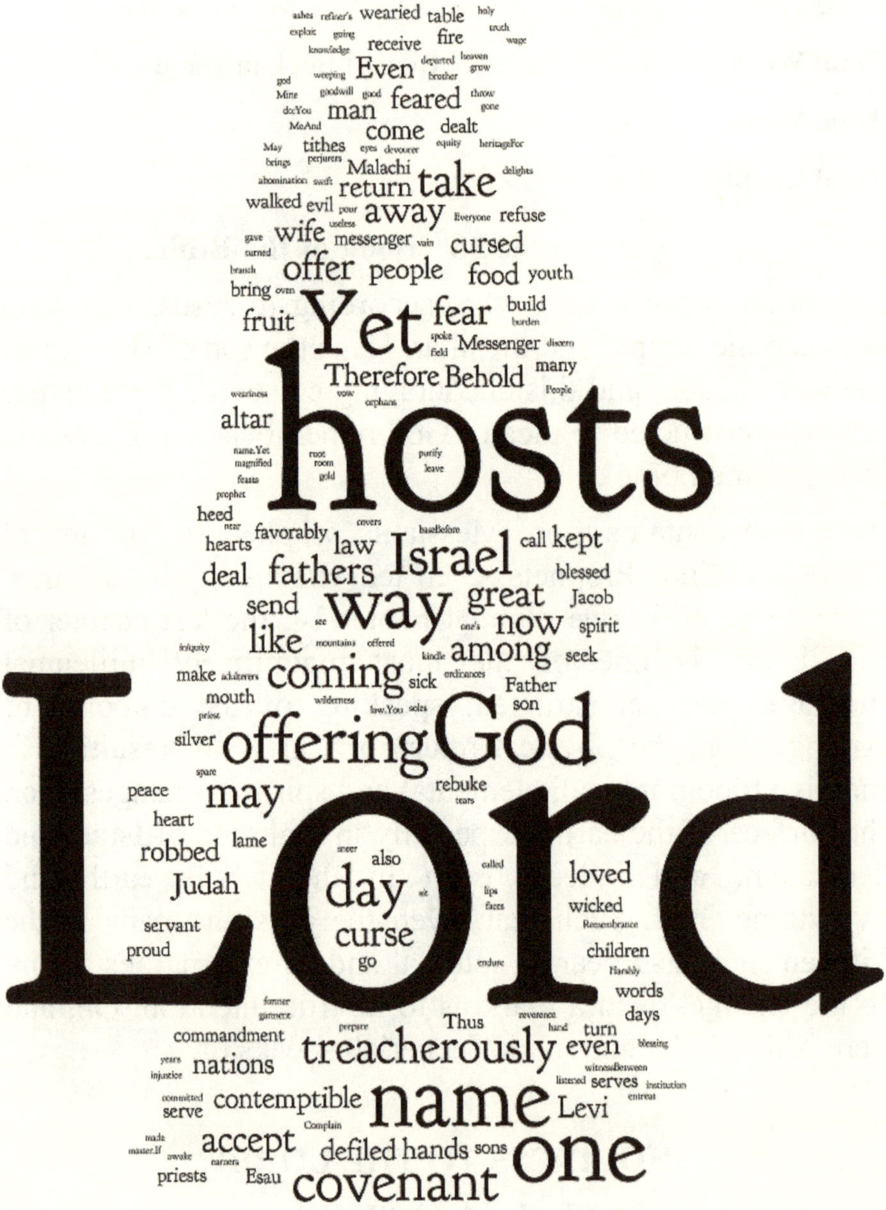
wearied
table
fire
receive
Even
feared
man
come
dealt
tithes
Malachi
take
return
walked
evil
away
refuse
wife
messenger
cursed
offer
people
food
youth
bring
Yet
fear
build
fruit
Messenger
Therefore Behold
many
altar
hosts
heed
hearts
favorably
law
Israel
call
kept
deal
fathers
blessed
send
way
great
Jacob
like
now
spirit
among
seek
make
coming
sick
Father
mouth
son
silver
offering
God
peace
may
rebuke
heart
Lord
robbed
lame
also
loved
Judah
day
wicked
servant
curse
proud
children
go
words
Thus
days
commandment
turn
treacherously
even
nations
serves
contemptible
name
Levi
serve
accept
defiled hands
sons
one
priests
Esau
covenant

| MALACHI |

Bible Section | OLD TESTAMENT - THE MINOR PROPHETS

Total Words | 1,781 (The 52nd Biggest Book in The Bible)

Total Verses | 55

Total Chapters | 4

| This is the **39th B**ook of the Bible.

Malachi is the last book in the Old Testament, and until the arrival of John the Baptizer, Malachi is the last prophetic 'Messenger' (and that's what his name means) for the next 400 years. Apart from chastising the people for offering sick and second class sacrifices and then for robbing God in withholding their tithes and offerings, as well as finally challenging them over their practice of Israeli's divorcing practices, when old men traded in their older wives for newer models, again, Malachi looks centuries down the road and speaks specifically about John the Baptizer and Jesus saying, "Behold, I send My messenger, And He will prepare the way before Me. And the Lord, whom you seek, will suddenly come to His temple, even the Messenger of the covenant, in whom you delight. Behold, He is coming," says the Lord of hosts. (Mal 3:1 NKJV) This book is a message sign-off that says, "The next voice you shall hear will announce the coming of the Messiah!"

"THEY SHALL BE MINE," SAYS THE LORD OF HOSTS, "IN THE DAY THAT I MAKE THEM MY JEWELS" (Mal 3:17 NKJV)

| MALACHI | 39 of 66 |

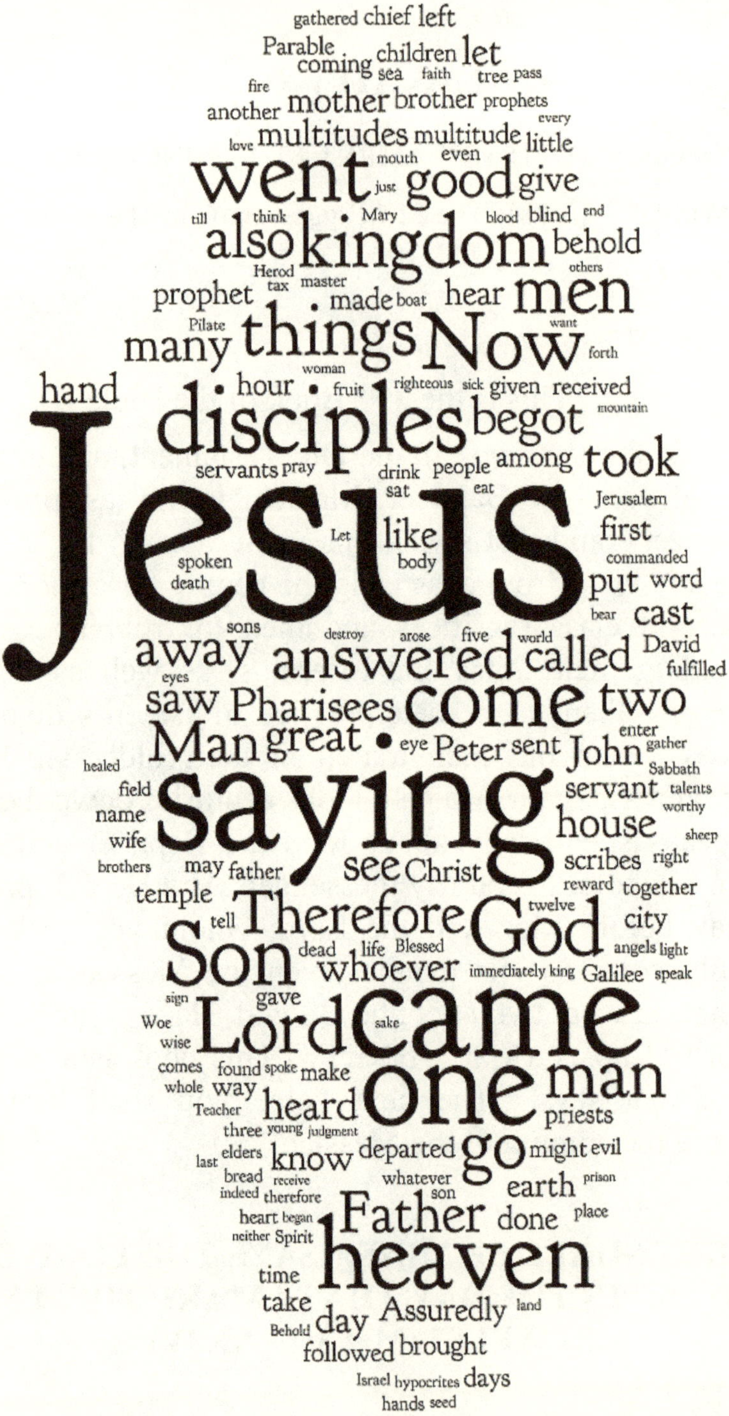
gathered chief left
Parable children let
coming sea faith tree pass
fire
another mother brother prophets
every
love multitudes multitude little
mouth even
went just good give
till think Mary blood blind end
also kingdom behold
Herod others
tax master
prophet made boat hear men
Pilate want
many things Now
forth
woman
hand hour fruit righteous sick given received
mountain
Jesus
disciples begot
servants pray drink people among took
sat eat
Jerusalem
Let like first
spoken body commanded
death put word
bear cast
sons destroy arose five world
away answered called David
eyes fulfilled
saw Pharisees come two
enter
Man great eye Peter sent John gather
healed Sabbath
field saying servant talents
worthy
name house
sheep
wife
brothers may father see Christ scribes right
reward together
temple
twelve
tell Therefore God city
Son dead life Blessed angels light
whoever immediately king Galilee speak
sign gave
Woe Lord came
sake
wise
comes found spoke make
whole way one man
Teacher heard priests
three young judgment
last elders know departed go might evil
bread receive whatever prison
indeed therefore son earth
heart began Father done place
neither Spirit
time heaven
take
land
Assuredly
Behold day
followed brought
Israel hypocrites days
hands seed

| MATTHEW |

Bible Section | NEW TESTAMENT - THE GOSPELS

Total Words | 23, 684 (The 04th Biggest Book in The Bible)

Total Verses | 1,071

Total Chapters | 28

| This is the **40th Book of the Bible.**

Matthew is the first book of the New Testament.

Remember, that for 400 years God has been silent - there has been NO WORD from Heaven whatsoever, until the angel Gabriel appears to an old priest, and picking up the theme of Malachi, says to him, "Do not be afraid, Zacharias, for your prayer is heard; and your wife Elizabeth will bear you a son, and you shall call his name John… He will also go before Him in the spirit and power of Elijah … to make ready a people prepared for the Lord." NKJV

Matthew is written by a converted, apostolic Tax Collector formerly called Levi. It's the first of four Gospels presenting the different aspects of the life and times of Jesus the Messiah.

Matthew is the book of 'the Kingdom of Heaven, come down to earth, for Matthew presents to us JESUS as 'The King' arriving to set up His kingdom.

THEREFORE, "REPENT, FOR THE KINGDOM OF HEAVEN IS AT HAND."

(Matt 3:2 & 4:17 NKJV)

| MATTHEW | 40 of 66 |

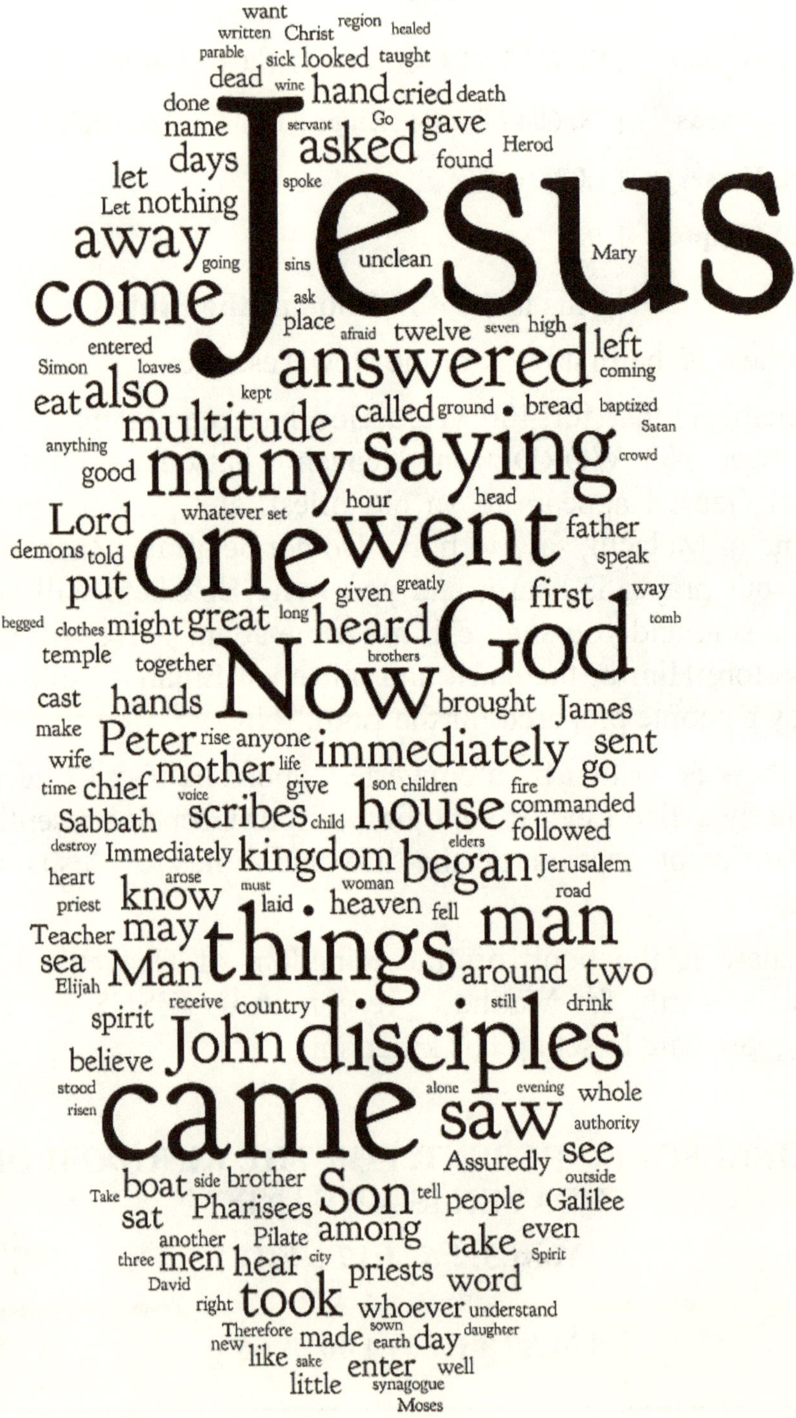

want
written Christ region healed
parable sick looked taught
dead wine hand cried death
done servant Go gave
name asked Herod
days found
let spoke
Let nothing
Jesus
away
going sins unclean Mary
come
ask
place afraid twelve seven high
entered left
Simon loaves answered coming
eat also kept
called ground bread baptized
multitude Satan
anything saying crowd
good many
hour head
Lord whatever set
father
demons told one went speak
put given greatly first way
begged clothes might great long heard God tomb
temple together brothers
cast hands Now brought James
make Peter rise anyone immediately sent
wife life go
time chief mother give son children fire
voice commanded
Sabbath scribes child house followed
destroy Immediately kingdom elders
heart arose began Jerusalem
priest know must woman road
laid heaven fell
Teacher may man
things
sea Man around two
Elijah
receive country still drink
spirit
believe John disciples
stood alone evening whole
risen came saw authority
Assuredly see
boat side brother outside
Take Son tell people Galilee
sat Pharisees
another Pilate among take even
three men hear city Spirit
David priests word
right took whoever understand
Therefore sown daughter
new made earth day
like sake well
enter
little synagogue
Moses

| MARK |

Bible Section | NEW TESTAMENT - THE GOSPELS

Total Words | 15,166 (The 23rd Biggest Book in The Bible)

Total Verses | 678

Total Chapters | 16

| This is the **41st Book of the Bible.**

Mark is written by John Mark, the nephew of Barnabas, who failed miserably in the eyes of Paul when he 'lost his bottle' and deserted them at Perga on the first missionary journey.

Like Peter, John Mark got his act together after his fall. Indeed, many theologians believe that Mark was a disciple of Peter and got much of his information and active action lifestyle and method of communication, right from him.

Mark certainly gets straight to the point in his writing; he's a tabloid head-liner, and consequently, Mark is an 'ACTION' Gospel, and McGee says that, 'Mark was written by a busy man for busy people about a busy Person.'

So Mark is all about headline action and deeds of daring and wonder, and all their associated emotions, and as John is his Hebrew name, Mark, being his Roman name, is emblematic of the primary audience to whom he is writing, - and you know the last human being to speak in this Gospel of Mark is a Roman Centurion speaking about Jesus saying,

"TRULY THIS MAN WAS THE SON OF GOD."

(Mark 15:39 NKJV)

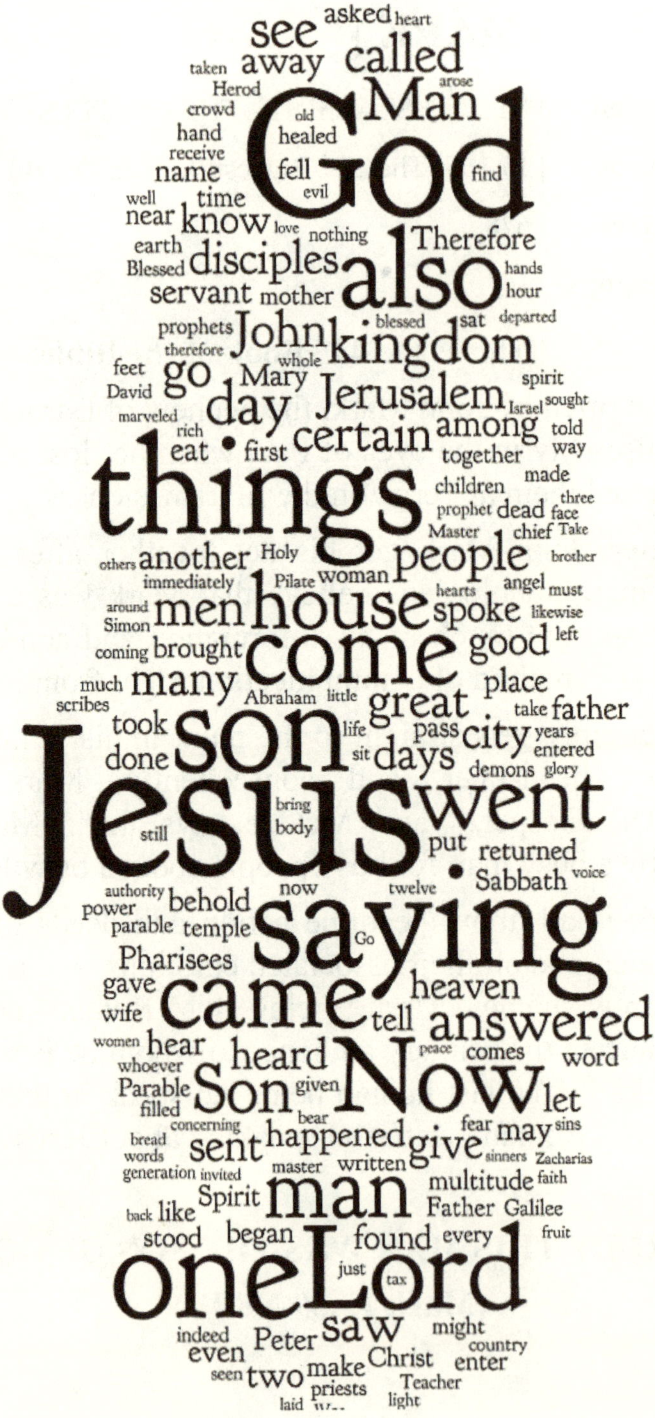

asked heart
see
taken away called
Herod arose
crowd Man
old
hand healed
receive
name God
fell find
well time evil
near know love
earth nothing Therefore
Blessed disciples also hands
servant mother hour
prophets blessed sat departed
therefore John kingdom
feet whole
go Mary spirit
David Jerusalem
day Israel sought
marveled rich among told
eat first certain way
together
things made
children three
prophet dead face
Master chief Take
Holy people
others another brother
immediately Pilate woman hearts angel must
around men house spoke likewise
Simon left
coming brought come good
much many place
scribes Abraham little great
took take father
son life pass city years
done sit days entered
demons glory
Jesus went
bring
still body put returned
Sabbath voice
authority now twelve
power behold
parable temple saying
Go
Pharisees
gave heaven
wife came
tell answered
women hear
peace comes
whoever heard word
Parable given Now
Son let
filled
concerning bear fear may sins
bread sent happened give
words master written sinners Zacharias
generation invited multitude faith
Spirit man
back like Father Galilee
stood began found every fruit
one Lord
just
tax
indeed saw might
Peter country
even make Christ enter
seen two priests Teacher
laid light

| LUKE |

Bible Section | NEW TESTAMENT - THE GOSPELS

Total Words | 25,939 (The 10th Biggest Book in The Bible)

Total Verses | 1,151

Total Chapters | 24

| This is the **42nd Book of the Bible.**

Luke is written by a doctor, indeed Colossians 4:14 refers to Luke as the "beloved physician." More than that thought, Luke was quite the historian and an accomplished and trained writer. He was also best buddies and travelling companion of the apostle Paul.

It's likely that Luke is probably not a Jew and seems therefore to be just the person to present certain aspects of Jesus which would be important for the caring, non-Jewish, pagan mind, and so Luke 'the witness,' is a medical scientist, a true humanitarian, and his gospel focuses on real people and how Jesus the perfect man, the 'God-man,' the man from heaven, related so superbly to them.

Indeed, Luke is the only one to record the parable of 'The Good Samaritan' and the parable of 'The Prodigal Son,' because he obviously cared for people, and after examining Jesus close-up, he presents to us Jesus as the perfect man from Heaven.

"BEHOLD THE MAN"

(John 19:5 NKJV)

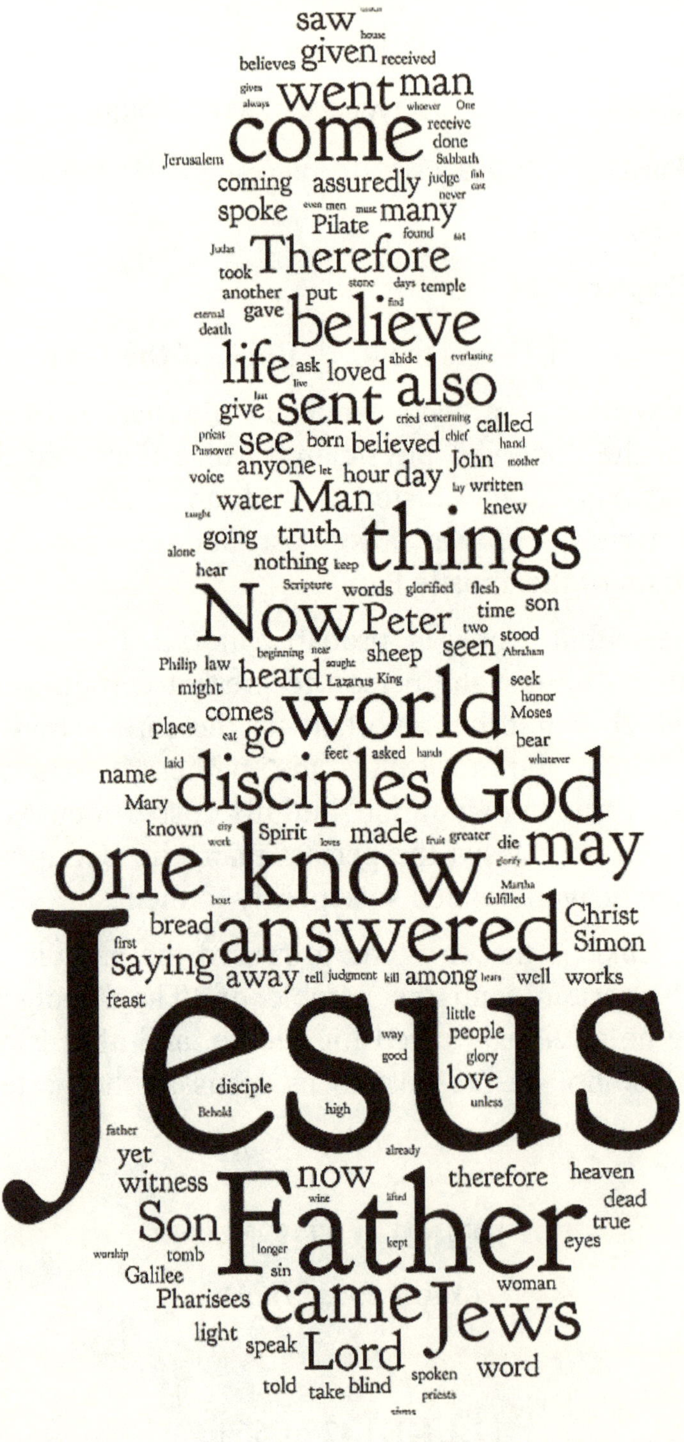
saw
house
believes
given
received
gives
went
man
always
whoever
One
come
receive
done
Jerusalem
Sabbath
coming
assuredly
judge
fish
never
spoke
even
men
must
many
Pilate
found
Judas
Therefore
took
another
put
stone
days
temple
eternal
gave
find
death
believe
life
ask
loved
abide
everlasting
live
also
last
give
sent
cried
concerning
called
priest
chief
Passover
see
born
believed
hand
anyone
let
hour
John
mother
voice
day
lay
written
water
Man
knew
taught
going
truth
things
alone
nothing
keep
hear
Scripture
words
glorified
flesh
Now
Peter
time
son
two
stood
beginning
near
sheep
seen
Abraham
Philip
law
sought
heard
Lazarus
King
seek
might
honor
comes
world
Moses
place
eat
go
bear
feet
asked
hands
laid
whatever
name
disciples
God
Mary
known
city
Spirit
made
fruit
greater
die
work
loves
may
glorify
one
know
Martha
boat
fulfilled
Christ
bread
answered
first
Simon
saying
away
tell
judgment
kill
among
hears
well
works
feast
Jesus
little
way
people
good
glory
love
disciple
Behold
high
unless
father
already
yet
now
therefore
heaven
witness
wine
lifted
dead
Son
Father
true
worship
tomb
longer
kept
eyes
Galilee
sin
woman
Pharisees
came
Jews
light
speak
Lord
word
told
take
blind
spoken
priests

| JOHN |

Bible Section | NEW TESTAMENT - THE GOSPELS

Total Words | 19,094 (The 19th Biggest Book in The Bible)

Total Verses | 879

Total Chapters | 21

| This is the **43rd Book of the Bible.**

John is the most theological, God-packed of all of the four Gospels.

Written by the brother of James, John 'The Apostle,' is also the writer of the epistles of John and the book of the Revelation of Jesus Christ. Indeed, that is this Gospel's very theme, 'The Revelation of Jesus Christ as the son of God, the promised Messiah of the Old Testament.

To that end, John gives us detailed insider information in chronological order, with great geographical reference, and subsequently it has a design of literary unity which has made it become the Gospel of the masses.

Because of John's emphasis on the unified and mystical relationship of the Son to the Father and the great prominence of love as the vital element of Christian character, it has become the canon of the common people, even the cup of rejoicing for the believer.

"WRITTEN THAT YOU MAY BELIEVE THAT JESUS IS THE CHRIST, THE SON OF GOD, AND THAT BELIEVING, YOU MAY HAVE LIFE IN HIS NAME." (John 20:31 NKJV)

| JOHN | 43 of 66 |

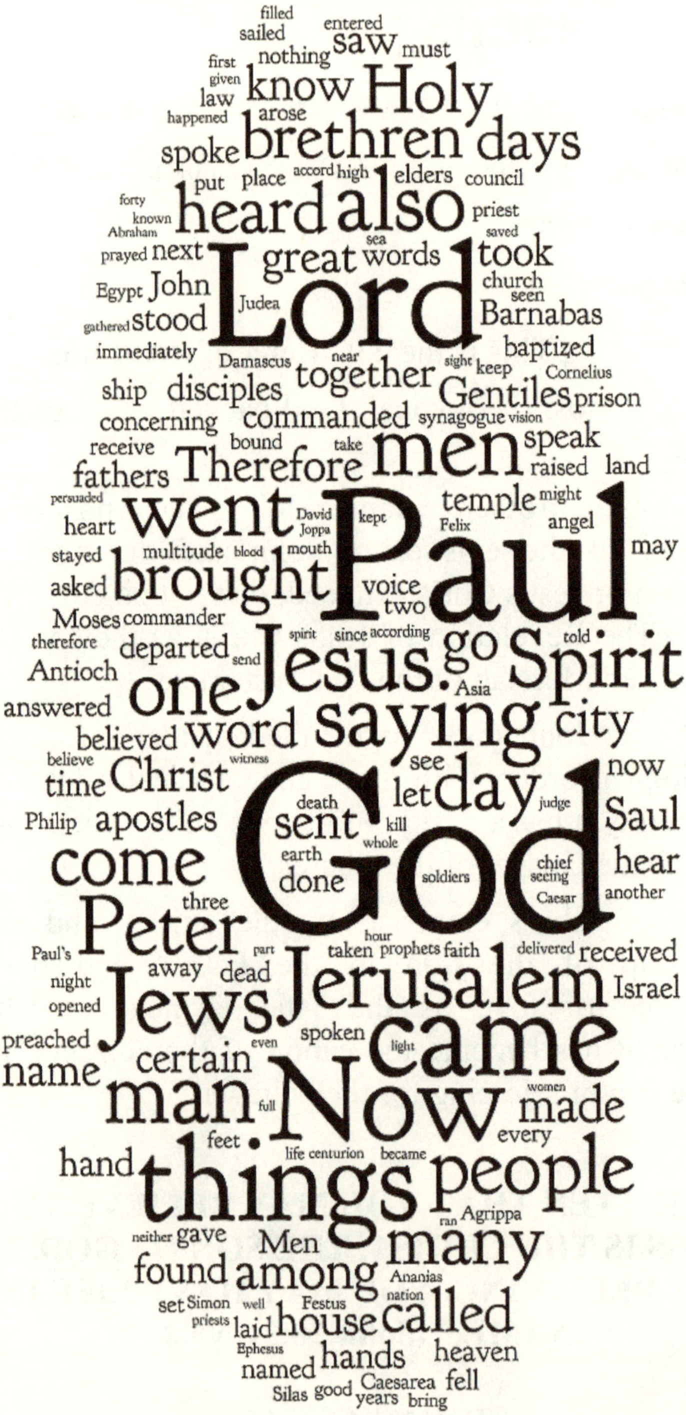
filled
entered
sailed
saw
must
first
nothing
given
know
Holy
law
happened
arose
brethren
spoke
days
accord
high
put
place
elders
council
forty
known
heard
also
priest
Abraham
saved
sea
prayed
next
great
words
took
Lord
Egypt
John
church
seen
Judea
gathered
stood
Barnabas
immediately
baptized
Damascus
near
sight
keep
Cornelius
together
ship
disciples
Gentiles
prison
concerning
commanded
synagogue
vision
receive
bound
take
men
speak
fathers
Therefore
raised
land
persuaded
temple
might
went
David
kept
heart
Joppa
Felix
angel
Paul
stayed
multitude
blood
mouth
may
asked
brought
voice
two
Moses
commander
therefore
spirit
since
according
told
departed
send
go
Antioch
Jesus.
Spirit
one
Asia
answered
saying
city
believed
word
believe
witness
see
now
time
Christ
let
day
death
judge
Philip
apostles
sent
kill
Saul
whole
God
come
earth
chief
hear
done
soldiers
seeing
three
Caesar
another
Peter
hour
Paul's
part
taken
prophets
faith
delivered
received
away
dead
night
Jerusalem
Israel
opened
Jews.
preached
spoken
even
light
came
certain
name
women
man
Now
full
made
every
feet
life
centurion
became
hand
things
people
ran
Agrippa
neither
gave
Men
many
found
among
Ananias
set
Simon
well
nation
Festus
priests
laid
house
called
Ephesus
hands
heaven
named
Caesarea
fell
Silas
good
years
bring

| ACTS |

Bible Section | NEW TESTAMENT – HISTORICAL BOOK

Total Words | 24,245 (The 14th Biggest Book in The Bible)

Total Verses | 1,007

Total Chapters | 28

| This is the **44th Book of the Bible.**

“It was necessary for the Christ to suffer and to rise from the dead the third day, and that repentance and remission of sins should be preached in His name to all nations, beginning at Jerusalem. And you are witnesses of these things. Behold, I send the Promise of My Father upon you; but tarry in the city of Jerusalem until you are endued with power from on high." (Luke 24:46-49 NKJV) ‘ACTS’ is this treatise, this formal and systematic discourse of Dr. Luke; it is really the continuation of the Gospel of Luke, and covers about thirty years of early church history and maybe the real title should be, ‘The Acts of certain apostles and that is Peter and Paul in particular.’

Peter, being the main apostle to the Jews, and Paul as the main apostle to the non-Jews means that in this way Acts is the Genesis of the New Testament church, even the beginnings of where we are and of how and where we go. It’s all very exciting!

THIS BOOK IS AN ENCOURAGEMENT FOR ALL THE LOVERS OF GOD TO PRESS ON!

| ACTS | 44 of 66 |

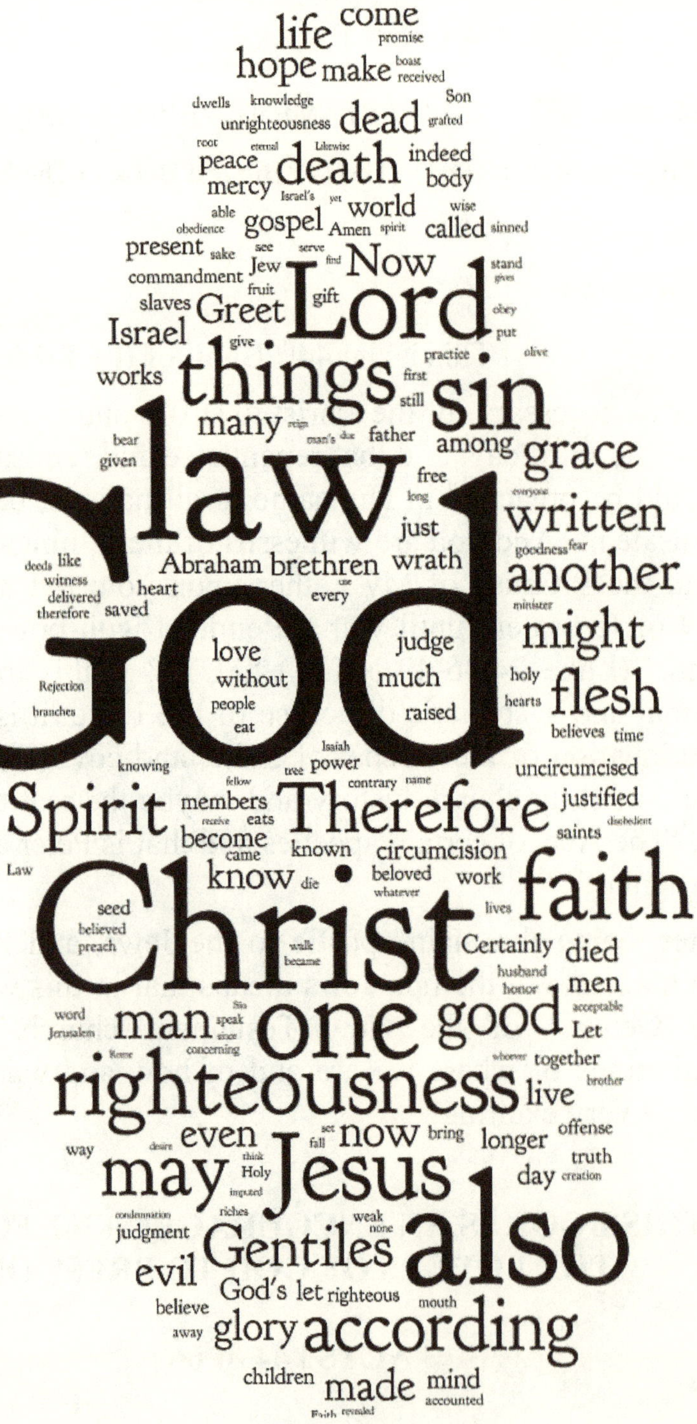

life
come
promise
hope
make
boast
received
dwells
knowledge
Son
unrighteousness
dead
grafted
root
eternal
Likewise
peace
death
indeed
mercy
Israel's
body
able
world
wise
obedience
gospel
Amen
spirit
called
sinned
present
sake
see
serve
Now
commandment
Jew
find
stand
fruit
gives
slaves
Greet
gift
Lord
obey
Israel
give
put
works
things
practice
olive
first
sin
still
many
reign
man's
due
father
bear
among
grace
given
law
free
everyone
long
written
just
goodness
fear
deeds
like
Abraham
brethren
wrath
another
witness
heart
use
delivered
every
therefore
saved
minister
God
might
love
judge
without
much
holy
Rejection
people
flesh
hearts
branches
raised
eat
believes
time
Isaiah
knowing
tree
power
uncircumcised
fellow
contrary
name
justified
Spirit
members
Therefore
receive
eats
disobedient
become
saints
came
known
circumcision
Law
know
die
beloved
work
faith
whatever
seed
lives
believed
preach
Christ
walk
Certainly
died
became
husband
men
honor
acceptable
word
speak
man
one
good
Jerusalem
since
Let
concerning
Rome
whoever
together
righteousness
live
brother
way
desire
even
set
now
bring
longer
offense
fall
think
truth
may
Holy
Jesus
day
creation
imputed
condemnation
riches
weak
judgment
none
also
Gentiles
evil
God's
let
righteous
mouth
believe
away
glory
according
children
made
mind
accounted
Faith
revealed

| ROMANS |

Bible Section | NEW TESTAMENT – THE PAULINE EPISTLES

Total Words | 9,422 (The 29th Biggest Book in The Bible)

Total Verses | 433

Total Chapters | 16

| This is the **45th Book of the Bible.**

Paul, the Moses of the New Testament, wrote this masterpiece of the New Testament to the Christians in the city of Rome.

This is a new way of God communicating, not in narrative style or poetry or historical narrative, but in a personal letter received by each individual in a very personal way, all stamped and addressed to you!

Chapters 1-8 are teaching truths which deal with 'how God makes bad men good' or 'justification by faith.'

Chapters 9-11 deal with Israel's Past, Present & Future, and

Chapters 12-16 deal with the duty of those saved.

Remember, that neither Paul nor Peter had directly founded this church in Rome, if anyone, it was Aquila and Priscilla, maybe; but Paul longed to be in that city which was the then hub of the world for which Christ had died. The gravitational force of Rome sucked Paul into its all-consuming center from which the great apostle eventually passed from earth to heaven.

IT'S ALL ABOUT THE RIGHTEOUSNESS OF GOD!

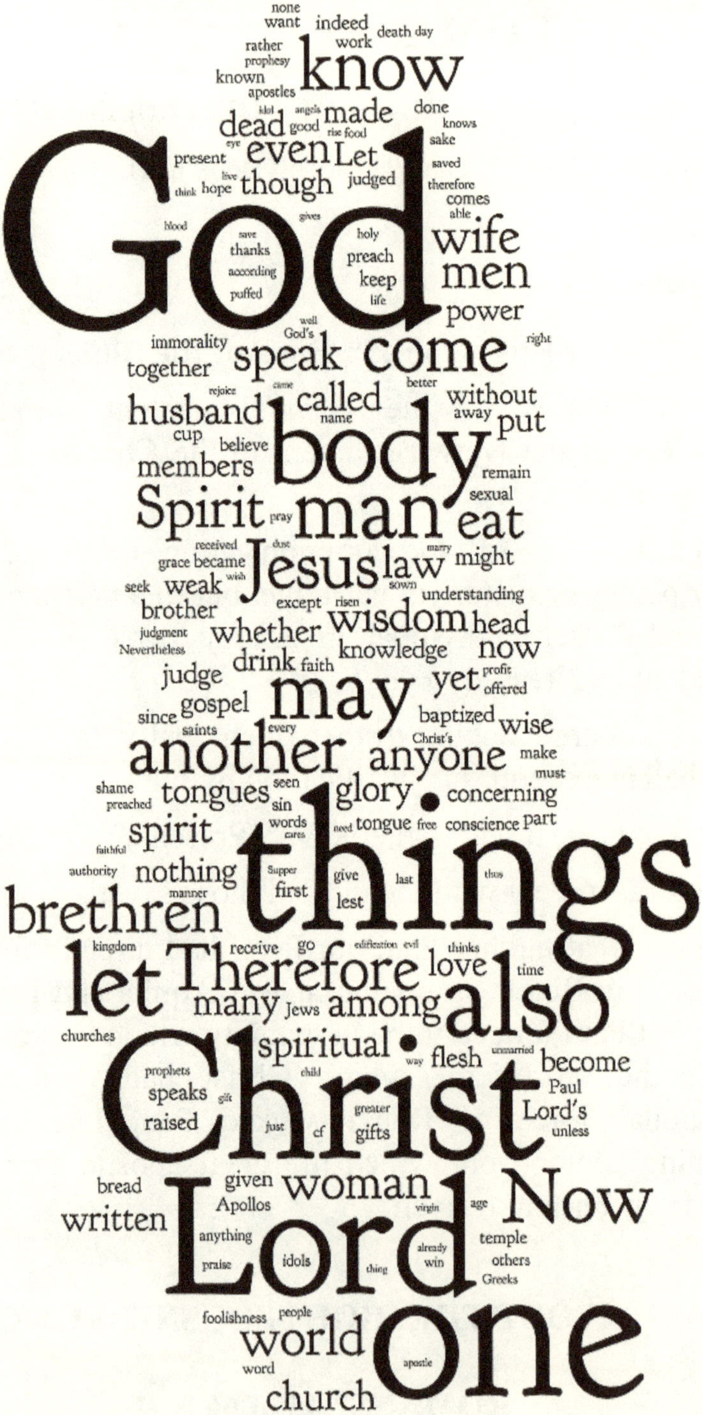
none
want
indeed
death day
rather
work
prophesy
know
known
apostles
done
made
dead
good
knows
even
Let
sake
God
present
saved
hope
though
judged
therefore
comes
able
blood
wife
holy
thanks
preach
men
according
keep
puffed
life
power
God's
immorality
right
speak
come
together
better
without
husband
called
away
name
put
cup
believe
body
members
remain
sexual
Spirit
pray
man
eat
received
dust
marry
grace
became
Jesus
law
might
seek
weak
sown
understanding
brother
except
risen
wisdom
head
judgment
whether
Nevertheless
knowledge
now
drink
faith
judge
yet
profit
offered
may
gospel
baptized
since
saints
every
wise
Christ's
another
anyone
make
must
shame
tongues
seen
glory
concerning
preached
sin
spirit
words
tongue
free
conscience
part
faithful
authority
nothing
Supper
give
last
thus
things
manner
first
lest
brethren
kingdom
receive
go
edification
evil
thinks
let
Therefore
love
time
many
Jews
among
also
churches
spiritual
unmarried
way
flesh
become
prophets
child
Christ
Paul
speaks
gift
greater
Lord's
raised
just
cf
gifts
unless
bread
given
woman
Now
Apollos
virgin
age
written
anything
temple
already
praise
idols
thing
win
others
Greeks
Lord
foolishness
people
world
one
apostle
word
church

1 CORINTHIANS

Bible Section | NEW TESTAMENT - THE PAULINE EPISTLES

Total Words | 9,462 (The 28th Biggest Book in The Bible)

Total Verses | 437

Total Chapters | 16

| This is the **46th Book of the Bible.**

I think 1 Corinthians is the second of three letters (the first of which is believed to be a lost letter) and it's written to the people of God located in 'Party Town', where 'Sex in the City' was par for the course.

The Corinthian church had obviously written and rewritten to Paul asking him lots of questions and this letter is Paul's Yahoo "Answers Home page" to all of those questions. And they needed answers! For this church was a pagan mess that was never the less so awash with spiritual gifts, that the cocktail of ignorance and spiritual gifting led to such an unholy disorder, that God had begun to injure and kill His own children and they were scratching their heads as to the reason why.

Amidst all of Paul's answers stand the mountains of love and practical holiness and how, without these twin peaks in view, the end of all our walking is a messy death.

CAREFUL NOW

| 1 CORINTHIANS | 46 of 66 |

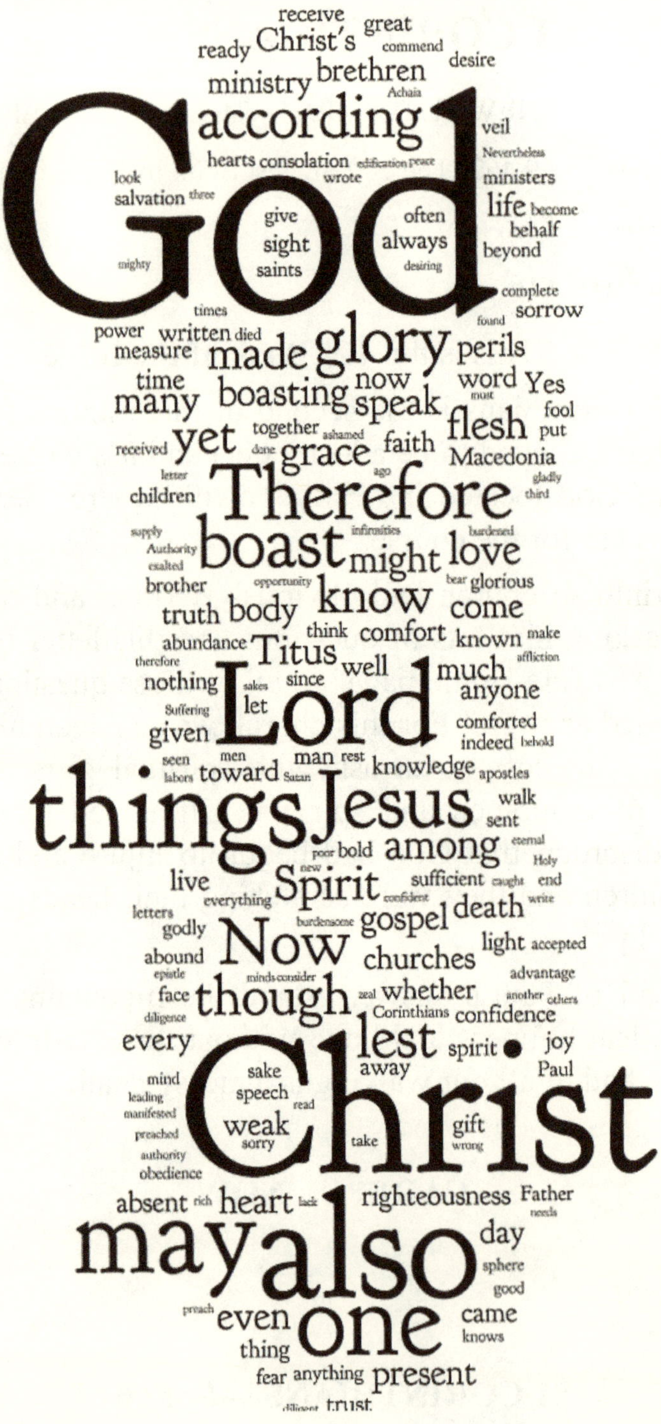
receive
great
ready
Christ's
commend
desire
ministry
brethren
Achaia
God
according
veil
hearts
consolation
edification
peace
Nevertheless
look
wrote
ministers
salvation
three
life
become
give
often
behalf
sight
always
beyond
mighty
saints
desiring
complete
times
sorrow
found
power
written
died
glory
perils
measure
made
time
now
word
Yes
must
many
boasting
speak
fool
together
flesh
ashamed
put
received
yet
done
grace
faith
Macedonia
letter
ago
gladly
children
Therefore
third
supply
infirmities
burdened
Authority
boast
might
love
exalted
brother
opportunity
bear
glorious
truth
body
know
come
think
comfort
make
abundance
known
therefore
Titus
affliction
nothing
well
much
sakes
since
anyone
Suffering
let
Lord
comforted
given
indeed
behold
seen
men
man
rest
knowledge
labors
toward
Satan
apostles
things
Jesus
walk
sent
poor
bold
among
eternal
new
Holy
live
Spirit
sufficient
caught
end
everything
confident
write
letters
death
godly
burdensome
gospel
light
accepted
abound
Now
churches
epistle
minds
consider
advantage
face
though
zeal
whether
another
others
diligence
Corinthians
confidence
every
lest
spirit
joy
away
Paul
sake
mind
speech
leading
read
Christ
manifested
weak
gift
preached
sorry
take
wrong
authority
obedience
absent
rich
heart
lack
righteousness
Father
needs
may
also
day
sphere
good
preach
even
one
came
thing
knows
fear
anything
present
diligent
trust

| 2 CORINTHIANS |

Bible Section | NEW TESTAMENT - THE PAULINE EPISTLES

Total Words | 6,065 (The 33rd Biggest Book in The Bible)

Total Verses | 257

Total Chapters | 13

| This is the **47th Book of the Bible.**

Titus had arrived to meet Paul in Philippi and brought word about their reaction to the letter we call 1st Corinthians. Paul responds to their positive reception with a tender and vulnerable openness not seen in any other letter. Here, the apostle Paul allows the Corinthians into his heart, showing them not only his high spirituality and religious authority but his absolute humanity as well, when he confesses his weakness and his wounds, the weight of his ministry; his struggles and his personal wishes for the future.

Indeed, the Corinthians applied his initial injunction in ejecting the man who was sleeping with his father's wife, but now needed his encouragement to forgive and take that same bloke back into fellowship as he had now repented of his sin; and of course, all of this is done in the context of constant and grueling spiritual warfare or, as we call it, 'general church life,' where we all need,

THE COMFORT OF CHRIST.

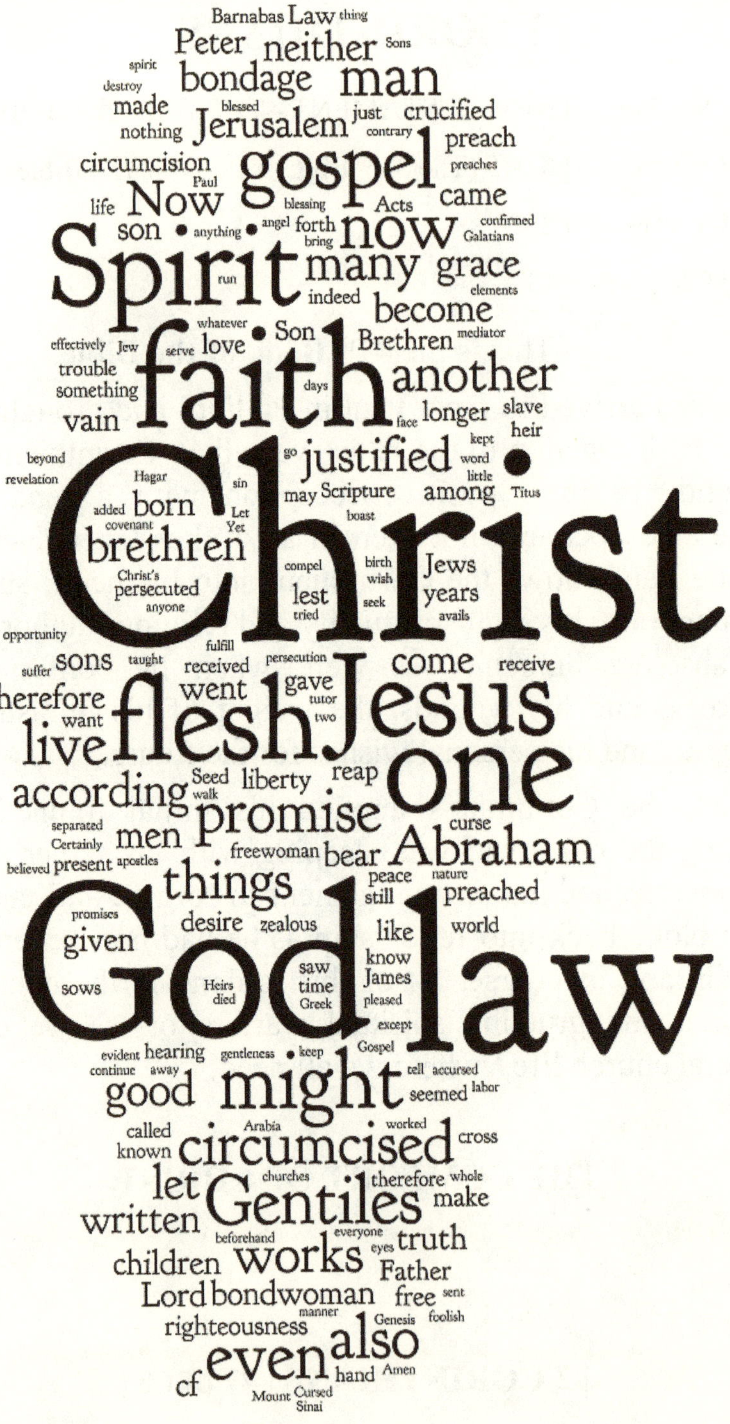

Barnabas Law thing
Peter neither Sons
spirit
bondage man
destroy
made blessed just crucified
nothing Jerusalem contrary preach
circumcision gospel preaches
Paul
life Now blessing Acts came
son anything angel forth now confirmed
bring Galatians
Spirit many grace
run
indeed elements
become
whatever Son mediator
effectively Jew serve love Brethren
trouble
something faith another
days
vain longer slave
face heir
kept
beyond go justified word
revelation Hagar little
sin may Scripture among Titus
added born Let
covenant Yet boast
brethren
Christ
compel birth Jews
Christ's wish
persecuted lest seek years
anyone tried avails
opportunity
fulfill
suffer sons taught received persecution come receive
Therefore went gave
want flesh tutor Jesus
two
live
according Seed liberty reap one
walk
promise
separated curse
Certainly men Abraham
freewoman bear
believed present apostles
things peace nature
still preached
promises
desire zealous world
given like
know
saw
God law
James
sows Heirs time
died Greek pleased
except
Gospel
evident hearing gentleness keep
continue away tell accursed
good might seemed labor
Arabia worked
called cross
known circumcised
churches therefore whole
let
Gentiles make
written
beforehand everyone truth
eyes
children works Father
Lord bondwoman free sent
manner
righteousness Genesis foolish
also
even
hand Amen
cf
Mount Cursed
Sinai

| GALATIANS |

Bible Section | NEW TESTAMENT - THE PAULINE EPISTLES

Total Words | 3,084 (The 40th Biggest Book in The Bible)

Total Verses | 149

Total Chapters | 6

| This is the **48th Book of the Bible.**

This letter was sent to all the churches in the region of Galatia which Paul had visited on each of his three missionary journeys and it was Paul's last word to these unstable gentile churches plucked from paganism.

This book should most certainly be read with the book of Romans, indeed, if you wanted a letter sandwich, with Ephesians as the Salami, then Romans and Galatians would be the whole meal bread slices into which you would sink your hungry teeth.

Paul always had false apostles following him around, legalistic Judaisers that sowed lies among his truth saying: 'you don't just need the unmerited favor of God shown to undeserving sinners to be saved, you need the law as well and circumcision as that particular sign of adherence to the Jewish law.' Paul showed no mercy to this grace-killing teaching and writes with an excessive warning encouraging these false apostles to go the whole way and make themselves eunuchs, if you know what I mean!

THE CHRISTIAN LIFE: IT'S ALL ABOUT GOD'S GRACE

| GALATIANS | 48 of 66 |

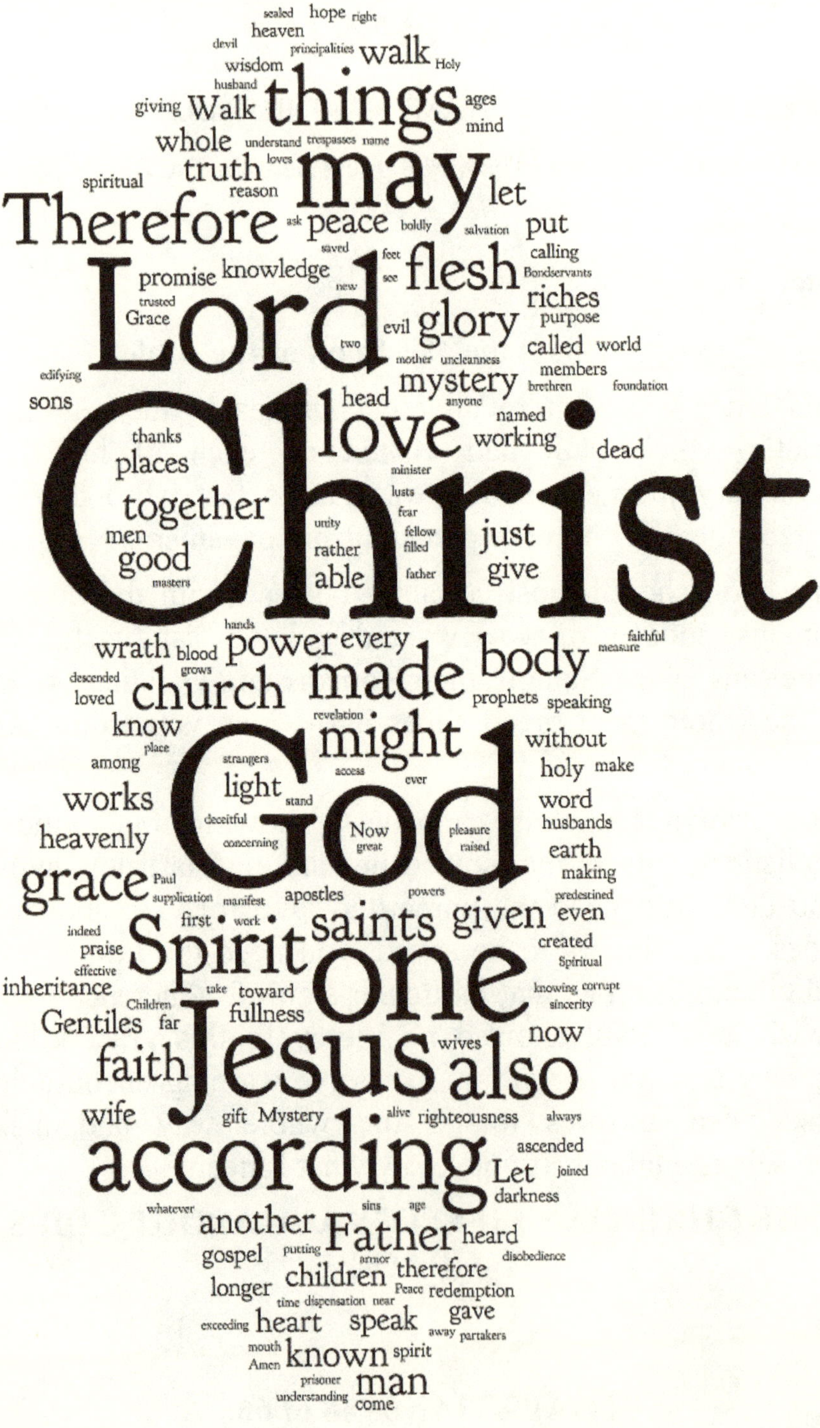
sealed hope right
heaven
devil principalities walk Holy
wisdom
husband
giving Walk things ages
mind
whole understand trespasses name
truth loves
spiritual may
reason let
Therefore ask peace boldly salvation put
saved
feet calling
Lord flesh
promise knowledge see Bondservants
new
trusted riches
Grace glory purpose
evil
two called world
mother uncleanness
edifying members
mystery brethren foundation
head
sons anyone
Christ
named
thanks love working
dead
places
minister
lusts
together
fear
unity
fellow
men just
filled
rather
good give
able father
masters
hands
faithful
wrath blood power every measure
grows body
descended made
church
loved prophets speaking
revelation
know
might without
place
among strangers holy make
access ever
light
works stand word
deceitful husbands
God
Now pleasure
heavenly concerning great raised earth
Paul making
grace supplication manifest apostles powers predestined
first work given even
indeed saints
praise created
Spirit
effective Spiritual
one
inheritance take toward knowing corrupt
Children sincerity
Gentiles far fullness
now
wives
faith Jesus also
wife gift Mystery alive righteousness always
ascended
according
Let joined
darkness
whatever sins age
another
Father heard
gospel putting armor disobedience
therefore
children
longer
Peace redemption
time dispensation near
gave
exceeding heart speak
away partakers
mouth
known spirit
Amen
prisoner
man
understanding come

| EPHESIANS |

Bible Section	| NEW TESTAMENT - THE PAULINE EPISTLES
Total Words	| 3,022 (The 41st Biggest Book in The Bible)
Total Verses	| 155
Total Chapters	| 6

| This is the **49th Book of the Bible.**

Ephesians is the first of four prison Epistles written from Rome where Paul is under house arrest while waiting for his appeal trial before Caesar.

Paul loved Ephesus as a place and with an open door of ministry, he spent his longest time based there and consequently he loved the Ephesian church even more.

This book presents to us the church of the living God, a mysterious "body" not revealed in the Old Testament, but a new thing, even more glorious than the temple, because it is made up of "living stones." Also it describes the church as,

A Body knit together.

A soon-to-be Bride, and presently,

A Battle-hardened warrior.

Paul begins this great description of the church by describing its Master, Jesus Christ, who is Lord over the entire created order, both seen and unseen, past present and future; inside and outside of time, even now extending Himself and His desire into the world via,

"THE CHURCH, WHICH IS HIS BODY."

| EPHESIANS | 49 of 66 |

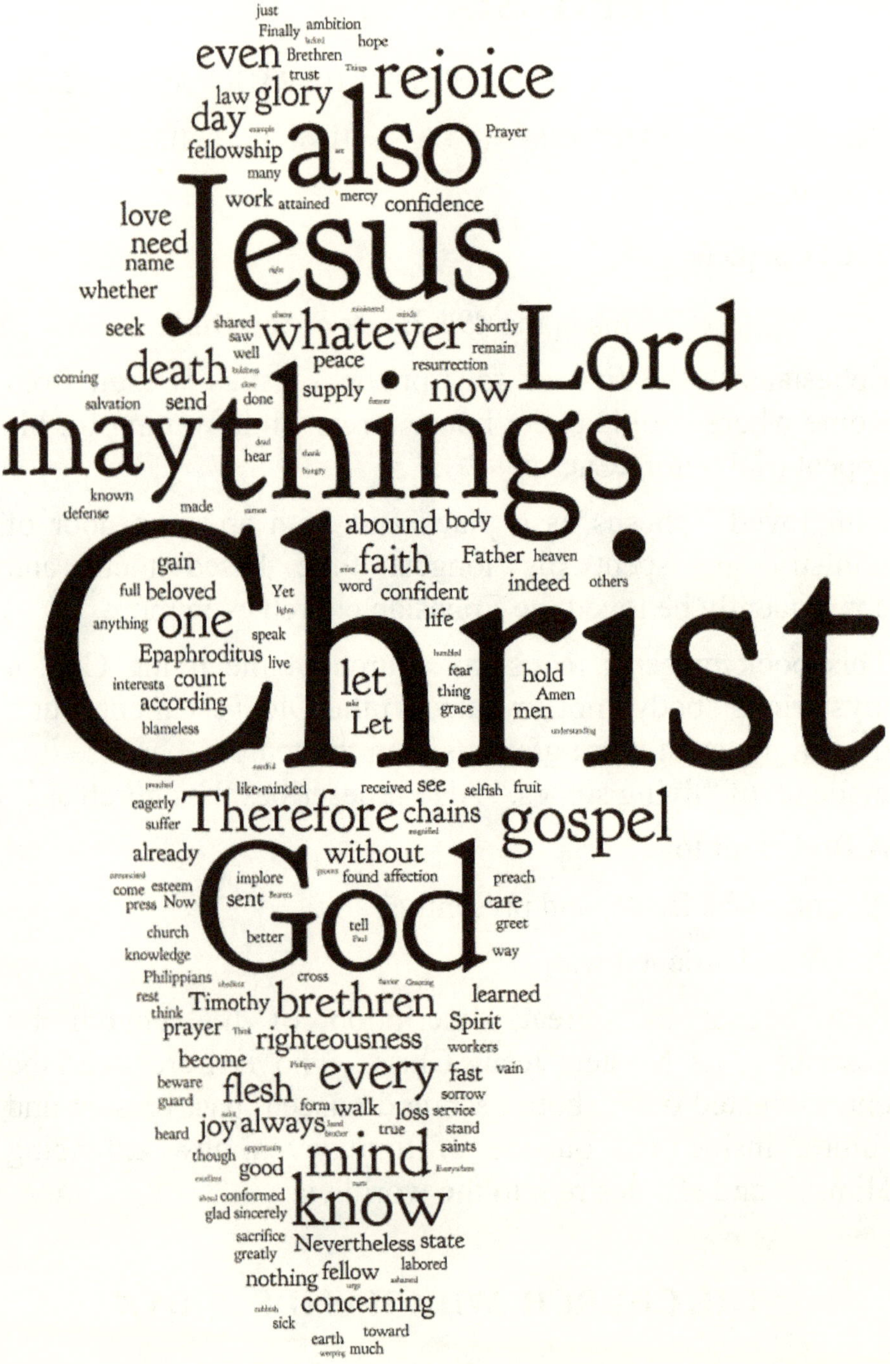

just
Finally
ambition
hope
even
Brethren
rejoice
trust
law
glory
day
also
Prayer
fellowship
many
Jesus
work
attained
mercy
confidence
love
need
name
whether
seek
shared
saw
whatever
shortly
remain
Lord
well
death
peace
resurrection
coming
salvation
send
done
supply
now
may
things
hear
known
defense
made
abound
body
Christ
gain
faith
Father
heaven
full
beloved
Yet
word
confident
indeed
others
anything
one
life
speak
Epaphroditus
live
interests
count
let
fear
hold
according
thing
Amen
grace
men
Let
blameless
like-minded
received
see
selfish
fruit
eagerly
Therefore
chains
gospel
suffer
already
without
God
implore
found
affection
preach
come
esteem
press
Now
sent
care
church
better
tell
greet
knowledge
way
Philippians
cross
rest
Timothy
brethren
learned
think
Spirit
prayer
righteousness
workers
become
beware
flesh
every
fast
vain
guard
sorrow
form
walk
loss
service
heard
joy
always
true
stand
though
mind
saints
good
conformed
know
glad
sincerely
sacrifice
Nevertheless
state
greatly
nothing
fellow
labored
concerning
sick
earth
toward
much

| PHILIPPIANS |

Bible Section | NEW TESTAMENT - THE PAULINE EPISTLES

Total Words | 2,183 (The 48th Biggest Book in The Bible)

Total Verses | 104

Total Chapters | 4

| This is the **50th Book of the Bible.**

Philippians is second of four prison Epistles sent from Rome, where Paul is waiting for his appeal trial before Caesar.

Philippi was a Roman Retirement Colony and this was one of the more 'well to do churches' and it had been a great financial patron for Paul. This was one of the churches he had 'robbed' to be able to minister to others.

Paul's love for this church and their love and support of him, makes me think that Phillip was maybe Paul's adopted home church.

For sure, when they found out he was in 'the clink,' they sent Epaphroditus there with money and much love. This letter is a pastoral reply to that most generous visit.

Of course, Paul also deals with the Pastoral problem of those two battling women, 'Odious' and 'Soon Touchy,' but more than that, out of his personal concerns, struggles and burdens, Paul also instructs them on the acquiring and maintenance of joy.

"SO, AGAIN I SAY – REJOICE"

| PHILLIPIANS | 50 of 66 |

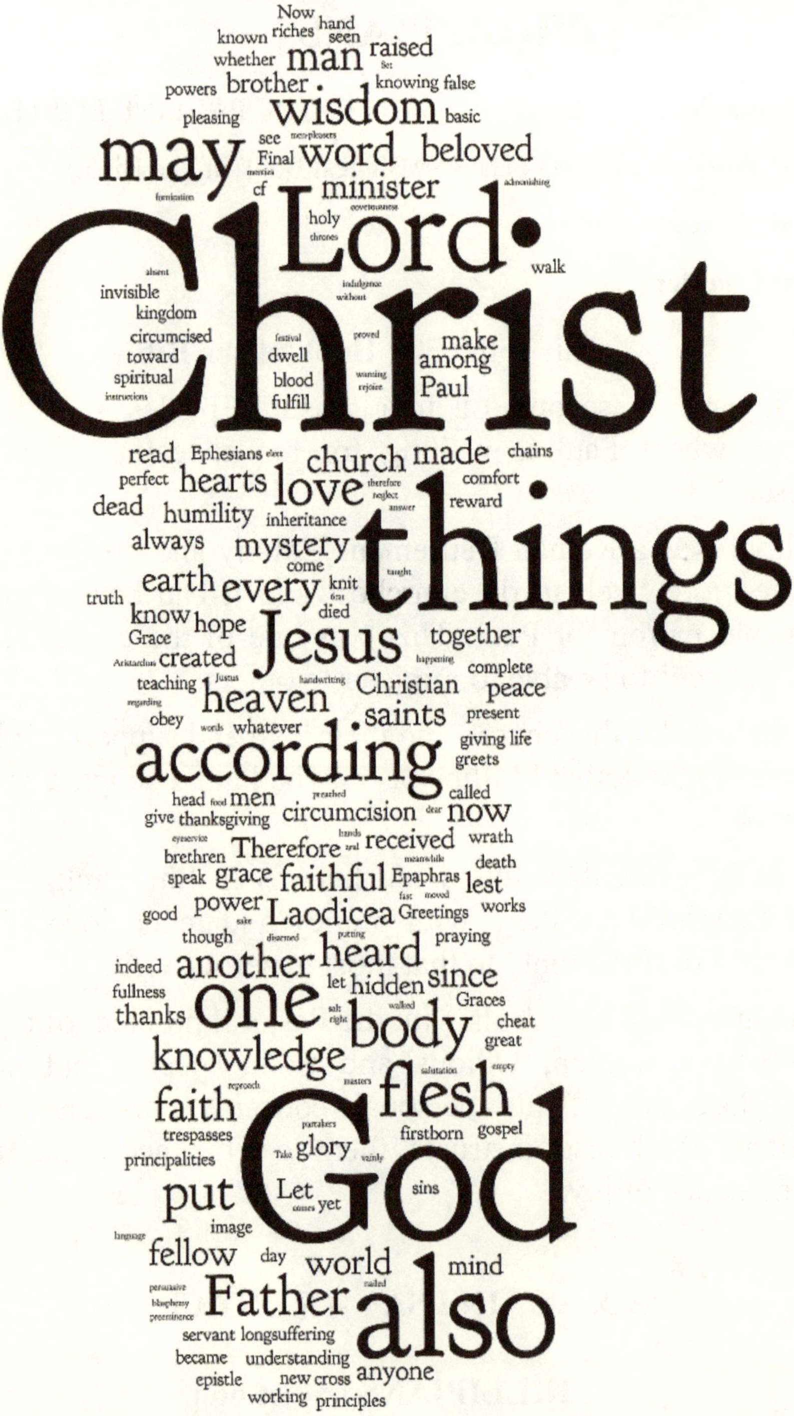
Now
known riches hand seen
whether man raised
powers brother knowing false
pleasing wisdom basic
may see Final word beloved
cf minister
Lord holy
Christ
walk
invisible
kingdom
circumcised
toward
spiritual
dwell
blood
fulfill
make
among
Paul
read Ephesians church made chains
perfect hearts love comfort
dead humility inheritance reward
always mystery things
earth every knit
truth know hope died
Grace Jesus together
created
teaching complete
Christian peace
heaven
obey whatever saints present
according giving life
greets
head men called
give thanksgiving circumcision now
Therefore received wrath
brethren death
speak grace faithful Epaphras lest
good power Laodicea Greetings works
though praying
indeed another heard
fullness hidden since
thanks one Graces
body cheat
great
knowledge
faith flesh
trespasses firstborn gospel
principalities glory
put Let God sins
yet
image
fellow day world mind
Father also
servant longsuffering
became understanding
epistle new cross anyone
working principles

| COLOSSIANS |

Bible Section | NEW TESTAMENT - THE PAULINE EPISTLES

Total Words | 1,979 (The 50th Biggest Book in The Bible)

Total Verses | 95

Total Chapters | 4

| This is the **51st Book of the Bible.**

Colossians is the third of four prison Epistles sent from Rome where Paul is waiting for his appeal trial before Caesar.

Paul had never been to Colossae, but it lay about 100 miles east of Ephesus and was awash with Gnostic mysticism, a bit like our own age really! That's right, false teaching had taken root in Colossae, and Paul calls this "idiotic and empty deceit."

The letter focuses on the head of the body, the Word Himself, Jesus Christ the Lord and Paul points to the only knowledge of Christ being found 'in that Word of God,' the Creator of all things visible and invisible, even the pre-eminence and fullness of the person of "Christ filling all in all," which in turn, forces a song of praise out of Paul because he sees Jesus as the most powerful person both on and off the planet.

The best way to counteract false teaching is to get a grip on the greatness of Jesus! "Let the word of Christ dwell in you richly" for,

HE IS THE HEAD OF THE BODY.

(Col 3:16 NKJV)

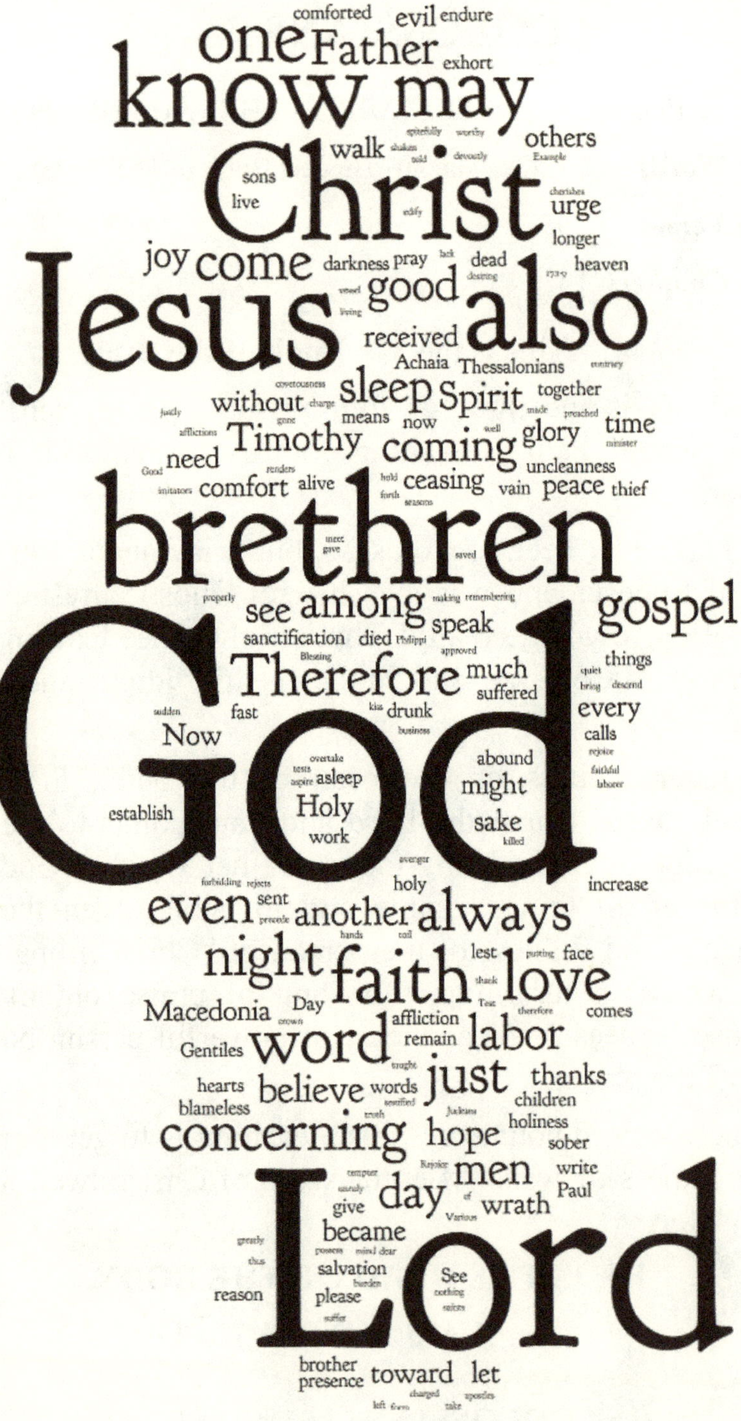

comforted
evil
endure
one
Father
exhort
know
may
walk
others
sons
live
Christ
urge
longer
joy
come
darkness
pray
dead
heaven
Jesus
good
also
received
Achaia
Thessalonians
without
sleep
Spirit
together
means
now
time
Timothy
coming
glory
need
uncleanness
comfort
alive
ceasing
vain
peace
thief
brethren
see
among
gospel
speak
sanctification
died
Therefore
much
things
suffered
fast
drunk
every
Now
calls
God
abound
asleep
might
establish
Holy
sake
work
holy
increase
even
sent
another
always
night
lest
face
faith
love
Macedonia
Day
affliction
comes
Gentiles
word
remain
labor
hearts
believe
words
just
thanks
blameless
children
concerning
hope
holiness
sober
men
write
day
Paul
give
wrath
became
salvation
reason
please
See
Lord
brother
presence
toward
let

| 1 THESSALONIANS |

Bible Section | NEW TESTAMENT - THE PAULINE EPISTLES

Total Words | 1,837 (The 52nd Biggest Book in The Bible)

Total Verses | 89

Total Chapters | 5

| This is the **52nd Book of the Bible.**

1 Thessalonians is Probably the first of Paul's letters, written to a Roman Colony, named after the half-sister of Alexander the Great.

Remember Paul was only in Thessalonica about a month, yet, as this book answers some questions relating to his discipleship, we know that he gave them "meat" and not "milk" which made them so heavenly minded, that they are of immense earthly use, and so much so, that this church becomes an example to every other in patience, faith, love and hope. The church at Thessalonica became a legend in its own lunchtime!

However, remember also that Paul is writing as well to correct errors; errors of misunderstanding of original teaching and errors which had been brought in from the outside.

So every preacher, no matter how spiritual and Biblically grounded, will have a necessary ministry in correcting misunderstanding. Get used to it! Meanwhile,

"COMFORT ONE ANOTHER WITH THESE WORDS" (1Thess 4:18 NKJV)

| 1 THESSALONIANS | 52 of 66

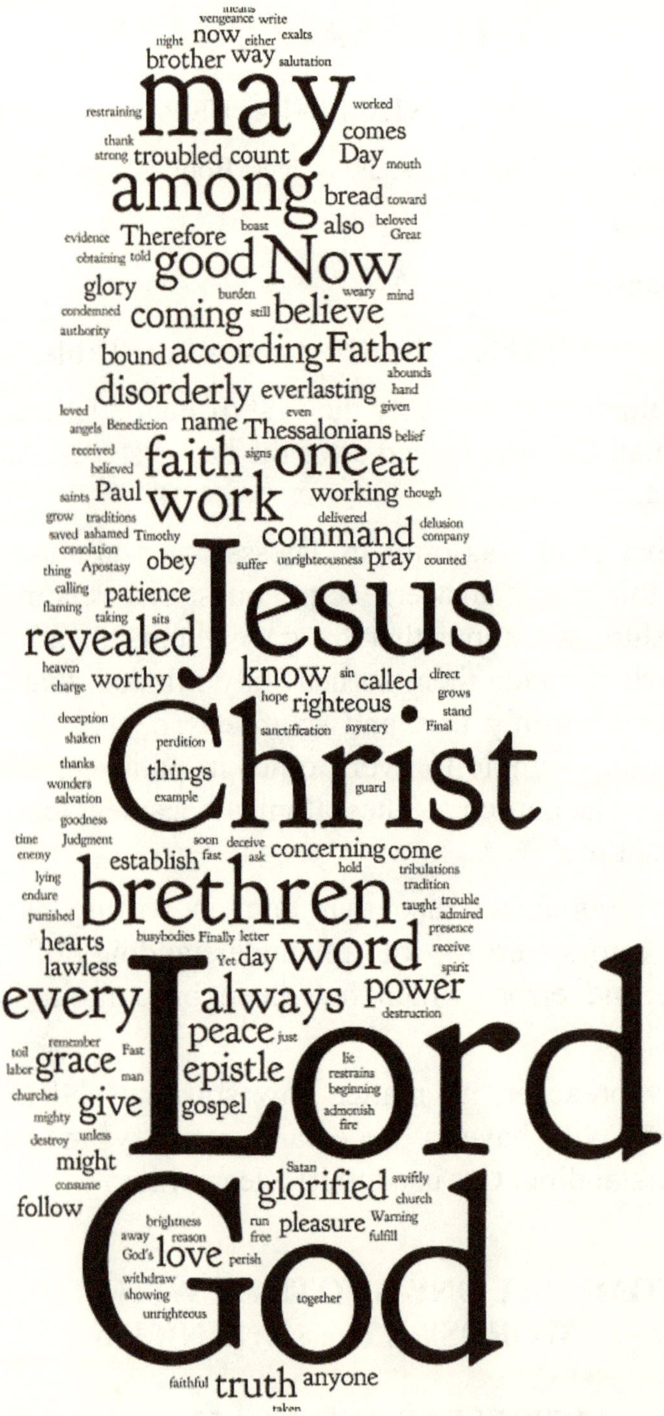

vengeance
write
night
now
either
exalts
brother
way
salutation
restraining
may
worked
comes
thank
strong
troubled
count
Day
mouth
among
bread
toward
evidence
Therefore
boast
also
beloved
Great
obtaining
told
good
Now
glory
burden
weary
mind
condemned
coming
still
believe
authority
bound
according
Father
abounds
disorderly
everlasting
hand
loved
even
given
angels
Benediction
name
Thessalonians
belief
received
signs
faith
one
eat
believed
saints
Paul
work
working
though
grow
traditions
delivered
delusion
saved
ashamed
Timothy
command
company
consolation
thing
Apostasy
obey
suffer
unrighteousness
pray
counted
calling
patience
flaming
taking
sits
revealed
Jesus
heaven
charge
worthy
know
sin
called
direct
hope
righteous
grows
stand
deception
sanctification
mystery
Final
shaken
perdition
thanks
things
Christ
wonders
guard
salvation
example
goodness
time
Judgment
soon
deceive
enemy
establish
fast
ask
concerning
come
hold
tribulations
lying
tradition
endure
brethren
taught
trouble
punished
admired
busybodies
Finally
letter
presence
hearts
receive
lawless
Yet
day
word
spirit
every
always
power
destruction
peace
remember
just
toil
Fast
labor
grace
man
epistle
lie
restrains
beginning
churches
give
gospel
mighty
admonish
fire
destroy
unless
Lord
might
Satan
consume
glorified
swiftly
church
follow
brightness
run
pleasure
Warning
away
reason
free
fulfill
God's
love
perish
withdraw
showing
together
unrighteous
God
faithful
truth
anyone
taken

| 2 THESSALONIANS |

Bible Section | NEW TESTAMENT - THE PAULINE EPISTLES

Total Words | 1,022 (The 60th Biggest Book in The Bible)

Total Verses | 47

Total Chapters | 3

| This is the **53rd Book of the Bible.**

Written pretty quickly after 1st Thessalonians, this second letter is written to refute false teachings that had seemingly been delivered either by word or by letter, as if from Paul. Astonishing really.

So, Paul writes to them to refute this disinformation placed among them. Bottom line is that these persecuted Christians believed that **the day of the Lord** had come and they had been left behind to suffer in the Great Tribulation period.

This letter delivers all Christians both from the shallow optimism and the deep despair which comes when regarding future events that we believe might be unfolding in the present. So, Paul in general terms outlines some happenings around the return of Christ FOR His church, followed by ' The Day of the Lord,' the removal of 'The Restrainer,' the great falling away from the faith, the revelation of the man of sin, and much, much more besides which were the common discourse of new Christians some 2,000 years ago! Again, astonishing! This great book is all about,

CONCERNING THE COMING OF OUR LORD JESUS AND OUR GATHERING TO HIM.

| 2 THESSALONIANS | 53 of 66 |

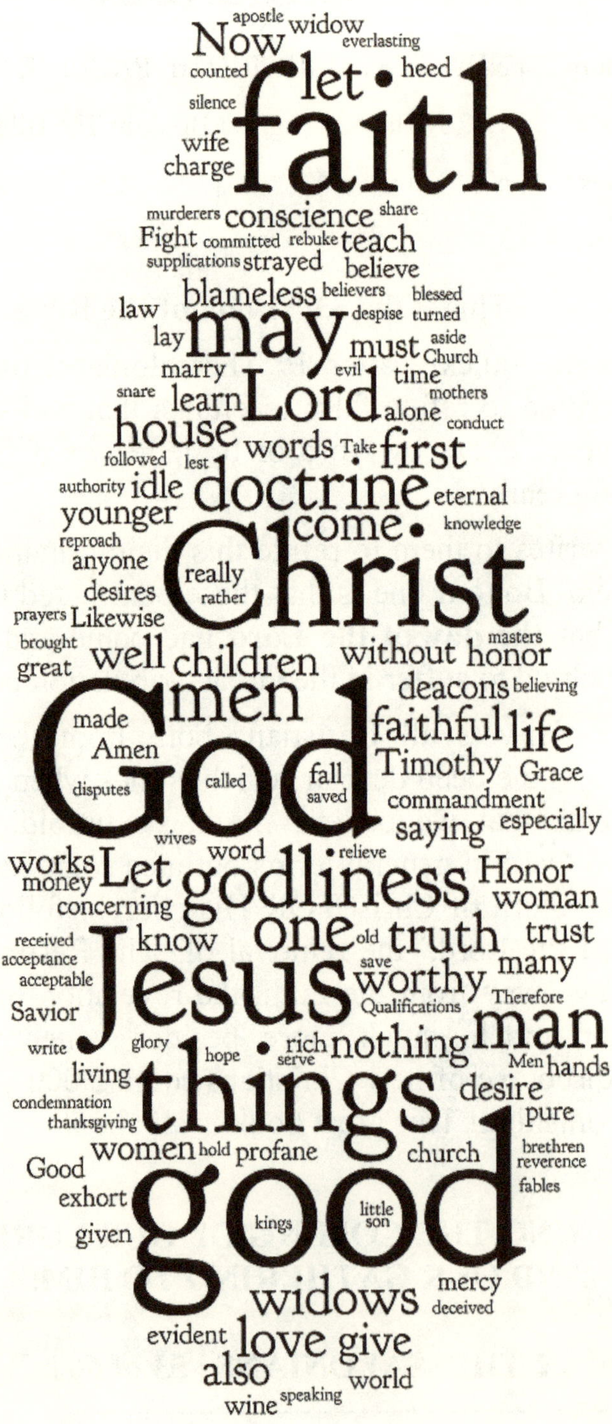
apostle
widow
Now
everlasting
counted
let
heed
silence
faith
wife
charge
murderers
conscience
share
Fight
committed
rebuke
teach
supplications
strayed
believe
blameless
believers
blessed
law
may
despise
turned
lay
must
aside
Church
marry
evil
time
snare
learn
Lord
mothers
alone
house
conduct
words
Take
first
followed
lest
authority
idle
doctrine
eternal
younger
come
knowledge
reproach
anyone
really
Christ
desires
rather
prayers
Likewise
brought
masters
well
children
without
honor
great
deacons
believing
men
made
God
faithful
life
Amen
Timothy
Grace
called
fall
disputes
saved
commandment
saying
especially
wives
word
relieve
works
Let
godliness
Honor
money
woman
concerning
received
know
one
old
truth
trust
acceptance
save
acceptable
Jesus
worthy
many
Therefore
Savior
Qualifications
man
write
glory
rich
hope
serve
nothing
living
Men
hands
things
desire
condemnation
thanksgiving
pure
women
hold
profane
church
brethren
reverence
Good
fables
exhort
good
little
kings
son
given
mercy
widows
deceived
evident
love
give
also
world
wine
speaking

| 1 TIMOTHY |

Bible Section | NEW TESTAMENT - THE PAULINE EPISTLES

Total Words | 2,244 (The 47th Biggest Book in The Bible)

Total Verses | 113

Total Chapters | 6

| This is the **54th Book of the Bible.**

1st Timothy is the first of three 'Pastoral Letters,' so named because they have specific reference to matters relating to the local church in terms of: Order, Gender, General Living, Laziness, and Leadership, Goodliness, Good Teaching and Good works!

This letter is written to Paul's spiritual son in the faith and his partner in mission, Timothy, who had been left in Ephesus to put a church in disarray back on right display, by correcting false teaching and getting in some new leadership.

In verse one of this letter Paul says he is an, "apostle… by the COMMANDEMENT of God" and this carried a great authority from which he authorizes and empowers 'timid Timothy' to take authority and take hold of these slippery snakes and remove them and their poison from the church. It's time to clean house. What a book!

RIGHT WORDS FOR RIGHT LIVING

| 1 TIMOTHY | 54 of 66 |

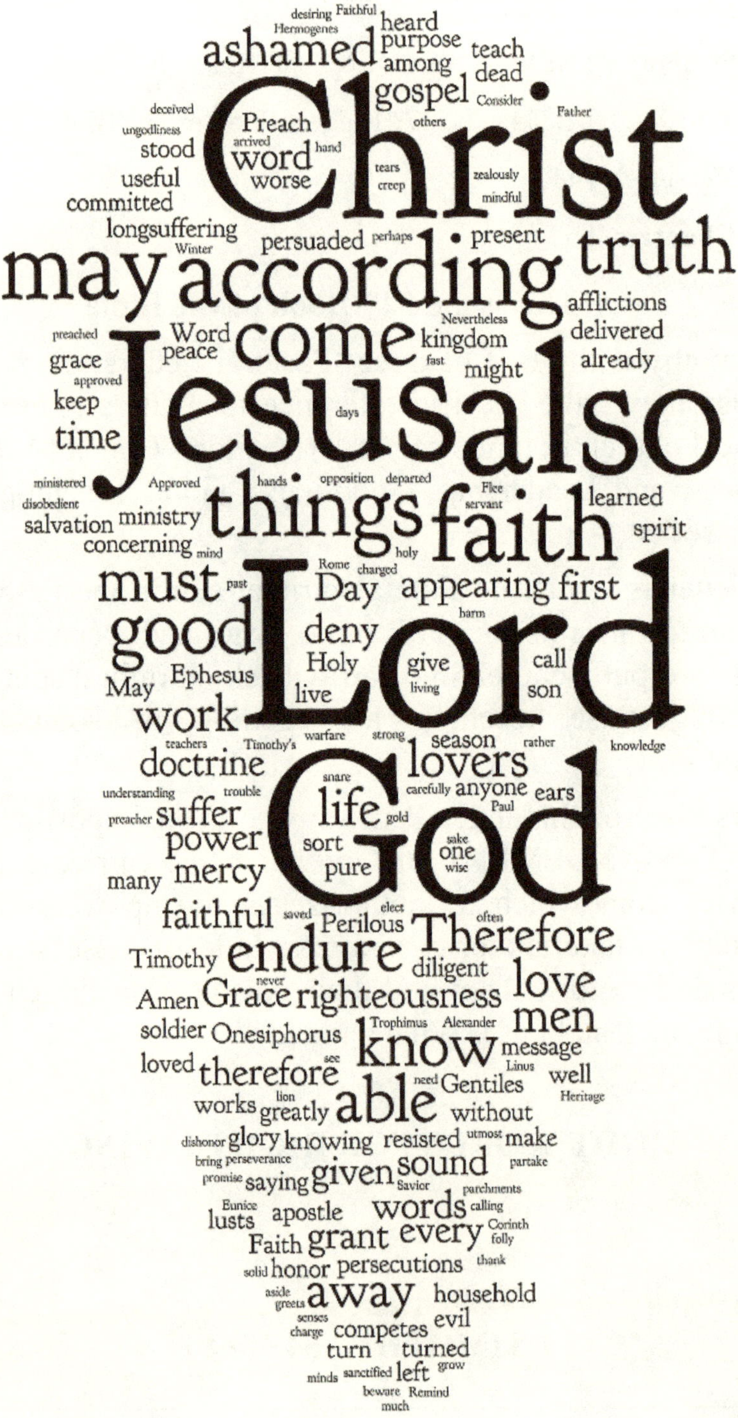
desiring Faithful
heard
Hermogenes
purpose
teach
ashamed
among
dead
gospel
Consider
deceived
Christ
Father
Preach
others
ungodliness
arrived
hand
stood
word
useful
tears
worse
zealously
creep
committed
mindful
longsuffering
perhaps
present
Winter
persuaded
truth
may
according
afflictions
Nevertheless
preached
Word
come
kingdom
delivered
peace
grace
fast
already
might
approved
keep
days
Jesusalso
time
ministered
Approved
hands
opposition
departed
Flee
disobedient
servant
learned
salvation
ministry
things
faith
spirit
concerning
mind
holy
Rome
charged
must
past
Day
appearing
first
harm
good
deny
Lord
Holy
give
call
May
Ephesus
live
living
son
work
teachers
Timothy's
warfare
strong
season
rather
knowledge
doctrine
lovers
understanding
trouble
snare
carefully
anyone
ears
preacher
suffer
life
gold
Paul
power
God
sort
sake
one
many
mercy
pure
wise
elect
faithful
saved
Perilous
often
Therefore
Timothy
endure
diligent
never
love
Amen
Grace
righteousness
Trophimus
Alexander
men
soldier
Onesiphorus
know
message
see
loved
therefore
Linus
well
need
Gentiles
lion
Heritage
works
greatly
able
without
dishonor
glory
knowing
resisted
utmost
make
bring
perseverance
sound
partake
promise
saying
given
Savior
parchments
Eunice
words
calling
lusts
apostle
every
Corinth
Faith
grant
folly
thank
solid
honor
persecutions
aside
away
household
greets
senses
evil
charge
competes
turn
turned
minds
sanctified
left
grow
beware
Remind
much

| 2 TIMOTHY |

Bible Section | NEW TESTAMENT - THE PAULINE EPISTLES

Total Words | 1,666 (The 53rd Biggest Book in The Bible)

Total Verses | 83

Total Chapters | 4

| This is the **55th Book of the Bible.**

2nd Timothy is the second of three 'Pastoral Letters,' so named, because they are matters relating to the local church.

Now remember Paul, arrested in Jerusalem, three years later now arrives in Rome where he is under house arrest and going to trial. He was probably acquitted, released, travelled further and wrote the letters to Timothy and Titus. He was obviously arrested later again and finally, before he departs from the scene, he writes Second Timothy, the final words of Paul; last words spoken; his most personal and heartfelt words, important words, peppered with pathos and powerful victory declarations.

But, most terribly, Paul speaks of perilous times which shall come upon the church in the 'Last Days' and this peril is a departure from the Word of God, good teaching and sound doctrine. It is deliberate departure as well; and it is heresy that gives birth to a superfluous ignorance of the things of God. God help us! Timothy,

"I HAVE FOUGHT THE GOOD FIGHT; I HAVE FINISHED THE RACE; I HAVE KEPT THE FAITH."

(2 Tim 4:7 NKJV)

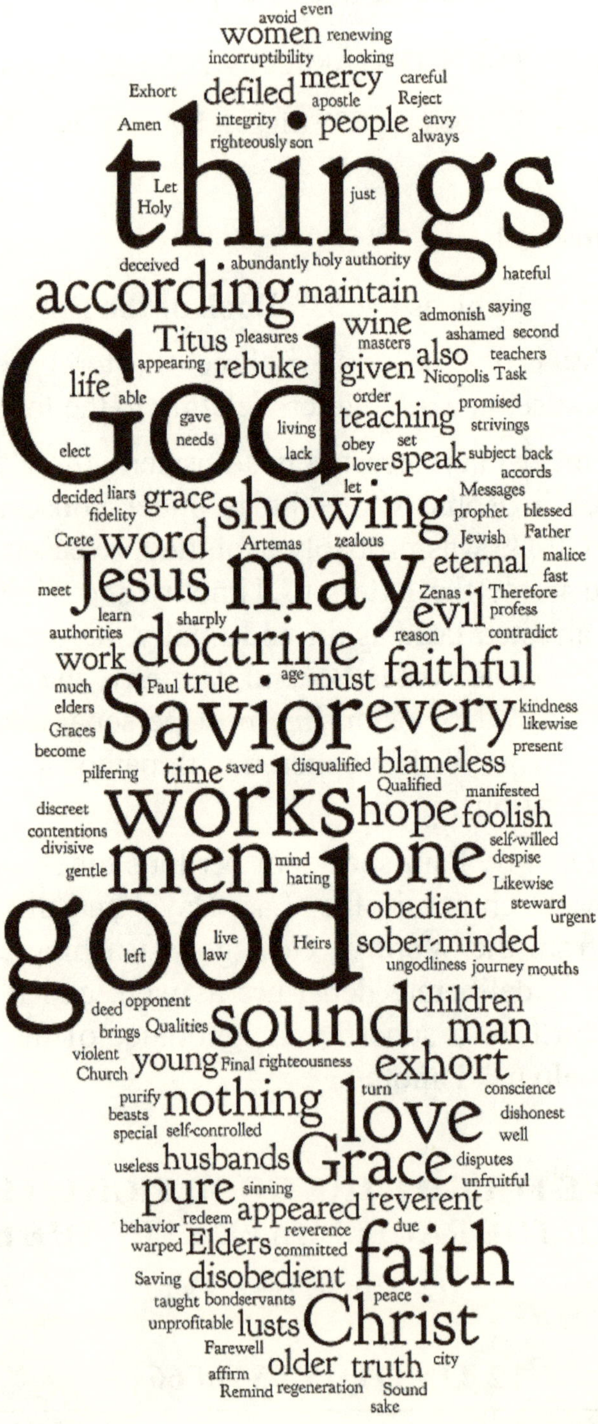
avoid even
women renewing
incorruptibility looking
Exhort defiled mercy careful
apostle Reject
Amen integrity people envy
righteously son always
things
Let Holy just
deceived abundantly holy authority hateful
according maintain
admonish saying
Titus pleasures wine masters ashamed second
appearing rebuke given also teachers
life able Nicopolis Task
God
order promised
gave needs living teaching strivings
elect lack obey set
lover speak subject back accords
let
decided liars grace showing Messages
fidelity prophet blessed
Crete word Artemas zealous Jewish Father
Jesus may eternal malice fast
meet Zenas Therefore
learn sharply evil profess
authorities reason contradict
work doctrine
much Paul true age must faithful
elders Savior every kindness likewise
Graces present
become
pilfering time saved disqualified blameless
Qualified manifested
discreet works hope foolish
contentions self-willed
divisive mind despise
gentle men hating one Likewise
good
obedient steward urgent
live left law Heirs sober-minded
ungodliness journey mouths
deed opponent children
brings Qualities sound man
violent
Church young Final righteousness exhort
purify turn conscience
beasts nothing love dishonest
special self-controlled well
useless husbands Grace disputes
unfruitful
pure sinning reverent
behavior redeem appeared
reverence due
warped Elders committed faith
Saving disobedient
taught bondservants peace
unprofitable lusts Christ
Farewell
affirm older truth city
Remind regeneration Sound
sake

| TITUS |

Bible Section | NEW TESTAMENT - THE PAULINE EPISTLES

Total Words | 896 (The 61st Biggest Book in The Bible)

Total Verses | 46

Total Chapters | 3

| This is the **56th** Book of the Bible.

Titus is the last of the three Pastoral Letters, relating to matters concerning the local church.

This letter to another of Paul's spiritual son's, Titus, on the island of Crete, lays out the principle organization of that living organism, the local church:

The local church must have male Elders.

The local church must be sound in good teaching.

The local church must be pure in living, ready for every good work.

The local church must be ready to help people physically, beginning with its own members first of all, and only then reaching out to others; investing always in living stones; investing in flesh and blood, which is always preferable to bricks and mortar.

As to the insubordinate idle-talking deceivers, those rude, crude and lying, fat-mouthed slobs, well, they need to have their 'gobs' shut for them and the best way to do it is to sharply rebuke them. The church must,

GIVE NO QUARTER TO LIES.

| TITUS | 56 of 66 |

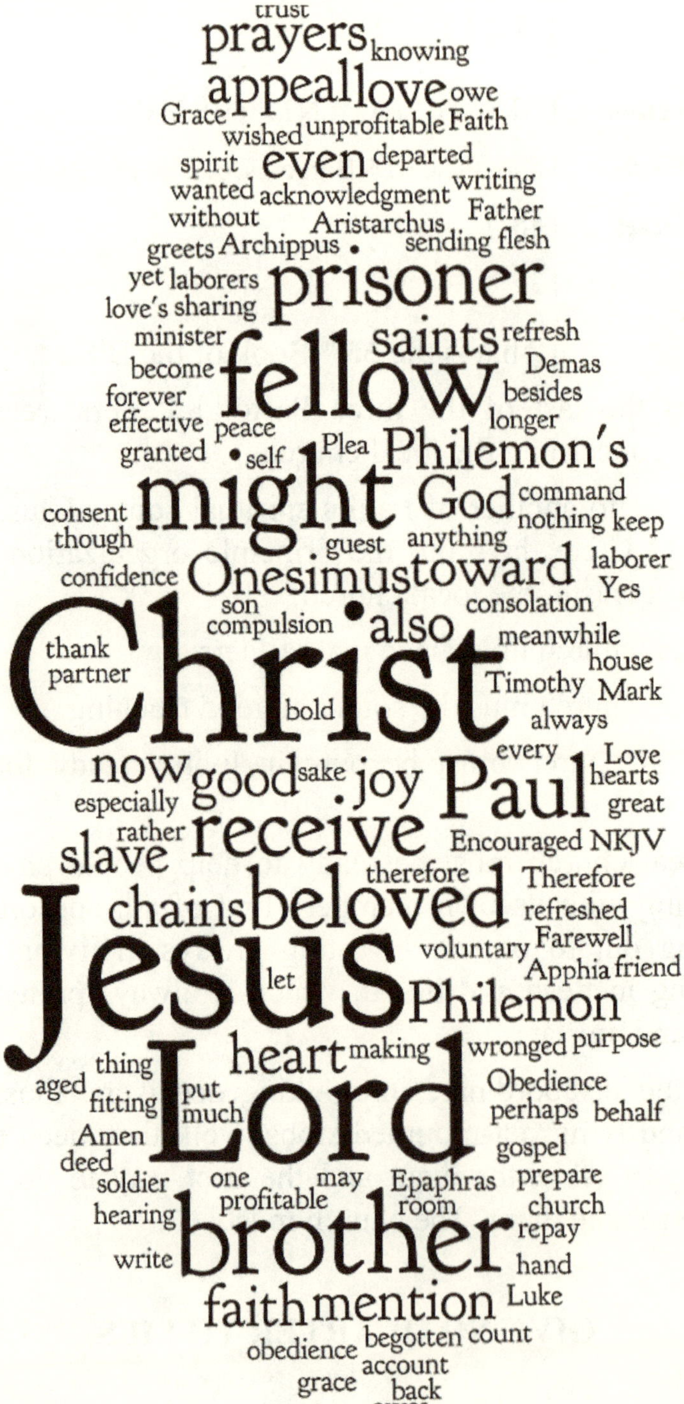
trust
prayers knowing
appeal love owe
Grace wished unprofitable Faith
spirit even departed
wanted acknowledgment writing
without Aristarchus Father
greets Archippus sending flesh
yet laborers prisoner
love's sharing
minister saints refresh
become fellow Demas
forever besides
effective peace longer
granted self Plea Philemon's
might God command
consent nothing keep
though guest anything
confidence Onesimus toward laborer
son Yes
compulsion also consolation
thank meanwhile
partner Christ house
Timothy Mark
bold always
now good sake joy every Love
especially Paul hearts
rather great
slave receive Encouraged NKJV
therefore Therefore
chains beloved refreshed
voluntary Farewell
Jesus let Apphia friend
Philemon
heart making wronged purpose
thing Obedience
aged put
fitting much Lord perhaps behalf
Amen gospel
deed
soldier one may Epaphras prepare
profitable room church
hearing repay
write brother hand
faith mention Luke
begotten count
obedience account
grace back
owes

| PHILEMON |

Bible Section | NEW TESTAMENT - THE PAULINE EPISTLES

Total Words | 430 (The 64th Biggest Book in The Bible)

Total Verses | 25

Total Chapters | 1

| This is the **57th Book of the Bible.**

Philemon is the last of the four prison letters, delivered by the hand of Onesimus, a returning runway slave, to his master Philemon.

I love this letter because of Paul's arm-twisting churchmanship, as he reconciles these two Chrisitan brothers. Laying it on thick, Paul says:

"I'm not just Paul, but Paul the aged, and did I tell you I've been in prison for Jesus; have you Philemon? No, I didn't think so. Oh and by the way, if Onesimus owes you anything put it to my account, even though you know I'm dirt poor. But you do owe me your very spiritual life anyway, and did I tell you I am old and have been in prison for Jesus, and I am coming to visit you to make sure you do even more than I ask. I know you will. And lastly Epaphrus, Aristarchus, Demas and Luke all send their love. Yes, they have read the letter as well."

No pressure there then Paul eh?

"C'mon Philemon," says Paul,

REFRESH MY HEART.

| PHILEMON | 57 of 66 |

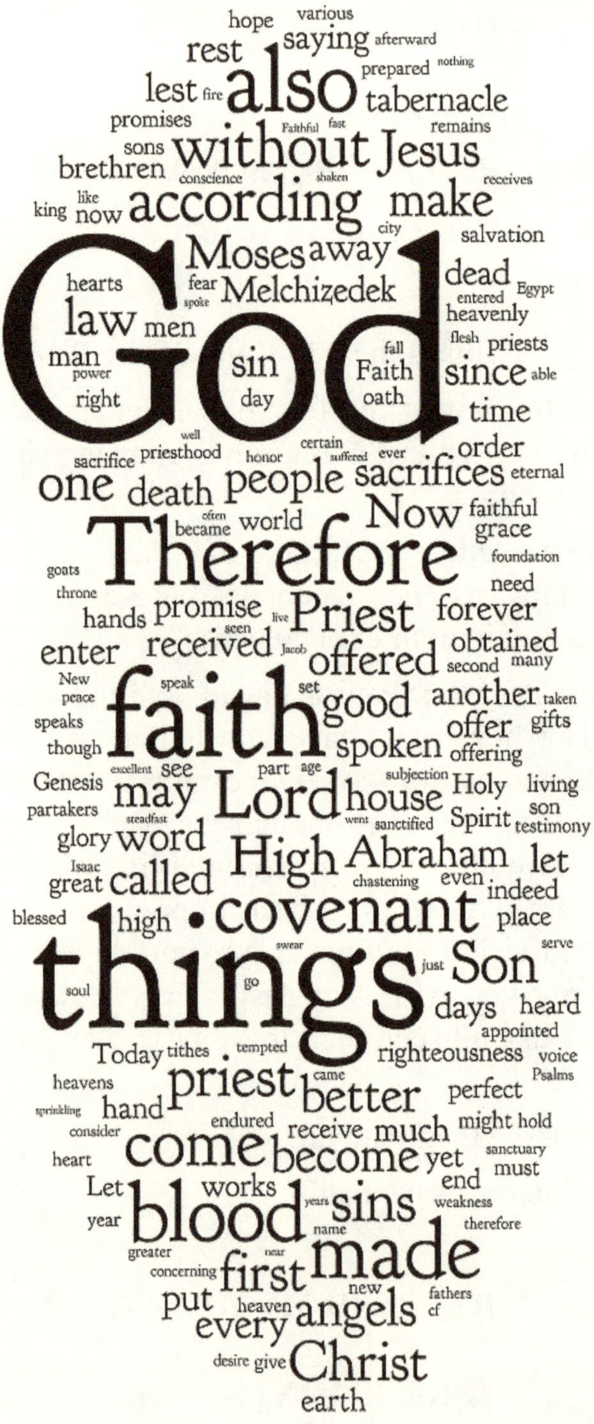
hope
various
saying
afterward
rest
nothing
prepared
lest
fire
also
tabernacle
promises
Faithful
fast
remains
sons
without
Jesus
brethren
conscience
shaken
receives
like
king
now
according
make
city
salvation
Moses
away
God
dead
hearts
fear
Melchizedek
Egypt
spoke
entered
law
men
heavenly
flesh
priests
man
fall
power
sin
Faith
since
able
right
day
oath
time
well
certain
priesthood
suffered
ever
order
sacrifice
honor
one
death
people
sacrifices
eternal
Now
faithful
often
became
world
grace
Therefore
goats
foundation
throne
need
promise
Priest
forever
hands
seen
live
enter
received
Jacob
offered
obtained
second
many
New
speak
set
peace
another
taken
speaks
faith
good
offer
gifts
though
spoken
offering
excellent
see
part
age
subjection
Genesis
Holy
living
partakers
may
Lord
house
son
steadfast
went
sanctified
Spirit
testimony
glory
word
Isaac
High
Abraham
let
great
called
chastening
even
indeed
blessed
high
covenant
place
swear
serve
things
just
Son
soul
go
days
heard
appointed
Today
tithes
tempted
righteousness
voice
heavens
priest
came
Psalms
better
perfect
sprinkling
hand
endured
might
hold
consider
receive
much
heart
come
become
yet
sanctuary
must
Let
works
end
year
years
blood
sins
weakness
name
therefore
greater
near
made
concerning
first
new
fathers
put
heaven
angels
cf
every
desire
give
Christ
earth

| HEBREWS |

Bible Section	| NEW TESTAMENT - THE PENTATEUCH
Total Words	| 6,897 (The 31st Biggest Book in The Bible)
Total Verses	| 303
Total Chapters	| 13

| This is the **58th Book of the Bible.**

Hebrews is the book which presents the 'much more,' 'far better' superiority of Jesus, in every single aspect of His person and work, and therefore clothes itself with unparalleled importance to the Christian. What a book!

Hebrew's initial read audience were persecuted Hebrew believers who rode the rapids of the transition from,

Old Testament to New Testament., Old Covenant to New Covenant, Olive tree to Vine, and it says to them, 'Your new faith gives you Christ, and in Christ is all that you and your fathers sought. Believe in Him with all your heart, with a faith in the unseen future as strong as that of the saints of old, patient under present troubled times and prepared for coming woe, full of energy, and hope, and holiness, and love. For in Jesus you have an all-sufficient Mediating Savior, who is nearer to the Father than the angels, better than Moses, more sympathizing, powerful and prevailing than any earthly high priest, and whose Sabbath rest awaits you in His eternal city in heaven.'

"So, c'mon guys," says the writer,

PRESS ON!

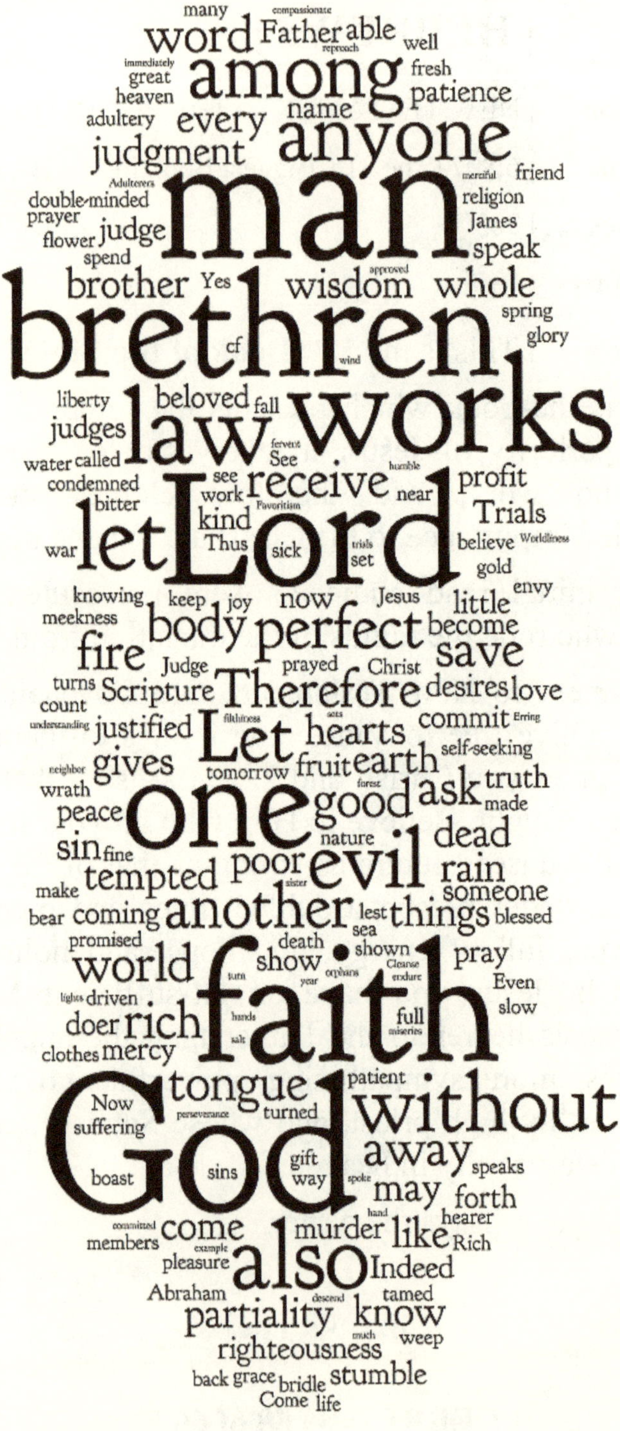

many
compassionate
word
Father
able
reproach
well
immediately
great
among
fresh
heaven
patience
name
adultery
every
anyone
judgment
Adulterers
merciful
friend
man
double-minded
religion
prayer
James
judge
flower
speak
spend
approved
brother
Yes
wisdom
whole
spring
brethren
glory
cf
wind
liberty
beloved
fall
works
judges
law
fervent
water
called
See
humble
condemned
see
receive
profit
work
near
bitter
Favoritism
kind
Trials
let
Lord
war
Thus
sick
trials
believe
Worldliness
set
gold
knowing
keep
joy
now
Jesus
envy
little
meekness
body
perfect
become
fire
save
Judge
prayed
Christ
turns
Scripture
Therefore
desires
love
count
understanding
justified
filthiness
sets
commit
Erring
Let
hearts
self-seeking
neighbor
gives
fruit
earth
tomorrow
forest
truth
wrath
ask
made
peace
one
good
dead
nature
sin
fine
poor
evil
rain
tempted
make
sister
someone
bear
coming
another
lest
things
blessed
sea
promised
death
shown
world
pray
show
Cleanse
turn
orphans
year
endure
Even
lights
driven
slow
faith
hands
full
doer
rich
salt
miseries
clothes
mercy
patient
tongue
Now
without
perseverance
turned
suffering
God
away
gift
speaks
boast
sins
way
spoke
may
forth
hand
hearer
committed
come
murder
members
like
Rich
example
pleasure
also
Indeed
Abraham
descend
tamed
partiality
know
much
weep
righteousness
back
grace
bridle
stumble
Come
life

| JAMES |

Bible Section	| NEW TESTAMENT – GENERAL EPISTLES
Total Words	| 2,304 (The 46th Biggest Book in The Bible)
Total Verses	| 108
Total Chapters	| 5

| This is the **59th Book of the Bible.**

James is not just the first of what are known as the General Epistles, but probably the very first book of the New Testament to have been written, and is written by James, the half-brother of Jesus, to the scattered early church, which was mostly Jewish! The key thrust of the book is to encourage believers saved by faith to be doers of the word and not hearers only. Its emphasis is on faith that produces works of faith, so it says,

By faith, rejoice in your trials.

By Faith, overcome your temptations.

By faith, hear and do the word.

By faith, don't engage in social or financial discrimination.

By faith, practice pure religion.

By faith, tame that world of iniquity, your tongue.

By faith, take a good look at yourselves.

By faith, rescue the wayward.

By faith, wait patiently for God, for remember,

FAITH THAT SAVES IS NOT ALONE!

| JAMES | 59 of 66 |

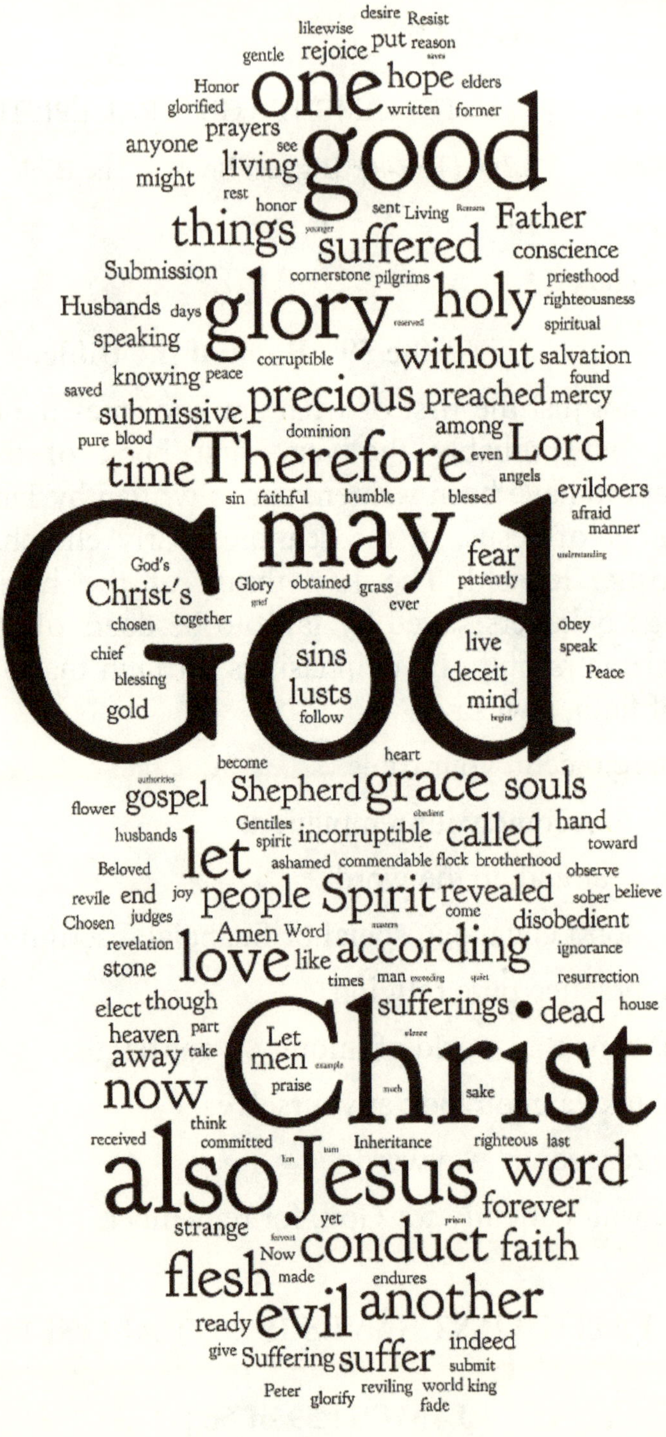
desire Resist
likewise
gentle rejoice put reason
Honor one hope elders
glorified written former
prayers
anyone see good
living
might
rest
honor sent Living Father
things suffered
conscience
Submission
cornerstone pilgrims priesthood
Husbands days glory holy righteousness
spiritual
speaking
corruptible without salvation
knowing peace found
saved preached mercy
submissive precious
dominion among
pure blood
time Therefore even Lord
angels
sin faithful humble blessed evildoers
afraid
may manner
God's fear
Christ's Glory obtained grass patiently
ever
chosen together obey
chief live speak
sins Peace
blessing deceit
lusts mind
gold follow
God
become heart
gospel Shepherd grace souls
flower
Gentiles hand
husbands let spirit incorruptible called toward
Beloved ashamed commendable flock brotherhood observe
revile end joy people Spirit revealed sober believe
Chosen judges come disobedient
Amen Word
revelation love according ignorance
stone like
times man resurrection
elect though sufferings dead house
heaven part Let
away take men
now praise sake
Christ
think
received committed Inheritance righteous last
also Jesus word
forever
strange yet
Now conduct faith
flesh made endures
ready evil another
indeed
give Suffering suffer submit
Peter glorify reviling world king
fade

| 1 PETER |

Bible Section | NEW TESTAMENT – GENERAL EPISTLES

Total Words | 2,476 (The 45th Biggest Book in The Bible)

Total Verses | 105

Total Chapters | 5

| This is the **60th Book of the Bible.**

Written by the apostle Peter from Babylon, in that place of relative shelter from the persecution of that 'nutter' Nero and the all-pursuing Jews, Peter himself was in a time of trial, and in full knowledge of his own impending death whilst writing to Christians in a great time of trial themselves!

Peter's great theme is 'HOPE IN SUFFERING – JOY IN TRIALS,' and the most frightening thing is that he is trying to get his readers ready for worse things to come! Yes, even more savage and fiery trials which will cost many of them their lives. Therefore these folk needed HOPE.

This hope Peter talks about is a living hope that fills and thrills the present with the happiness of such a real and solid, perfect and wonderful future, that present trials can be endured with a patience and joy that passes any present understanding. Now that's a miracle of staggering proportions, and I tell you, that is both a sign and a wonder.

Remember, Peter writes,

"SO THAT YOUR FAITH AND HOPE ARE IN GOD"

(1 Peter 1:21 NKJV)

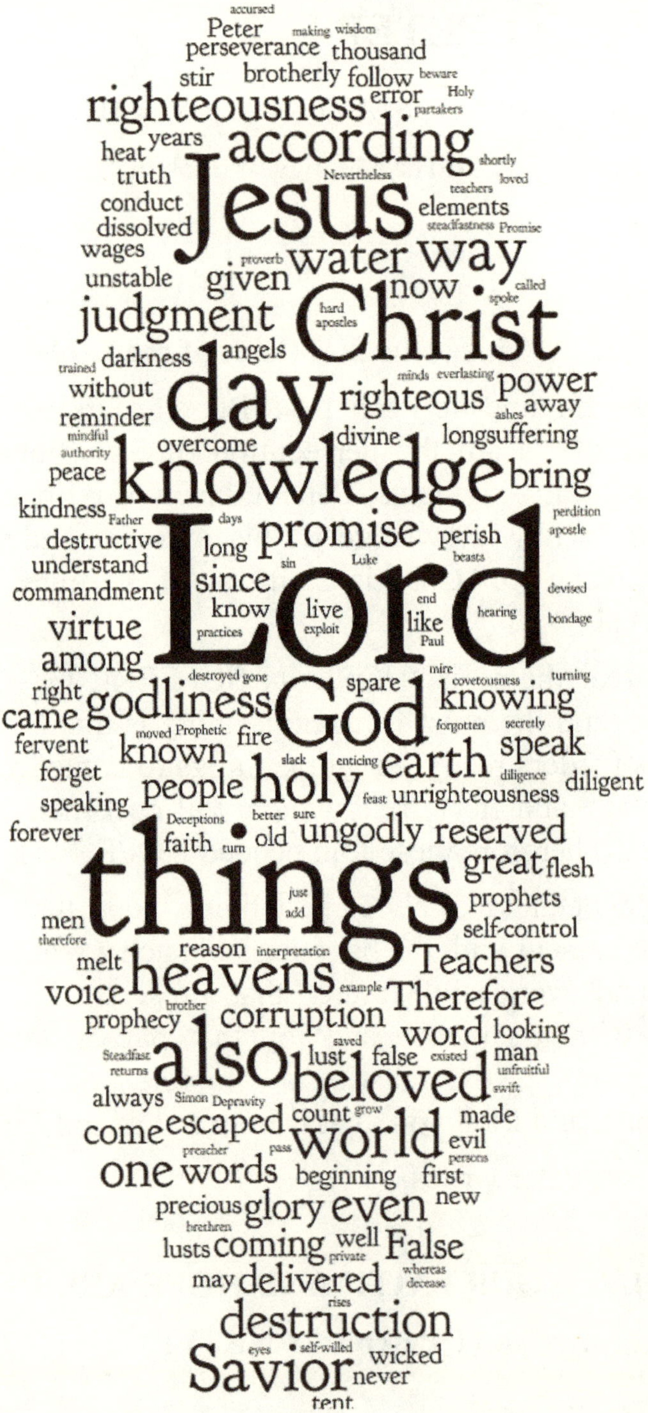
accursed
Peter
making
wisdom
perseverance
thousand
stir
brotherly
follow
beware
righteousness
error
Holy
partakers
heat
years
according
shortly
truth
Nevertheless
loved
Jesus
teachers
conduct
elements
dissolved
steadfastness
Promise
wages
proverb
water
way
unstable
given
now
called
spoke
judgment
hard
apostles
Christ
darkness
angels
trained
minds
everlasting
without
day
power
righteous
ashes
away
reminder
mindful
divine
longsuffering
authority
overcome
peace
knowledge
bring
kindness
Father
days
perdition
destructive
promise
perish
apostle
understand
long
sin
Luke
beasts
commandment
since
Lord
devised
know
end
live
hearing
virtue
practices
exploit
like
bondage
Paul
among
mire
destroyed
gone
covetousness
turning
right
spare
came
godliness
God
knowing
moved
Prophetic
forgotten
secretly
fervent
fire
known
speak
forget
slack
enticing
earth
diligence
speaking
people
holy
feast
unrighteousness
diligent
forever
Deceptions
better
sure
faith
turn
old
ungodly
reserved
great
flesh
things
just
prophets
men
add
self-control
therefore
reason
interpretation
melt
Teachers
heavens
voice
example
Therefore
brother
prophecy
corruption
saved
word
looking
Steadfast
existed
man
returns
also
lust
false
unfruitful
beloved
swift
always
Simon
Depravity
count
grow
made
come
escaped
world
evil
preacher
pass
persons
one
words
beginning
first
new
precious
glory
even
brethren
lusts
coming
well
private
False
may
delivered
whereas
decease
rises
destruction
eyes
self-willed
wicked
Savior
never
tent

| 2 PETER |

Bible Section | NEW TESTAMENT – GENERAL EPISTLES

Total Words | 1,553 (The 55th Biggest Book in The Bible)

Total Verses | 61

Total Chapters | 3

| This is the **61st Book of the Bible.**

2nd Peter is Peter's "swan song" before his martyrdom, for he knew that the moving tent he pitched that was a day's march nearer home each evening; was about to be put off once and for all, and like Paul, aware of the coming storm of the great falling away from the faith, with hurricane hawsers, he now secures the great ship of the church alongside that more sure word of prophecy, the Bible.

Aware that false prophets shall come spouting denying and destructive heresies, Peter not only points us to the precious promises of the Scriptures, but at the same time, pressurizes us to make our calling and election sure, that is, he insists we examine ourselves to see if we are in the faith by testing ourselves regarding our spiritual possessions.

Have we faith, virtue, knowledge, self-control, perseverance, Godliness, brotherly kindness and love? Or, do we possess only expediency, insider lies and internal despising? If it's the latter – then we are lost. Look now, the true sign of faith is the fruit of

"GROWING IN THE GRACE AND KNOWLEDGE OF JESUS"

| 2 PETER | 61 of 66 |

righteous
Son
toward
confesses
knows
receive
true
whatever
went
abide
ask
greater
love
Therefore
lust
loves
commits
let
message
Little
every
murderer
need
believes
eternal
write
revealed
little
beginning.I
world
written
spirit
many
lawlessness
old
beginning
young
commandment
brethren
manifest
overcomes
flesh
Antichrist
begotten
liar
wicked
hears
God
Father
everyone
Obedience
last
perfected
bear
Now
coming
given
fellowship
hates
heart
now
perfect
born
truly
testimony
loved
sinned
Word
three
Holy
death
devil
water
might
known
blood
Truth
John
whoever
made
anointing
works
things
abides
Spirit
fear
name
practices
unrighteousness
also
eyes
darkness
commandments
anyone
overcome
fathers
new
keep
Whoever
Love
life
passing
propitiation
Beloved
heard
Jesus
One
manifested
walk
truth
lie
just
righteousness
already
word
believe
may
children
leading
keeps
know
away
hour
Test
believed
confess
Faith
Another
confidence
sees
concerning
sent
sins
brother
deceive
sin
declare
practice
men
come
whole
witness
Christ
denies
another
one
light
Knowing
seen

| 1 JOHN |

Bible Section | NEW TESTAMENT – GENERAL EPISTLES

Total Words | 2,516 (The 44th Biggest Book in The Bible)

Total Verses | 105

Total Chapters | 5

| This is the **62nd Book of the Bible.**

Written by a former "son of Thunder" who had become just 'John the aged apostle of love,' this is a family newsletter to everyone who has God as their Father, and there are six real reasons for writing, even six "so that's." Look now, John writes,

"So that you can have fellowship with us, the Father, and Jesus."

"So that your joy may be full."

"So that you don't sin."

"So that you know you have eternal life."

"So that you may believe on the name of the Son of God."

"So that you might know the truth."

The letter is all about light, life and love but, most importantly, it is about knowledge. This book has the sound of a spiritual building site and the hammering of six inch nails is heard and felt as great truths are pounded home, having been stated, repeated, enlarged and applied. Know this though: the children of the devil hate the children of god. However, the children of God

LOVE THE CHILDREN OF GOD.

| 1 JOHN | 62 of 66 |

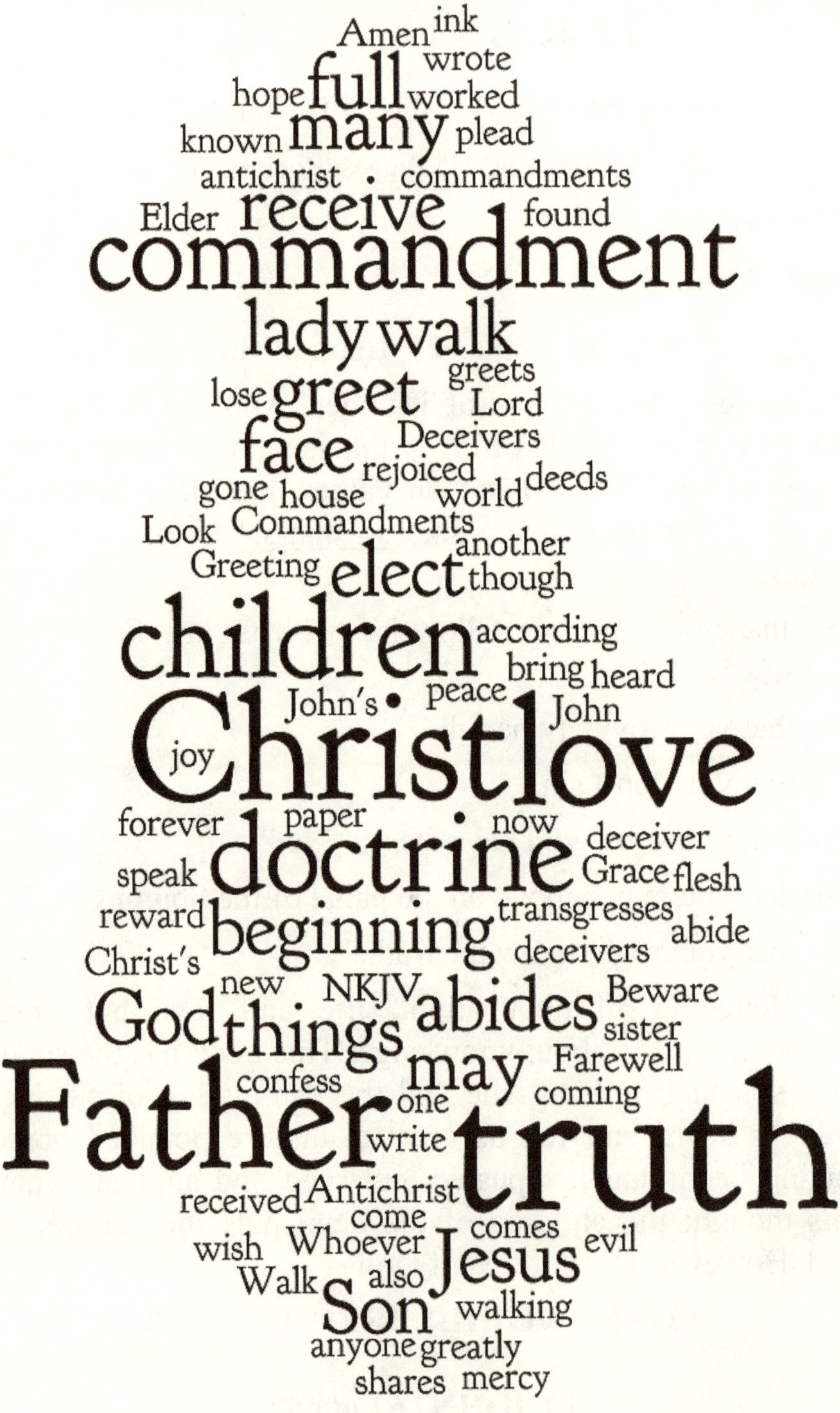
Amen ink
wrote
hope full worked
known many plead
antichrist commandments
Elder receive found
commandment
lady walk
greets
lose greet Lord
face Deceivers
rejoiced
gone house world deeds
Look Commandments
another
Greeting elect though
children according
bring heard
John's peace John
joy Christ love
forever paper now
deceiver
speak doctrine Grace flesh
reward transgresses
beginning abide
Christ's deceivers
new NKJV Beware
God things abides sister
Farewell
may
confess coming
Father one
write truth
received Antichrist
come
comes evil
wish Whoever Jesus
Walk also
Son walking
anyone greatly
shares mercy

| 2 JOHN |

Bible Section | NEW TESTAMENT - GENERAL EPISTLES

Total Words | 298 (The 65th Biggest Book in The Bible)

Total Verses | 13

Total Chapters | 1

| This is the **63rd Book of the Bible.**

2 John is a personal letter written to someone called "The Elect Lady," that is, Lady Electa and her children whom John hoped to visit shortly. The 'Elect Lady' could be a Euphemism for the church, and her children could refer to its members? Either way it does not matter, for it does not take away from either the letter's point or power.

2 John is all about love and truth.

We must walk in the truth of God's word and love those who walk in the truth of God's word.

Those however, who do not walk in the truth are NOT Christians and loving them, especially in terms of extending hospitality, provision prayers and pulpit time is not love! On the contrary, it is a sharing in their evil deeds.

Where love is not balanced with truth, the child of God falls off his little bike.

Love is to be placed and applied according to truth. Remember,

TRUTH TRUMPS LOVE- ALWAYS.

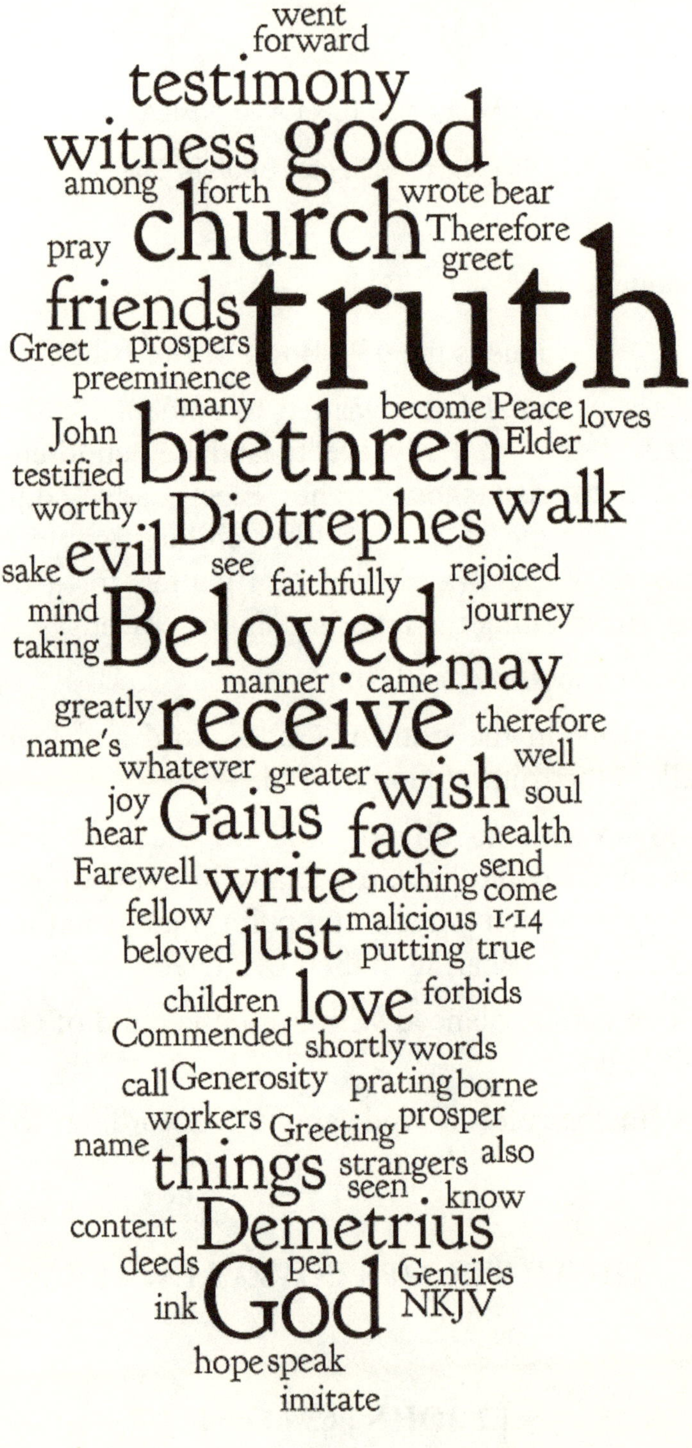
went
forward
testimony
witness good
among forth wrote bear
church Therefore
pray greet
friends truth
Greet prospers
preeminence
many become Peace loves
John brethren Elder
testified
worthy Diotrephes walk
sake evil see rejoiced
faithfully
mind journey
taking Beloved
manner came may
greatly receive therefore
name's well
whatever greater wish
joy soul
hear Gaius face health
Farewell write nothing send
come
fellow malicious 1-14
beloved just putting true
children love forbids
Commended shortly words
call Generosity prating borne
workers Greeting prosper
name things strangers also
seen know
content Demetrius
deeds pen Gentiles
ink God NKJV
hope speak
imitate

| 3 JOHN |

Bible Section	| NEW TESTAMENT – GENERAL EPISTLES
Total Words	| 294 (This is the Smallest Book in The Bible)
Total Verses	| 14
Total Chapters	| 1

| This is the **64th Book of the Bible.**

3 John is a personal letter to Gaius, whom John had probably himself discipled; a man 'sound through and through' and whom John hoped to visit shortly.

John commends Gaius, and prays for him as he might not have been in the best of health whilst hammering home the necessity to "walk in the truth." Indeed, this letter is all about walking in the truth.

'Dyostrophies the dictator,' seemed to either have to rule of ruin. He was the prize 'prat' who refused to receive the apostles and the Apostle John in particular. He also excommunicated those Christians who did entertain them! Love had opened the door to error, and now it had come and made the house its own.

I wonder if John is sending a 'not so subtle eviction notice' with this letter to a bailiff whose name was 'Demetrius,' the man of apostolic selection set to mash the megalomaniac of Dyostrophies?

Trouble's brewing in this letter because it's

TIME TO CLEAN HOUSE

| 3 JOHN | 64 of 66 |

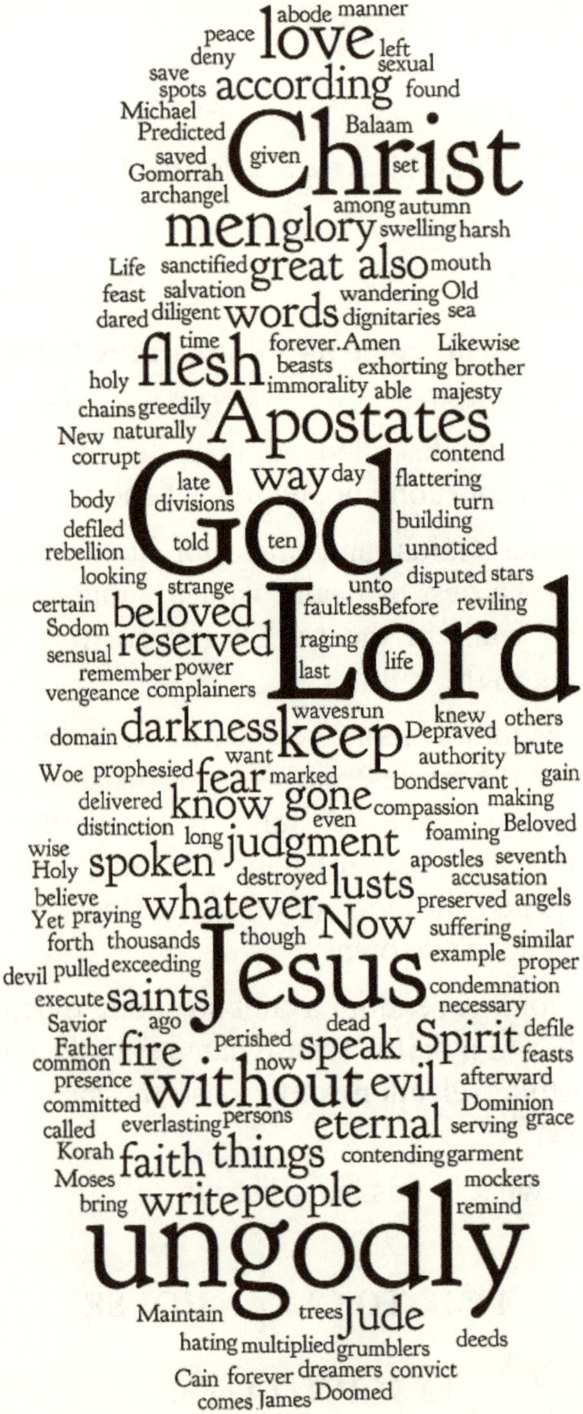
abode manner
peace love left
deny sexual
save
spots according found
Michael
Predicted Balaam
saved given Christ
Gomorrah set
archangel
among autumn
men glory swelling harsh
Life sanctified great also mouth
feast salvation wandering Old
dared diligent words dignitaries sea
time forever.Amen Likewise
flesh beasts exhorting brother
holy immorality able majesty
chains greedily
New naturally Apostates
corrupt contend
late way day flattering
body divisions turn
defiled God building
rebellion told ten unnoticed
looking strange unto disputed stars
certain faultlessBefore reviling
Sodom beloved
sensual reserved raging
remember power life
vengeance complainers last Lord
wavesrun knew others
domain darkness keep Depraved brute
want authority
Woe prophesied fear marked bondservant gain
delivered know gone compassion making
distinction even foaming Beloved
wise long judgment
Holy spoken apostles seventh
destroyed accusation
believe lusts preserved angels
Yet praying whatever
forth thousands though Now suffering similar
devil pulled exceeding example proper
execute saints Jesus condemnation
necessary
Savior ago dead defile
Father fire perished speak Spirit feasts
common now
presence without evil afterward
committed Dominion
called everlasting persons eternal serving grace
Korah faith things contending garment
Moses mockers
bring write people remind
ungodly
Maintain trees Jude
hating multiplied grumblers deeds
Cain forever dreamers convict
comes James Doomed

| JUDE |

Bible Section | NEW TESTAMENT – GENERAL EPISTLES

Total Words | 608 (The 63rd Biggest Book in The Bible)

Total Verses | 25

Total Chapters | 1

| This is the **65th Book of the Bible.**

Written by the half-brother of Jesus, who was burdened with a driving necessity to write about the need to contend with 'all your might for that faith once delivered to the saints, for false teachers, having roots in the demonic, had already successfully sown poisonous and aggressive, spiritually genetically modified tares amongst the wheat!'

Yes, the fallen angels; rebellious Israel; killer Cain; erring Balaam and big-mouthed Korah, are all brought as examples of aspects of heresy, all of whom are gifted but faithless, self-consuming and selfish, murdering and muttering, mocking and malevolent megalomaniacs, that are unleashed and unaccountable, all swollen up with words but empty of truth. They are all dangerous reefs set with vultures that are ready to pick you clean of your faith. Jude was having quite the rabid rant against them!

Look now, for Jude says that only God can keep you from falling before such smiling and malevolent monsters so, "pray in the spirit, keep your selves in the love of God and build yourselves up in your most holy faith."

TO HIM WHO IS ABLE.

| JUDE | 65 of 66 |

Satan
hand bowl made
angel number creature days
Now three
cried elders wine
saying works sword
power full sits
torment open
called glory eat sea
sounded clothed
worshiped rest
midst Church given written death
testimony names take
came horns
God
hour horse
write
time right pit
Almighty loud
harm mark anymore creatures mighty
night
waters twelve
day fell
one great ear
prophecy church
forever honor water looked
thousand golden
know heard
twenty-four ten
fine
sound new
earth
kings life angels
sharp
sun
third fear give Bowl
fallen woman must hear churches
dragon
wrath saw throne
gold tree
true men
saints behold seven fire became
ever found
people One
Lamb sealed
let opened every
stars servants book place
smoke fourth
away
beast heaven Book
went
Come Jesus poured seal scroll repent
standing gates Lord voice Trumpet
many little bottomless
make
see city Blessed heads
like living
image Behold
tribe
first white Spirit Life
rich authority quickly
things come prophets
hundred
another feet
lives
altar worship Seal dwell plagues First
sat blood mouth overcomes
holy
name
fornication eyes may world
cast nations temple second
Amen
stone
flesh Christ four coming killed
gave two also
words Babylon dead
anyone
war

| REVELATION |

Bible Section | NEW TESTAMENT - PROPHECY

Total Words | 11,995 (The 25th Biggest Book in The Bible)

Total Verses | 404

Total Chapters | 22

| This is the **66th & Last Book of the Bible.**

Revelation is a letter written by John the apostle whilst exiled on the Isle of Patmos, to suffering Christians, and despite its vast canvas from eternity past to eternity future, all painted with symbols, it is at its heart, a book all about Jesus. Indeed, it is the REVELATION OF JESUS CHRIST, and a very special blessing is promised to the readers of it.

The first three chapters of the book, are written to seven local, historical and geographical churches having only direct application to them, but also might apply to and define the seven 'spiritual states' that each church and even Christian individual might find themselves in from time to time. Indeed, the first three chapters could also represent the different 'spiritual states' of the whole church as it has progressed through space and time until now.

The rest of the book from Chapter 4 onwards, however, is prophetic and futuristic in that it has yet to come to pass. In this way, Revelation could be the only prophetic book of the New Testament! In any event, Revelation is all about Jesus and with the very last words of this book He says,

"BEHOLD I AM COMING SOON!"

| REVELATION | 66 of 66 |

MORE ABOUT 'THE 66 BOOKS MINISTRY'

Over the next 25 years, by the grace of God and according to His will and favor, The 66 Books Ministry shall be preaching consecutively from each of the 66 Books of the Holy Bible, the Gospel of the Lord Jesus Christ in 16,500 of the most influential cities of the world on an annual and ongoing basis!

We do not underestimate the quality teams of trained people that this will take, together with the need for vast amount of materials and finances which will also have to be raised. However, as most futurists indicate that the growing global population will be gathered mostly in major world cities in the coming years, there is a necessity laid upon the church to present and proclaim the God of the whole Bible, through the primacy of preaching in these cities. We are convinced that this is a paramount and pressing concern.

"For since, in the wisdom of God, the world through wisdom did not know God, it pleased God through the foolishness of the message preached to save those who believe" 1 Corinthians 1:21NKJV

"Preach the Word! Be ready in season and out of season. Convince, rebuke, exhort, with all longsuffering and teaching." 2 Timothy 4:2NKJV

The church is looking for a revival. The 66 Books Ministry, however, is trying to start a revolution of a return to the preached Word, from the whole of the Bible as a precursor to any and all coming revival.

For "whoever calls on the name of the Lord shall be saved." How then shall they call on Him in whom they have not believed? And how shall they believe in Him of whom they have not heard? And how shall they hear without a preacher? And how shall they preach unless they are sent? As it is written: "How beautiful are the feet of those who preach the gospel of peace, Who bring glad tidings of good things!" Romans 10:13-15 NKJV

We are unashamedly looking for and seeking to foster a massive, huge, releasing, transformative, and exceptionally disruptive reversal and revolutionary change, both within the church and then in the world. We are not just another mission trying to do the same as every other mission. We are intent on revolution!

To this revolutionary end, we have no fear of seeming failure and will cultivate that audacious atmosphere within our ministry. We want to attract grass roots people who are people of faith risk takers, for we believe it is people of such life hazarding attitudes that are used by God to make breakthroughs in the world for the Kingdom of God. Hanging back for fear of seeming failure, hanging back and waiting for the trained professionals, both wastes the time of the church time and kills the spirit of victory.

In that spirit then, we therefore are believing that this task can be accomplished by such people in the 25 year time frame we have given ourselves.

Fully assured then, that we are in full obedience with the great commission of our great God and Savior Jesus Christ, we do, with great confidence in Him, turn ourselves happily to this so great a task in the hope that, like a happy hound straining at the leash to be let loose, we believe that many other people will smile along with us and be part of this brand new grass roots 21st Century Global City Mission.

If you want to know more and want to be part of what we are doing then go to www.The66BooksMinistry.com or call us in the USA on 855 662 6657, or email V.R. directly on vr@The66BooksMinistry.com

THE MISSION STATEMENT OF THE 66 BOOKS MINISTRY

Our Mission is:

1. "To proclaim Jesus, the Savior of the whole world, from the whole Bible, because He is wonderful!"

2. Indeed, we are constrained by the love of God, to communicate the rawness of the Bible to real people, in real ways, and our driving and major project of '66Cities' shall take us to the 66 most influential cities of the 250 nations of the world in the next 25 years. That's 16,500 cities!

3. We are aiming to build relationships with grass roots, real people, that is, ordinary people, who, in their own countries and cities, want to do extraordinary things for Jesus and the Kingdom of God, to bring a Biblical Gospel message that is relevant to now, in a world that has come to believe that Jesus is irrelevant to their lives.

If you would like to partner with us in this great task. Then we want to hear from you! Contact me today on vr@66books.tv

AUTHOR BIO | VICTOR ROBERT FARRELL

Victor Robert Farrell (1960-Now & still alive and kicking) was born in Chesterfield England to Scottish parents with Irish grandparents, which is an obvious recipe for writing and emotional disaster, if ever there was one!

He grew up a culturally excluded Roman Catholic (his parents were divorced,) which is one of the reasons why he hates religion with a passion, and that's an interesting enough fact by itself, because he is also an ordained protestant minister to boot.

V.R. became a Christian whilst serving on board a Polaris Submarine at the end of the cold war. He has gone on to do many things, including being a broadcaster, App developer, performance poet, and the long-time author of 'Night Whispers,' which is read in over 100 counties and is also translated into Spanish (see www.Night-Whispers.com)

Currently, V.R. is also President of The 66 Books Ministry: a grass roots global city mission endeavor. I suppose it is this concoction of background and experience which means V.R's communication is always raw and emotive. After all, "If Christianity can be relevant on a Monday morning, several hundred feet underneath an unknown ocean, in a pornographic sewer pipe carrying enough nuclear weapons to destroy a continent, whilst hiding from the Russians, then it can be relevant anywhere and everywhere!"

V.R. sees himself as a servant of the Word of the Lord, and communicating the God of the whole Bible, proclaimed in very real terms, to real people, is both his burden and his passion.

AN INTRODUCTION TO 'PURPLE ROBERT'

Now, before I go any further, this guy comes with warning shots! The opening parts of his currently seven volumes pf poetic works says quite clearly, "If you are easily offended by low level expletives...Go no further. Do not read this book! If you are prudish in any way ...Go no further. Do not read this book! If you do not want to be challenged...Go no further. Do not read this book! If you want to be stroked into unchanging sleep and into the stupor of remaining as you are...Go no further. Do not read this book! If you hide under the respectable covers of a comfortable religion...Go no further. Do not read this book! If you are frail in faith and dishonest about life under this sun...Go no further. If you have no real integrity regarding the state of your own heart, then do not read this book! If however, you are grown up, honest and have a basic human integrity, ENJOY!" So, there you go, you have been warned!

Purple Robert is a Perforamce Poet and a Metaphysical Biblical Realist. If you want to hear some of his work and get hold of the 66 Poems each of the Seven volumes contain, then go to www.PurpleRobert.com and purchase them today.

www.ingramcontent.com/pod-product-compliance
Lightning Source LLC
Chambersburg PA
CBHW020000050426
42450CB00005B/263
9781910686843